CARGOES

The schooner *Emma Claudina,* the first Matson vessel. About 1882.

CARGOES

Matson's First Century in the Pacific

WILLIAM L. WORDEN

A KOLOWALU BOOK
THE UNIVERSITY PRESS OF HAWAII | *Honolulu*

Library of Congress Cataloging in Publication Data

Worden, William L.
  Cargoes: Matson's first century in the Pacific.

  (A Kolowalu book)
  Bibliography: p.
  Includes index.
  1. Matson Navigation Company—History. 2. Shipping—
Hawaii—History. I. Title.
HE753.M3W67   387.5'09969   80–21666
ISBN 0–8248–0708–1

My half of this project
is dedicated to
Mary Lasher Worden
who did the other half herself

—W. L. W.

CONTENTS

PREFACE

Owners of ships generally are, or would like to be, in business for a profit; and many of them would ask nothing more if their financial rewards equalled those of pickle packers or sellers of plastic pipe. But ships frequently produce more headaches than profits, more romance than dividends, and history instead of capital gains.

Shiplines may be born of careful financial planning, politics, or pure greed; but they are shaped as much by bearded skippers with square-faced bottles of gin as by budgetary experts. Luck brings them to disaster or saves them from it. Sober management must deal with lady stowaways and idiosyncratic plumbing as well as with bankers and stockholders. Timid men adrift in small boats perform heroics because there is no reasonable alternative. Pratfall comedy never is far away, nor is the threat of tragedy. The sea remains undefeated.

In nearly a century of serving Hawaii and other ports, Matson Navigation Company has established unique relationships with the islands. Their histories have become intertwined almost beyond separating, politics sometimes nibbling profits, and corporate stumbles shaking the island economy. In good seasons, they have served each other well; and thus far neither has found a suitable substitute for the other.

In a society so close, very little could be independent. The history of Matson has been shaped by extraneous business and government developments, as a river is shaped by its tributaries. Apparently diverse, these stories are in fact essential to an understanding of the whole.

Matson has had moments of glory, high-minded policies, and many men of stature. It also has had its share of corporate warts, made wrong guesses, stewed over trivia, experienced true adventures and—like any seagoing enterprise at any time or place—stored up many a tall tale. Not all of these happenings may be history in the strict academic sense, but every one is a part of the Matson story. The only pity is that not all can be included here.

ACKNOWLEDGMENTS

Where possible, materials for this book have been obtained from participants in the events described. In addition to those mentioned elsewhere as interviewees or letter writers, many others contributed to the project.

We are especially grateful to the staff members (not always known by name) of the Seattle and San Francisco public libraries, the California State Library at Sacramento, the Bancroft Library at the University of California (Berkeley), the University of Hawaii libraries, the San Francisco Historical Society, the San Francisco Maritime Museum (now the National Maritime Museum), the Hawaiian Mission Children's Society, the Hawaii State Archives, the San Mateo, California, County Recorder's Office, and the museum ship *Falls of Clyde;* also Harry Avery, Joyce Curry, Edna Duryee, Jeanne Boothe Johnson, Gwen Hemila, B. Marian Marquardt, Gary Reese of the Tacoma Public Library, Robert M. Richardson (for precise editing as well as information), Jan Smith, Jean Vandervelde, and personnel of Matson Navigation Company and Alexander & Baldwin, Inc.

Within the Matson company, Dudley Burchard initiated the history project at the request of Robert J. Pfeiffer. Fred A. Stindt not only made available carefully conserved company records and photographs but provided essential cooperation throughout, and is responsible for the basic ship lists. Charles Regal, public relations manager, devoted weeks to correspondence, collection of materials, fact checking and sharp editing. Additional help was provided by Gregg Perry, John Spaulding, Mark Zeug, and Carol Sander of the Alexander & Baldwin public relations staff.

THE FOUNDER
AND ONE SMALL OPENING
(1849–1882)

William Matson said he had been born on October 18, 1849, in Lysekil, a village on Sweden's Skagerak coast near Göteborg. There is no reason to doubt his statement but confirmation is difficult. Swedish mid-century birth and church records perhaps noted that a son of Matt had been born or baptized and named William; but there were many Matts, not necessarily of the same or related families. Since family names were not used in the modern manner, the family effectively ceased to exist once siblings or cousins were dispersed or died, unless someone kept private records.

Matson's daughter, Mrs. William P. Roth, visited Lysekil after her father's death and located a church where he said he had been baptized, but even with expert Swedish help could learn no more. "We could find nothing," she reported. "I don't think my father had any brothers or sisters, but if there were other relatives he didn't know and didn't want to find out. His father and mother were killed in an accident. I think it had something to do with a mine, an explosion. He was taken by an aunt. He probably didn't care for that much so he ran away to sea when he was twelve years old. In his early years he never wanted to go back to Sweden. Later, he did want to go, but illness prevented him from doing it.

"I don't think he ever went to school, ever. So his education was from his Bible and what books he could gather. I wouldn't say he was overreligious, but he had his Bible and he taught himself. He had to. He sailed down the coast, I think it may have been to South America, and finally got to a ship for New York."

Exactly this much and no more is known about the childhood of the youth who arrived in New York on the Nova Scotia vessel *Aurora* in 1863. Obviously, his lifelong habit—never to go back, never look back, don't even talk about the past—was formed early. He left no autobiography, and if he told others more about his youth they did not record it. No one has an explanation of how a fourteen-year-old, landing in the midst of a bitter war and with what could only have been rudimentary English, survived the next four years.

Various biographers have agreed that he reached San Francisco in 1867, after a trip around Cape Horn on the sailing ship *Bridgewater,* probably as a seaman; but the record of the next fifteen years is cloudy and confused. The former Matson Navigation Company magazine, *Aloha,* in an article written long after Matson's death and disclosing no sources, reported that he shipped on the "old schooner *John J.*" to Puget Sound, transferred to the bark *Oakland* for another northern trip, then shipped on the scow schooner *William Frederick* "plying on San Francisco Bay" and after two years became captain of this vessel, chiefly engaged in carrying coal from Mount Diablo to the Spreckels sugar refinery in San Francisco. It added, "later he became captain of the schooner *Mission Canal*, which was used for the same purpose."

There are other versions of the story of Matson's years in the scow schooners. John E. Cushing, president of the Matson company in 1949, said: "The best job [Matson] could get was on a barge [that is, scow schooner] which plied San Francisco Bay, and it was while serving on barges and on the coal schooner *William Frederick* that he met, and liked, the men connected with the Spreckels sugar refinery."

John L. Peterson of Burlingame, California, in a letter circa 1960 said: "Captain Matson tried to interest my grandfather, Captain August Anderson, in starting a South Seas shipping service in 1872. Grandfather had to decline when he was struck down with crippling rheumatism."

In Matson's 1917 obituary, the *San Francisco Chronicle* reported: "His first independent investment was made in a scow schooner, with which he engaged in bay and river traffic in the early years. On one of his upriver trips he met the young woman who became his first wife. They were divorced thirty years ago and she afterwards died." The obituary named five children of this marriage: Arthur J., Walter, Theodore, Emily, and Ida.

There is no confirmation that Matson owned a scow schooner; but in a 1957 interview, Rod G. Fischer of Oakland, California, a grandson of Captain Charles Rock, told R. R. Olmsted: "In the seventies, Rock owned a scow schooner; and on one slow trip down to San Francisco with a load of sand, the crew as usual were playing poker in the cabin. Rock got into an argument with the cook, William Matson, over a 10-cent bet; and some harsh words passed between them, with the result that when they landed in San Francisco, Matson gathered his belongings and left, despite the fact that Rock had repented. . . . Matson found that he might command one of Spreckels' vessels, trading in the Hawaiian islands, if he could raise the money to buy an interest in her. Lacking the cash, he re-

turned to the scow and asked Rock to help him out. Rock put up $4,000. Rock continued to share in Matson enterprises: he went into the oil business with Matson, was a director of Honolulu Oil, and in later years was port captain for Matson."

Matson probably did meet some of the large Spreckels family while making deliveries to the refinery, but Mrs. Roth added: "He used to go on the Spreckels' yacht to help them sail, which probably was how they became good friends. That was the yacht *Lurline,* and it was because of the happy times he had on the Spreckels' yacht that he later named his ship the *Lurline.*" (Matson indeed was fond of the name, using it not only for a series of ships but also for his daughter. Mrs. Roth was christened Lurline Matson.)

The one photograph of Matson from this period shows an unlined face, a small mustache, wide mouth, and alert eyes. The suit looks too heavy for San Francisco, and the tie is oddly knotted. There is nothing to indicate burning ambition or unusual ability to inspire confidence in men with money or loyalty from generations of sailors, but the abilities and the ambition were there.

From Captain Rock or elsewhere, Matson obtained $5,000. Joseph Knowland, Otis J. Preston, John J. McKinnon, Charles Watson, and Peter A. Smith each added $2,500. The Spreckels family turned over to this group the new, $20,000 schooner *Emma Claudina,* of 198 tons, retaining a one-eighth interest in the name of A. Spreckels.

Only speculation is possible about the reasons the Spreckelses, already busy expanding their own shipline to Hawaii, not only permitted the partners to buy a ship that could compete with them but assisted the purchasers, then and later. After ordering her, they may have decided the *Emma* was too small for their needs. They could have been trying only to help a young man who had been a good unpaid hand on their yacht and represented no visible threat to their main businesses. On the other hand, it may have appeared only as sound business: let Matson and his partners run the ship, risking loss at sea or on the treacherous coast of the island of

Hawaii, while the Spreckels family made a profit as agents in supplying cargo.

At any rate, Captain Matson prepared to take out his first deep-sea command.* He also was taking his first step toward a fortune, even as the little schooner was establishing what would become Hawaii's most important single lifeline.

During 800 years before 1778, Polynesians in Hawaii enjoyed a society as independent as any on earth. Remarkable navigators had brought them some 2,000 miles north from the Society and Marquesas islands in outrigger canoes; and in the Hawaiian archipelago they had everything they needed or wanted. The climate was delightful; the waters teemed with fish; and men and the animals and plants they brought with them throve. Even the warriors managed to batter each other in tribal battles frequently enough to avoid boredom. If the sons and grandsons of those masterful navigators did not forget navigation, they avoided extensions of that ancient science, which could lead only to boredom, seasickness, and an oversupply of flying fish. What lay over the oceans, out of sight of their mountains, simply did not matter. That it still might not matter to them today if only haole explorers had gone somewhere else is an intriguing thought, although pointless.

The aliens did come, bringing alien tastes and alien toys. The independent society was doomed from the moment they landed. Captain James Cook and other explorers were followed by China traders, and sandalwood buyers by whalers. Crews coming ashore wanted fresh water, fresh foods, sails, rope, fuel for try-pots, and a thousand other items. They brought ashore the traditional delights: whiskey, guns, Bibles, and diseases. Hawaiians were not in a rush for more Bibles; but the firearms were handy for local arguments and the whiskey soon ran out.

The islands could not produce half the things the aliens wanted; and now the Hawaiians, too, wanted things they never had known, things that must come from beyond the oceans. For the first time, it was important that 2,400 miles of water separated the islands from California. A bridge of supply ships was essential.

More than 1,600 ships did visit Honolulu between 1823 and 1837. This traffic continued to grow, with whalers, casual merchantmen, and occasional foreign naval vessels competing for anchor room. Most of their crews came ashore briefly, then departed for a thousand other ports. The foreigners who did not leave, however, changed the islands forever.

A New England brig brought Protestant missionaries in 1820, the first of ten companies totalling 184 persons to arrive in a twenty-eight-year period. Many stayed, in or out of the church, including Abner Wilcox, patriarch of a family on Kauai; Amos Starr Cooke and S. N. Castle, Honolulu mission teachers and storekeepers later to establish their own merchandising, agency, and shipping business; and William P. Alexander and Dwight Baldwin, whose sons would expand sugar acreage into fortunes.

The British brig *Bordeaux* landed James Hunnewell, ship's officer, to sell its cargo and invest the profits. He established a company that eventually was bought by Captain Charles Brewer and still operates as C. Brewer & Company. R. C. Janion arrived from Liverpool; leased a store site for 299 years from the Hawaiian king; and finally sold the business to his clerk, Theophilus H. Davies. This company, Theo. H. Davies & Company, Ltd., also is still very much alive.

German-born Henry Hackfeld visited the islands as a supercargo on a ship sailing from Boston to China, and returned in 1849 with a stock of goods bought in Bremen to found Hackfeld & Company. This company was seized as alien property during World War I, renamed American Factors, and now operates as diversified Amfac, Inc. Benjamin Dillingham, a nineteen-year-old mate on the Union

---

*At the time, any man who owned a vessel or could convince its owners of his competence could become a sailing ship's captain with no further formality. So his move from cook or captain on scows to ocean skipper was not too unusual. Until 1898 no license for any tonnage of sailing vessel was required of the shipmaster.

ship *Southern Cross* when it was captured and burned by a Confederate raider, was put ashore in Brazil in the early 1860s. In 1865, again a ship's officer, he came ashore at Honolulu, only to fall off a horse and break his leg. Seeing absolutely no logic in more of such adventuring, he happily watched his ship sail and stayed in the islands to build railroads and several businesses.

All these men were influential from their arrival; and their power increased as the proud Hawaiian monarchy, never able to cope with the outsiders or their governments, stumbled toward its sad end, little more than a century after its king and commoners had learned there *were* outsiders. The foreign companies were mostly merchants or sugar planters, but the real source of their strength lay at anchor in the harbors. Without ships, neither foreigners nor Hawaiians now could survive. So the companies bought and chartered ships, connived for space in ships they did not control, and lobbied in Hawaii's palace and Washington congressional halls to get more ships.

Sometimes they were successful. Steamers still were rarities in the Pacific in 1866, but one named the *Ajax* (the ship that brought Mark Twain to Hawaii) briefly attempted a regular California–Honolulu run. In 1867 the U.S. Post Office awarded a mail contract to the California, Oregon & Mexico Steamship Company, promising $75,000 a year for monthly service. By contrast, the first successful steamship service from San Francisco to Sydney did not come until 1871, when the paddle wheeler *Nevada* splashed down to Australia.

For Hawaii, however, steamers were not yet the complete answer. Coal for the round trip had to be carried from California. Whereas westbound cargoes frequently filled ships, eastbound trips too often were in ballast. Hawaii's first important export had been sandalwood to China, but that soon was exhausted. The islands had served as a transfer point for sperm oil from whalers to merchant ships, and produced some hides, tallow, rice, and coconuts, plus bananas and other tropical fruits that occasionally reached California in edible condition. By the 1870s some 31,000 tons of sugar were produced

annually; but the islands developed no other major exports until the advent of canned pineapple.*

Hence, most nineteenth-century Hawaiian trade moved in sailing vessels, many owned by plantations or agencies. Castle & Cooke, C. Brewer & Company, Alexander & Baldwin, Inc. and other firms operated fleets of varying sizes, several of which were combined into the Planters Line fleet at the turn of the century. (The Spreckels ships were exceptions.) Castle & Cooke sold its interest in several vessels to purchase 731 shares of the new line's stock. Brewer also was a large holder, as was Welch & Company, a San Francisco firm active in the Hawaiian trade.

These ships represented a comparatively small investment and could, upon need, wait days or weeks for eastbound cargo. More important, they really did not need to make a profit so long as they helped the owners to do so in their shoreside businesses. This anomaly was to confuse the whole Hawaiian shipping picture for a century, and does so today.

For years before 1876, island sugar planters had been urging a reciprocal trade treaty that would remove an American import duty on sugar of two cents per pound. In return, the kingdom was willing, just possibly at the suggestion of the merchants, to let American goods into Hawaii duty free and to allow establishment of a U.S. Navy coaling station at Pearl Harbor. Unfortunately for treaty advocates, Hawaiian bases and business meant little to American politicians or businessmen; and one of the latter, the influential and combative Claus Spreckels, was violently opposed. Spreckels had other sources for his California sugar refineries and already was looking to production of beet sugar. With others, he managed to hold off the treaty for a decade. A farmboy from Hanover, Germany, Spreckels had been successively an immigrant baker's helper, grocery owner, brewer, and sugar

---

*Fast ships and modern refrigeration have made possible increasing shipments of fresh pineapple and papaya in recent years, but in 1977 a shipping official reiterated, "If a thing can't be made of lava, coral, air or semitropical plants, then the chances are Hawaii must import it, or the things from which it is made."

refiner—and a winner in each of those fields. Signing of the 1876 reciprocity treaty represented a rare defeat; but the forty-eight-year-old "sugar king" reacted predictably by setting out immediately for Hawaii on the *City of San Francisco,* the ship that carried news of the treaty signing. Others had traveled to the islands to convert the heathen, to escape lives they didn't like, or to try for fortunes. Claus Spreckels went out to buy the place. In the next decade, he nearly succeeded.

For years, Boat Day automatically produced Honolulu celebrations complete with bands, flower leis, canoeists paddling around an arriving ship, and assorted noises. The news brought aboard the *City of San Francisco* increased the enthusiasm and racket, even among those who hadn't a clue about what the reciprocal treaty meant; but Spreckels wasted no time. He started buying sugar. For plantations that barely had survived lean years, this was dream stuff: a man who wanted the whole crop. Within three weeks, he had signed contracts for more than half of the 1877 sugar production.

The writers of a history of Castle & Cooke, Inc., credited that company with blocking Spreckels' effort to corner the market. The company sent a letter to plantations, saying:

"Mr. Claus Spreckels is in town. He is known in California as the sugar king and wishes to contract for the whole of the crop of 1877. So far he has expressed himself unwilling to take half of the plantations' sugar crop.

"It seems to us that if Mr. Spreckels is willing to take half . . . it might be best for the planters to compromise with him, but to give him the whole we cannot see the justice of the measure, either to our California or Oregon friends."

So Spreckels missed on his initial effort but on few other matters. Within two years, he had a lease on 20,000 acres of crown land on Maui and was digging an ambitious irrigation ditch from the slopes of Mount Haleakala to water the new sugar plantings. Samuel T. Alexander and H. P. Baldwin, operating the Haiku plantation almost next door to the Spreckels lease, had started a ditch to their property

somewhat earlier but had to rush it to completion when they discovered Spreckels would get certain of their water rights if they didn't.

Spreckels also bought land on the island of Hawaii and established a Honolulu sugar agency and other businesses, first with George H. MacFarlane, who was a Scottish aide-de-camp to King Kalakaua, and later with William G. Irwin. Details of the relations of Spreckels and his partners to the Hawaiian monarchy required many chapters in other histories.

Beginning in 1879, the California shipyard of Matthew Turner was kept busy building a Spreckels fleet of brigs, barkentines, and schooners: the *Claus Spreckels, John D. Spreckels, W. H. Dimond, Anna, W. G. Irwin, Consuelo, Selina, Emma Augusta,* and *Emma Claudina.* The Oceanic Steamship Company was incorporated in 1881, with John D. and Adolph B. Spreckels, sons of Claus, as principals. The 2,166-ton British steamer *Suez* was chartered for the year 1882, while two steamers were being built in the Cramp shipyard in Philadelphia on Oceanic's order. Thus, the family had a complete operation: its own sugar lands, agencies to buy sugar, ships to carry it, and the dominant refinery on the western mainland.

Persons who feuded with Spreckels (these were many) could get their supplies to Hawaii or ship their crops to the mainland via the island-owned Planters Line sailing vessels or the Pacific Mail Line steamers that had called at Honolulu since 1875 en route between San Francisco and Australia. Most of the whalers had vanished, thirty-three being destroyed in Arctic ice in 1871; but deepwater square-riggers of several nations still served the islands at their own convenience.

So Honolulu was reasonably served; Maui, as the center of the Spreckels and Haiku sugar operations, could attract enough ships, and even Kauai managed to get service. For a Johnny-come-lately in the shipping business, there were only a few small openings. William Matson on the three-masted schooner *Emma Claudina* slipped through one of them to Hilo on April 23, 1882.

The nature of his opportunity was indicated in

1953 in a pamphlet by C. J. Henderson, describing conditions that were general in the middle of the nineteenth century at outer-island plantations and mills. For the island of Hawaii, not much had changed by 1882. The pamphlet reads:

"Communication was by letter, labored in long hand, delivered, if at all, by a wandering missionary or a casual traveler. Currency was uncertain, dollars, pounds, pesos and script were exchanged as come by but always uncertainly because proper exchange rates were unknown. Supplies were optimistically ordered, often not delivered and sometimes damaged by salt water or below specifications. It took a long time to adjust a claim with a shrewd supplier six months away on the Atlantic Coast. If Honolulu seemed the end of the earth, Koloa on Kauai, Kohala on the island of Hawaii, as well as Lahaina and Haiku on Maui were like distant stars. . . . There were labor problems, mill parts performed badly, there was concern about the merits of cane species, costs of guano and manure. Financing was always difficult and so was the disposal of molasses. . . . shipping was of prime importance. Then as now, there was no local market for all the raw sugar produced, no regular scheduled shipping service. It was operated on a tramp basis in trades where the master's judgment dictated that the best cargoes could be found. If the China run looked more attractive than Hawaii's business, that's where the sea captain went."

Geography, volcanoes, and economics combined to delay development on the island of Hawaii. Agriculturists were reluctant to spend much effort or money in the shadows of volcanoes that had spewed lava down new channels seven times in less than forty years and frequently threatened to do it again. Too little rainfall on one part of the island and far too much elsewhere was discouraging. The island was off the main shipping lane from Honolulu to San Francisco; and its one large harbor, Hilo, lay on a treacherous coast, wide open to frequent storms and occasional tidal waves. Other tiny ports were so shallow that lighters were needed, as at Mahukona, or, like Kukuihaele, so precipitous that cargo could be handled only by overhead wire conveyors while a ship lay in an open roadstead.

No elaborate welcome was recorded when Captain Matson brought the *Emma Claudina* into Hilo for the first time, but obviously there was interest. His was a direct voyage from San Francisco, his general cargo not subject either to the delays or added costs of transshipment at Honolulu to tiny interisland vessels. Possible advantages of his operation were obvious, including the fact that eastbound cargo, what there was of it, might be delivered to the Pacific Coast at rates competitive with those charged Honolulu shippers. For importers of beans, tea, leather, and beer, as well as exporters of hides, fruit, and sugar, the prospects were pleasing, if only the shipmaster could be induced to come again, and regularly.

It wasn't much—just one small ship—but with luck Hilo could have its own bridge to the mainland. Not too surprisingly, Matson found local people willing to gamble with him against the seas and forbidding competition. Some of them got rich.

CHAPTER TWO

ONE SHIP TO A FLEET
(1882–1898)

Matson's early shipowning partnerships were short-term commitments, not unlike the one-voyage agreements under which fishing boat crews still trade their time and labor and bind themselves for a portion of the operating expenses in return for a share in the catch, if any. The *Emma Claudina* thus had numerous co-owners, but only Matson continued to invest and sail on each voyage.

He used the Oceanic Company's house flag and bills of lading, obviously getting much of his cargo through that company's agency; but he did not stay out of its way entirely. Four months after his first Hilo voyage in 1882, he loaded lumber at Eureka, California, and unloaded it at Kahului, Maui, the very center of the Spreckels operations. In a way, it was prophetic.

Hilo did remain his principal island port, however, and he served the Big Island's scattered plantations frequently. "My father," Mrs. Roth said, "used to do everything. He bought the horses, he bought needles, thread, mules, dress materials. . . . a floating store."

Business soon was good enough to require more cargo space. Matson chartered the bark *Julia Foard* and sent it down to Hilo in 1884, and the *Emma Claudina* continued to run through 1886. On November 6 of that year, the co-owners were George W. Chandler, three-eighths interest; William Matson, M. Mass, E. D. Allen, H. W. Jackson, and

Benjamin Sherburne, each with one eighth. John A. Scott, a Hilo district plantation manager, in 1910 remembered: "I first became acquainted with Captain Matson in 1884, he then being captain and owner [*sic*] of the schooner *Emma Claudina*. . . . Up to this time very little cargo was to be obtained [on the island of Hawaii, or Big Island] as very little sugar was produced in or shipped direct from Hilo.

"With the development of the Hilo plantations, the captain saw that he would require larger vessels . . . so he decided to place an order with Matthew Turner, shipbuilder . . . for the brigantine *Lurline,* which vessel was completed in the Spring of 1887. The captain induced several of his friends to take an interest with him in the vessel. It was then that I, along with C. C. Kennedy, joined him, and I have continued to have an interest with him in owning vessels that he or the Matson Navigation Company has bought or built up to the present day."

Matson could not wait for the *Lurline* so he chartered the schooner *John G. North* late in 1886 for at least one voyage. The brigantine *Selina,* chartered from the Oceanic Steamship Company, was unlucky. On her second voyage for Matson, she was becalmed off Paukaa, just north of Hilo, driven ashore by a heavy swell and wrecked on February 11, 1887. Miss Lillian Low, later to figure in Matson's personal life, was saved from a shipwreck at approximately the same time and place while en route to Hilo. Available records do not indicate whether it was the same ship.

The *Lurline,* of 389 gross tons and able to carry 640 tons of sugar, actually was built for the Spreckels family rather than for Matson, despite Scott's divergent memory. As with the *Emma Claudina,* however, the vessel was turned over to Matson upon completion.* Spreckels retained a one-third interest this time; Matson had one fourth, using his own or borrowed money; and Scott, Kennedy, and Captain Rock financed the remainder.

Peter Johnson, born at Hälsingborg, Sweden, about 175 miles from Matson's birthplace, had been first mate on the *John G. North* during her Matson charter and now was offered a job on the *Lurline.*

"When I got on the dock," he wrote in privately published *Memoirs,* "I met James Tyson, who was manager of the Charles Nelson Company, owners of the *North.* He told me I was making a big mistake and that I was first on the list to take command of a vessel. He also asked me if I had stopped to realize that Captain Matson had only one ship while the Nelson Company had a number. . . . someone would have to die before I could get a command in that [Matson] company. I replied that I would take my chances. . . .

"We [in the *Lurline*] loaded merchandise for Hilo; and the more I saw of Captain Matson the more I realized what a real man he was. He made friends wherever he went and was fair and just to them all. His two closest friends in Hilo were C. C. Kennedy and John A. Scott, both of whom were stubborn Scotsmen. Captain Matson had to use considerable diplomacy to keep them in line."

Matson's financial fortunes were improving, but he was less lucky in his personal life. Following a bitter divorce from his first wife, he married twenty-two-year-old Evadna M. Knowles, of San Mateo, on May 28, 1887, with the bride's brother and Walter D. K. Gibson, a business associate of Matson's, as

witnesses. The captain then was thirty-eight. A few weeks later, bride and groom sailed on the *Lurline*'s maiden voyage for their honeymoon. A Hilo newspaper reported: "The new brig *Lurline* came gaily sailing into the bay on Friday, the first instant [Friday, July 1, 1887] with flags flying and Captain Matson and his bride on board. She had all the appearance of a bridal yacht, as her hull was painted white and her sails were fresh and new, and a considerable amount of bunting flying."

Evadna Knowles Matson died at San Francisco on September 15, 1887. Until 1974, neither the current Knowles family nor Captain Matson's descendants were aware the marriage ever had occurred.

Captain Matson sailed the *Lurline* for another two years, but without complete satisfaction. Peter Johnson wrote: "After taking a load of sugar we sailed for San Francisco. About six hundred miles from port, we saw the smoke from a steamer approaching us and about nine that night she passed us. It was the Oceanic steamer *Zealandia.* Captain Matson and I were sitting on the bitt watching her when I noticed he became unusually quiet. After a while I asked him what he was thinking about but got no reply. Soon he swung around and said, 'I'll tell you what I was thinking. I was wondering whether I'd ever be able to run a steamship between the islands and San Francisco.' "

David Kanakeawe Richards, Sr., in 1941 told an interviewer: "Captain Matson borrowed me [in 1889] for one trip to be a cabin boy for him. . . . About two months later, we arrived back in Hilo. On that particular trip, Miss Low was one of the passengers. . . . I began to notice that Captain Matson was friendly with Miss Low [who] happened to be James L. Low's sister, and Mr. Low was head bookkeeper of the Hakalau plantation."

Captain Matson and Miss Lillian Low, twenty-five, were married on May 27, 1889. Lurline Matson, born in 1891, was their only child.

Mrs. Roth said: "My mother was a schoolteacher. . . . I think it probably was the plantation school at Hakalau. All those plantations had little private schools for children of the plantation people

---

*Matson sold the *Emma Claudina* late in 1887. She sailed for various owners until November 13, 1906, when she was wrecked off Moclips, Washington, the crew of eight escaping.

and the owners. . . . My mother was a dreadful
sailor. In those days they didn't have any seasickness
medicine. After they were married, my father never
took out another ship.''

Matson still operated with minimal organization,
such temporary or intermittent partners as he could
find, and ships he somehow could afford. The
twenty-year-old bark *Harvester,* of 754 tons, was the
third purchase. In 1891 she made a fourteen-day
run to Hilo with mixed cargo and four passengers.
There, Captain Peter Johnson (who really had not
needed to wait for somebody to die before he got a
command) had to lie four weeks, waiting for sugar.
''In those days,'' he wrote later, ''Hilo was a
mighty small place and I could have counted on my
two hands all the white people in town.''

Finally, the *Harvester* plowed back to San Francisco. Matson ordered a new deck, using, according
to Johnson, ''very green lumber, for when we got
into warmer weather the deck dried out and began
to leak. In spite of my precautions to keep it wet, it
still was leaking on the way home, so I nailed canvas over the sugar and put buckets and tubs around
to catch the water. We took 430 bags out of the
hold to the deck, drying it as best we could, sewing
up the bags and replacing them. On our arrival . . .
Captain Matson came aboard and I told him my
troubles. . . . we went forward to the main hatch,
and looking down the 'tween decks we could see
the sun shining through a seam in the deck. That
convinced him. He had the deck calked, made some
other repairs I suggested, and then I felt I had a
real ship under me.

''I made four trips in the *Harvester* that year. As
far as I could tell, the ship was in good condition,
but I was still a little doubtful about her timbers,
for whenever we would run into bad weather she
would leak. I had the carpenter and the men rip off
two planks of sheeting [*sic*] between wind and water
so that we could get a good look at her timbers. . . . After one look and feeling the timbers
with my hands, I told the carpenter to put the
sheeting back. I went to San Francisco [from
Oakland] immediately to tell Captain Matson what I

had found. He said to keep quiet and he would see
about selling the *Harvester* as soon as he could.''

Johnson did keep quiet, at least until dictating
his memoirs; but he was not yet free of the rotting
Harvester. After one trip on another ship, he took
the *Harvester* again to Hilo in midwinter, waited
nearly two months for sugar, and came back to San
Francisco in March to learn that Matson was making
an unusual deal: he would sell the ship to the
Alaska Improvement Company, a salmon packer, if
the firm would keep Johnson as her skipper, bypass-
ing captains in its own organization. ''Not one ship
owner in a thousand would care what became of the
captain if he wanted to sell a ship,'' said Johnson.
''That is one of many such things [I saw] Captain
Matson do in the years I was in his employ. No
wonder his employees were 100 percent loyal.''

The Alaska buyers finally agreed to the deal.
Johnson took the ship, which had normal accommodations for ten passengers, to Karluk Bay at the entrance to Cook Inlet in April with cannery supplies,
forty Chinese cannery workers, some foremen, and
forty-five fishermen. He found the bay in a snowstorm, later made a summer run to San Francisco
with a load of canned fish, then returned to pick
up the crews and more fish, sailing south in a
''boisterous'' October sea.

Still, the *Harvester* held together; but Johnson
left her in San Francisco, without regrets, to return
to Matson's employ. Astonishingly, the *Harvester*
continued to sail for another quarter century, disappearing on a voyage from Tonga in the South
Seas on November 4, 1920.

Coincidentally with Johnson's Alaska adventure,
Matson bought the iron bark *Annie Johnson* and
the steel bark *Santiago.* The *Annie*, of 1,409 tons,
already was famous. Built as the British ship *Ada
Iredale* in 1872, she had sailed from Scotland in
1876 with a load of coal for San Francisco. The coal
caught fire after the ship had cleared the Strait of
Magellan. Abandoning ship, the captain, his wife,
and twenty-three crewmen sailed 1,900 miles to the
Marquesas islands in lifeboats.

The ship drifted nine months with the cargo

afire. Taken in tow by the French gunboat *Seigne-lay,* it was beached at Tahiti, where the coal smoldered for another year. When the fire finally died, the hull was found to be sound and was sold by the French government for 2,000 francs to James Crawford & Company, San Francisco. Captain Ignatius Thayer went to Tahiti, recruited native workers, rerigged the ship, and sailed it to San Francisco. Crawford obtained American registry for the rebuilt vessel and renamed it the *Annie Johnson.* It was bought by Spreckels, who sold it to—who else? —Matson and partners. Peter Johnson, taking her on her first trip to Hilo, hurried to take off the main and forward hatches, ''as I was anxious to show off the ship to the two principal owners,'' John A. Scott and C. C. Kennedy.*

The *Santiago,* a nitrate carrier between Chile and England, was bought by Matson during what appears to have been his only return trip to Europe in thirty years. When the ship reached San Francisco, side ports were cut for easier sugar loading; later, some passenger accommodations were added. Johnson called her ''the trimmest little sailing ship I had ever seen.''

The *Annie* could carry twice as much cargo as any vessel Matson had used before, but other ships were also needed for the 1893 and 1894 seasons. Four were chartered, and one was bought in haste: the 1,060-ton, thirty-eight-year-old wooden bark *Sumatra,* which had been gathering barnacles and seaweed in San Francisco Bay for years. Matson paid only $1,170 but likely got no bargain. Records show she was scheduled to load coal in Puget Sound in

*A conflicting story of the *Annie Johnson* was told by Philip M. Thayer, of Honolulu, in a letter to Matson Vice-President Hugh Gallagher in 1960. Thayer wrote: ''As a result of the efforts of my grandfather, it was arranged between him and Captain Matson that Captain Matson would have a three-fourths ownership in the *Annie Johnson* as long as he lived and that my grandfather would have a one-fourth interest and that neither party could sell his interest as long as the other lived. I feel quite sure of my facts as I have heard these first hand from my grandfather, Captain Ignatius Elms Thayer, and from my father, Philip R. Thayer. I have neglected to mention that my grandfather, Captain Thayer, performed all the salvage work himself.'' No confirmation of such an agreement has been found.

October 1894 and that she did arrive at Honolulu in ballast from Hilo on October 16. There she was sold to a local shipping line, laid up, then broken up a year later. Adventures and misadventures of the ship and her crew in a month or two of Matson service can only be guessed.

The *Roderick Dhu,* another English-built iron ship, of 1,534 tons, was added to the Matson fleet in 1896. Although twenty-two years old, she was described as the fastest-sailing vessel in the Pacific. Matson's addition of a seagoing electric light and cold storage plant also made her among the most modern. According to Captain Johnson, the ship impressed passengers and island people, but her modern conveniences caused some problems. He wrote:

''On one trip leaving Hilo, we had quite a number of passengers, including Judge Gardner Wilder. . . . one morning Judge Wilder complimented us on the fresh fish that had been served, so I invited him to come down with me and look at our plant . . . for preserving them. The plant was in the forward part of the ship. I was very particular about not letting any warm air get in, so, after opening the door and lighting a candle, I immediately closed the door after us. We were both dressed in lightweight clothes and it was not long before we felt the cold. I went to the door to open it but—lo and behold—the door was locked from the outside. We spent all of two hours in the chamber, the candles had burnt out and we were groping and hoping for some place to thaw out. Meanwhile, we tried to keep happy by singing all the old songs we could think of. . . . [finally] the cook did come down . . . and we could hear him in the next compartment. After loud hammerings we made him hear us and he opened the door from the outside. . . .

''I tucked the judge into his berth and told him to stay there for a while. . . . I brought him some medicine: a square-faced bottle of gin from which I filled a tumbler, telling him to drink it all. This he did, and I went to my room and took the same dose, and then went to bed also. By five o'clock that evening, I got up, just a little dizzy but apparently all right. When I went to see the judge, he thought that with another dose he would be all right.''

Johnson had other refrigeration problems. ''During all those trips,'' he wrote, ''the cold storage and electric plant behaved but my gasoline engine continued to balk and almost drove me crazy. . . . I was no engineer. . . . There was a man put aboard to teach me one trip, but he was so seasick . . . that he was no use to me. . . . What made me so mad was that after fiddling around with that engine, suddenly it would go, running smoothly as a top, and I wouldn't have the slightest idea what I had done to it. . . .

''From Hilo, I wrote to Captain Matson that I was finished with gasoline engines. [Later] he asked me what I would suggest and I told him to put in a steam engine. When I left San Francisco I had a steam engine to run the cold storage and electric plants. It meant that we had to keep up steam in the donkey boiler continuously [but] consequently we had steam power for the handling of the sails . . . which added to the speed of handling them and to the speed of the ship.''*

The *Roderick Dhu* averaged ten days from San Francisco to Hilo and once made it in nine days and three hours, dock to dock. The old *Harvester* had averaged seventeen days, and the *Santiago* usually needed fifteen.

A friend of C. C. Kennedy described Hilo arrivals of Matson ships: ''I got this story from Mr. C. C. Kennedy, also from Mr. John A. Scott, long-time associates of Captain Matson in his shipping ventures when I believe the so-called Matson ships were owned separately and in shares. Whenever the *Roderick Dhu* or the others arrived in Hilo Bay, Mr.

Kennedy and Mr. Scott always made haste to go out and 'greet the captain'; but the real purpose of their visit was to get hold of the manifest and see what the freight money amounted to.''

New ships permitted Matson to sell the smaller *Lurline* to the Hawaiian Commercial Company, a Spreckels firm, in 1896. The sale was beautifully timed. The brigantine left San Francisco late in the year, fought adverse winds for twenty-three days getting to Kahului, and unloaded her cargo of mixed merchandise and hay just in time to be caught at the dock in a raging gale and five-inch rainstorm on December 6. Driven ashore when a hawser parted, she was pulled off ten days later and towed to Honolulu by an interisland steamer that collected $5,000 for the salvage job.

The little vessel sailed for various owners in the next eighteen years but ran out of luck in 1915 while hauling railroad ties from Eureka, California, to Salina Cruz, Mexico. This time a storm at sea seriously disabled her. The steamer *Panaman* rescued the crew and took the *Lurline* in tow but had to cut her loose when the weather worsened.

Four days later, the U.S.S. *Annapolis* reported sighting the *Lurline*, with her lower mast still standing but her rudder gone. Eight months after that, the *San Francisco Commercial News* carried a Honolulu item saying that the *Lurline* had been sighted again, this time by the Japanese steamer *Komi Maru* in latitude 15°20′, longitude 109° west. This would mean that the derelict had been drifting almost due west, but very slowly. The value of this report suffers somewhat in that no ship named the *Komi Maru* was listed in Lloyd's Register of Shipping for the pertinent years.

The late Hugh Gallagher wrote in Matson publications that the ship had been sighted a third time—two years later and thousands of miles south, ''off Fernandos Donderos, near the Strait of Magellan.'' Unfortunately, he left no record of his source for that information; and no place named ''Fernandos Donderos'' appears in the sailing directions for South America or available encyclopedias. The island Juan Fernandez, site of Alexander

*Johnson's problems with cold storage would not have impressed the skipper of the brig *John D. Spreckels,* also in the Hawaii trade at the time but boasting no such modern gadgets. On one trip from the islands to San Francisco, one R. Ziegler, a passenger, died while the *John D. Spreckels* was still five days from port. The widow Ziegler would not allow burial at sea, so the desperate crew disemboweled the corpse and delivered it ashore—filled with sugar as a preservative.

Selkirk's marooning and the prototype for Robinson Crusoe's fictional island, lies off Valparaiso, Chile, more than 1,000 miles from the Strait of Magellan. Ocean currents in that area, however, run south to north, so a two-year drift in the opposite direction stretches credulity. Hard though it may be on the romantic history of the sea, the story doesn't hold water as well as the sound hull of the old *Lurline* kept it out. Too bad.

Operations of Matson ships to Hawaii were barely newsworthy in the last decade of the nineteenth century. Those islands were rocked with political upheavals leading inexorably to the kingdom's downfall; while offshore, powerful steamship companies wrestled for dominance of the whole Pacific Ocean, with Hawaii no more than a pawn in the larger struggles.

The Pacific Mail Steamship Company, which had been running steamers from Panama and Nicaragua to California since the gold rush, did put the steamer *Costa Rica* on the San Francisco–Hawaii run briefly in 1873 but gave up when the ship ran ashore and was badly damaged. The real prize, however, was the promising passenger and freight business between San Francisco and Australia/New Zealand and a healthy $210,000 annual subsidy that went with it. The *Nevada*, in 1871, was followed by sister ships *Nebraska* and *Dakota*. In 1875, Pacific Mail, already operating from California to the Orient under the U.S. mail subsidy, received a similar contract from the New Zealand government for South Pacific service.

This it attempted with several vessels, finally chartering the British steamships *Australia* and *Zealandia*, each of 2,737 tons. They did a good passenger business, carrying British colonists to the Antipodes and giving settlers a pleasant route back to England for holidays.

In 1883, the two 3,000-ton steamers ordered by the Oceanic line went into service between San Francisco and Honolulu. The *Mariposa*, arriving at Honolulu July 31, had on board, among others, Mr. and Mrs. Claus Spreckels, also a Mrs. Samuel Roth and four children. The youngest, William P. Roth,

would become Matson Navigation Company's third president years later. The ship was met by celebrating crowds, bands, salutes from a shore battery, and innumerable flowery speeches. J. D. and Adolph Spreckels, owners of the vessel, also were in evidence. The *Alameda* arrived on October 22 with less uproar but set a record the next March by lifting 2,990 tons of cargo, the largest load ever taken from the islands in one vessel.

The Spreckels brothers, however, had other things in mind for these ships. Pacific Mail's ten-year subsidy for the South Pacific service ended in 1885. A British group using the same vessels took over, but the Spreckels contrived a neat confrontation early in 1886. Fifty-two hours after the *Zealandia* left San Francisco for Sydney, the brothers dispatched the *Alameda* on the same route. The *Alameda* got there first by thirteen hours.

That was enough for the British operators, who quickly sold their two vessels to Oceanic, which promptly resold them to William G. Irwin, who equally quickly sold both to a John S. Walker, who secured Hawaiian registry for them and just as promptly chartered them to Oceanic. These merry-go-round maneuvers accomplished one purpose: the slow *Australia* and *Zealandia* now could operate from Hawaii (home country) to California. Rivals with American flag steamers could gnash their teeth at this breach of a comfortable little monopoly, but only to the advantage of their dentists. U.S. laws specified that foreign flags could serve the United States only from their own countries. In all, the Hawaiian monarchy gave registry to some 700 foreign vessels, qualifying them for the run to the United States; but this was the first instance of giving the Hawaiian flag to foreign steamers.

The *Alameda* and *Mariposa* were sent on the Antipodes run in 1890, with intermediate stops at Hawaii and a new $210,000 subsidy. The only blot on this painting was the insistence of the New Zealand and Australian governments that the Union Steamship Line, Ltd., of New Zealand, have a part as a joint venture. The Union management chartered the British liner *Arawa;* and the three-ship

Top Left: William Matson as a very young man. Date and place unknown.

Bottom Left: William Matson about 1882.

Below: Captain William Matson as a ship line owner.

Consul General Matson opening the Swedish Pavilion at San Francisco's 1915 Exposition.

William Matson as an amateur race driver. (Courtesy of the National Maritime Museum, San Francisco)

Commodore Peter Johnson assists William Matson down the gangplank from the S.S. *Maui* on her maiden voyage. Honolulu, 1916.

Right: The scow schooner *Annie Maria.* "Rugged, square-ended, broad of beam, and shallow of hold," these were hard-working craft. (Courtesy of the National Maritime Museum, San Francisco)

Below: The scow schooner *James McKenna* becalmed up-river with a load of hay. Matson served as cook and later as skipper on these picturesque vessels. (Courtesy of the National Maritime Museum, San Francisco)

Top: Honolulu Harbor just before the turn of the century.

Middle: Hilo, "a very small place," about 1904.

Left: Sailing vessels in Hawaii. A few of the more than 1,600 vessels that visited Honolulu in the fourteen years beginning 1823.

Above: The brigantine *Lurline,* first
of five Matson vessels so named,
entering San Francisco Bay.
(Courtesy of the National Maritime
Museum, San Francisco)

Right: The first *Lurline* docking at a
San Francisco sugar refinery.
(Courtesy of the National Maritime
Museum, San Francisco)

Above Left: The bark *Annie Johnson.* As the British bark *Ada Iredale* she drifted, abandoned and on fire, for most of a year before being towed into Tahiti. Purchased by Matson in 1895, she sailed under his flag for 31 years.

Above Right: The full-rigged iron ship *Falls of Clyde* was a Matson vessel 1897–1906. She was returned to Honolulu in 1968 and restored as a museum ship.

Left: Chinese cannery hands gamble on the fo'c's'le head as the wooden bark *Harvester* tows out of Cook Inlet, Alaska. Early 1890s. (Courtesy of the National Maritime Museum, San Francisco)

service continued until 1901, except for part of 1898 when the U.S. vessels were used briefly as troopships.

Mrs. R. L. Holman, of Los Angeles, in 1956 wrote to the Matson Navigation Company:

"With mingled thots and feelings I have been reading the last few days of the launching of the new *Mariposa.* Sixty-three years ago, in March, 1893, I was a passenger on the old *Mariposa,* coming from New Zealand to Chicago. . . . My parents and a brother and sister accompanied me.

"I was ten years old at the time but I can remember the voyage very clearly. My home [in New Zealand] was in Dipton, a small town. . . . We sailed first from 'The Bluff' and it took about a week to reach Auckland. The *Mariposa* had come on from Sydney. In about another week we arrived at Samoa and the *Mariposa* dropped anchor about a mile away from the island on account of the coral reefs. Robert Louis Stevenson and his wife got off there. I saw him and a lot of native canoes with native musicians, some native women wearing blue Mother Hubbard dresses. The *Mariposa* brought some native Samoans to the World's Fair. . . . I saw them sitting around on mats in the hold one day when my dad and I went down there. . . .

"I have the passenger list here, and the first name is 'Duchess of Buckingham & Maid.' Farther down is 'Mr. and Mrs. R. L. Stevenson.'"

Events ashore in Hawaii in the 1890s were more confused than anything at sea. Claus Spreckels' political power in the islands had declined by the late 1880s, and so had his power in his own family. Two sons, C. A. (Gus) and Rudolph, gained control of the Hawaiian Commercial & Sugar Company after filing suit against their father for various financial irregularities. The brothers promptly fired William G. Irwin & Company (once Spreckels & Irwin) as the plantation's Honolulu agency, hiring Hackfeld & Company in its place.

Four years later, in 1898, J. B. Castle, a member of the missionary-trader family but not then involved with Castle & Cooke, Inc., secretly obtained enough options to gain control of the Hawaiian Commercial & Sugar Company. These he traded to Alexander & Baldwin for a one-fourth interest in that company. Rudolph and Gus Spreckels, who had sold most of the options without recognizing what was happening, realized large profits but were tossed out of the company.

The Spreckels internal battles affected Matson less than might have been expected. The captain's particular family friends were John D. and Adolph, who owned the Oceanic line as well as J. D. Spreckels & Company, the shipping and commission firm that handled Matson business in San Francisco. Irwin continued to represent Oceanic and occasionally Matson in Honolulu.

The creaking Hawaiian monarchy fell on January 17, 1893, in an almost bloodless revolt—one policeman was shot. A provisional government composed mostly of American-born immigrants or their descendants took over and after eighteen months set up the Republic of Hawaii. Robert W. Wilcox, a part-Hawaiian who had been educated in an Italian military academy at the expense of the old monarchy, then organized a brief royalist insurrection; but this was put down with a few casualties. The republic's courts imposed some death sentences and long prison sentences on the insurrectionists; but no one was executed, and even Wilcox was jailed only briefly.

By a joint resolution of Congress, Hawaii was annexed as a U.S. territory on July 7, 1898, despite objections from many Hawaiians. For two years, however, the government operated without precise definitions of its powers, pending passage of an organic bill for the new territory. Although the congressional resolution had specified that the United States would be responsible for all Hawaiian international relations, the republic's consulates at San Francisco and Seattle continued to operate.

Like many shipowners, Captain Matson was primarily concerned with ship registrations. As early as 1897 several of these gentlemen were maneuvering to get more vessels under the Hawaiian flag, in the correct belief that such ships might end up with American colors under a blanket acceptance when and if the islands were annexed. This was vital. American registration of foreign vessels ordinarily was possible only when they were rebuilt in U.S. yards; foreign vessels could not (and still cannot) carry cargo or passengers between U.S. ports, which soon would include Hawaii.

Three of Matson's British-built ships already were safely under U.S. or Hawaiian flags; but his worry was the *Falls of Clyde,* built in Scotland and, at 266 feet in length, larger than anything in the Matson or Oceanic sailing fleets. A series of letters from Walter D. K. Gibson, of San Francisco, Matson's best man at his second wedding and an official of J. D. Spreckels & Company, unfolded the drama, bit by bit. They were written to Walter M. Giffard in Honolulu. On December 20, 1898, Gibson wrote:

"Another good Bristol [first-class condition] ship in which yours truly expects to be interested one of these days has been granted an Hawaiian provisional register in the name of Arthur M. Brown and will proceed to your port in a week or so for a permanent register. She is a fine four-master and ought to carry over three thousand tons of sugar. . . . You will understand that Matson is largely interested in this vessel but it must not be known on any account, at least for the present, that anyone is interested in her except Brown. . . . The name of the ship is *Falls of Clyde.*"

Eleven days later ("per *Falls Clyde*"), he added: "The bearer leaves for your port tomorrow, consigned to your good firm, and I trust may have a speedy run over. . . . Captain Matson has written you per '*Alameda*' and has suggested that the vessel be measured as soon as possible after arrival, in order that there may be the least delay should she be refused the flag."

There was reason for worry. The ship registration question had become sticky in 1897 when George MacFarlane (the onetime partner of Claus Spreckels) bought the British steamship *China.* The Hawaiian Republic's collector of customs refused the vessel

registration on the basis that MacFarlane was not a citizen of Hawaii and that the ship actually was controlled by C. P. Huntington and the Pacific Mail steamship line. MacFarlane sued, won in court, and subsequently registered the ships *Barracouta* and *Himalaya;* but the conflict was out in the open.

The system of obtaining temporary Hawaiian ship certificates from the republic's overseas consulates, these to be replaced by permanent papers when the ship first reached the islands, was well established; but shortly after July 1898 the executive branch of the Hawaiian government specifically told Charles Wilder and John C. Carter, Hawaiian consuls at San Francisco and Seattle, respectively, to write no more temporary registrations.

Obviously, these gentlemen did not hear well. They granted provisional certificates not only to the *Falls of Clyde* in late autumn but also to the *Star of Russia, Star of Italy,* and *Willscott.*

Arriving in Honolulu in December, A. M. Brown "resumed his duties as police chief of the country," according to a newspaper account, and averred that indeed he had a temporary registration for the *Falls,* which he personally had bought from a British firm with funds borrowed from John Buck, an investor in sugar plantations, at 5 percent interest. On January 23, 1899, he filed a writ of mandamus on the collector to force issuance of a permanent registration and testified that he was the vessel's owner, "and no one else is involved, directly or indirectly, in the ship nor do they come in for a share of the profits in any way."

Not everyone was impressed. Brown's note to Buck had been endorsed over to William Matson, and insurance on the vessel was payable to him as security for it. More to the point, the *Falls* had come back to Honolulu on January 20 under command of Captain Charles Matson, senior skipper of the Matson line, but not a relative of the owner.

Henry Cooper, the Hawaiian minister of foreign affairs, wrote to Wilder in San Francisco: "I am at a loss to account for your actions in regard to issuing of provisional certificates for foreign-built vessels. Your instructions prohibiting your issuing of such documents were certainly most explicit. . . . You are therefor positively forbidden to issue provisional registers to any vessel unless specifically authorized by me to do so. Any failure to observe this injunction will forfeit your position."

Wilder's reply, if any, has not survived; but the battle went on. Gibson wrote that Matson was in Washington "making a fight for the *Clyde*" in February. One of the early acts of the U.S. president in relation to Hawaii's new status as a territory was to forbid, on September 18, 1899, any further registration of vessels by Hawaii. The Organic Act, specifying what was to be the territorial government in 1900, first read: "All vessels carrying Hawaiian registers immediately prior to the transfer of sovereignty . . . shall be registered as American vessels."

When the act finally emerged from a Senate committee, however, this section read: "All vessels carrying Hawaiian registers on August 12, 1898, together with the following vessels claiming Hawaiian registry, *Star of France, Euterpe, Star of Russia, Falls of Clyde* and *Willscott,* shall be entitled to be registered as American, etc."

The record does not show just who did what, whether MacFarlane, Matson, Police Chief Brown, or the intractable Consul Wilder; but the *Falls of Clyde* and the others were safely under the Stars and Stripes. The *Falls* arrived in Hilo in June, carrying "616 bbls flour, 21 pkgs beer, 1,714 lbs sugar, 301 cs canned goods, 77 cs caps and hats, 2,382 ctls barley, 45 ctls wheat, 48 pkgs paints and oils, 157 pkgs groceries/provisions, 80 sacks middlings, 815 bales hay, 6,578 lbs bread, 70,162 ft lumber, 480 lbs lard, 1,080 sacks bran, 26 bales dry goods, 2,745 lbs cracked corn, 395 lbs hops, 1,083 lbs tobacco, 320 tons fertilizer, 200 bbls and 850 sacks lime, 11 tons coal, 20 cases whiskey, 18 cases boots and shoes, 7 rolls leather, 56 ctls corn, 20 cases drugs, 55 cases soap, 20 cases hardware, 3 tanks acid, 109 coils rope, 500 lbs dried fruit, 4 cases honey, 67 bbls salt, 1,688 lbs soda, 25 mules, 207 lbs cheese, 25 reels wire, 474 lbs codfish, 1 cow, 12 sacks potatoes, 28,789 lbs beans, 15 cases + 26 bbls salmon, 10 cases candles, 781 lbs butter, 15 cases meal, 500 lbs peas, 100 lbs tea, 10 crates onions."

She also carried William Matson, Lillian Low Matson, the child Lurline Matson, and eleven other passengers. Freight was valued at $44,211.84.

The vessel had cost Brown $25,000, according to his figures; and another $15,000 had been spent to change her rigging from ship to bark, to install a deckhouse and charthouse, and to rearrange passenger quarters. Just what Brown actually gained from his connection with the ship remains unclear. Correspondence indicates that he was shipped a horse on one voyage and a cow on another; but with those entries, he disappears from Matson records.

FROGS, OIL, AND QUAKES
(1898–1907)

Cholera in Honolulu interdicted interisland travel in 1895, and bubonic plague in early 1900 was much worse. Most of the Chinese section of Honolulu burned when spot fires in infected buildings got away from the fire fighters. Again, travelers and goods from Honolulu were barred from the other islands. Cut off, Hilo residents ordered so many emergency supplies from San Francisco that the *Falls of Clyde* could carry only part of them. Gibson wrote that Matson "has also chartered three schooners at a loss to him in order to accommodate the Hilo people." The Matson sailing fleet also was enlarged by purchases of the forty-four-year-old iron bark *Antiope*, and the iron sailing ships *Marion Chilcott* and *Monterey*, the last later being reduced to a barge.

Despite plague and other upsets, the Hilo trade was thriving. In the autumn of 1900 the *Roderick Dhu* delivered twenty vacuum pans, each weighing six and one half tons, for a new sugar mill on the Olaa plantation; and the *Annie Johnson, Santiago*, and *Falls of Clyde* were needed to carry the rest of its machinery. The *Falls* lifted $245,724 worth of sugar on an eastbound trip; and on a run to Hilo the ship had a full list of passengers, a large cargo of groceries, twenty-five Berkshire hogs, and a new launch for use of the Matson port people. Her name: *Lurline*.

In *Santiago*, Captain Peter Johnson had cargo of a different sort on one trip. Mrs. Roth, in 1974, remembered: "My maternal grandfather, who had been divorced for many years, off and on lived with us. He always went in for fads, which drove my father crazy, just crazy. After a while, Grandfather would be encouraged to find another place to live. Now, he had a friend—I think his name was Marchand—who owned a French restaurant in Oakland. They had these regular French frogs. Mr. Marchand gave my grandfather some of them and we put them in a pond at our place across the bay. We had this house near Mills College because my father had bronchitis and the air across the bay was good for him. . . . He couldn't sleep nights because of those frogs. . . . They were wonderful frogs, good to eat, but they made an awful lot of noise. I think Grandfather got orders to get rid of the frogs, so one of the captains took them down to Hilo and put them in the river. . . . That's where the famous Hilo frogs came from."

In his *Memoirs*, Johnson remembered details differently. He wrote: "Before we left Hilo, the two fish commissioners . . . called on me and wanted to know if I could bring down some live frogs . . . and I promised to get them. . . . We arrived in San Francisco on a Sunday and Captain Matson invited my wife and me to lunch. . . . His father-in-law,

Mr. Low, was building a frog pond, which reminded me of my promise. . . . Mrs. Matson said she knew a woman who lived in the foothills above Hayward who had some. . . . After I told the woman what I wanted, she asked what I was going to do with them.

"I told her I was taking them to Hilo. . . . She then wanted to know where Hilo was. . . . She inquired how to get there. I said, 'In a ship,' at which she held up her hands in horror, telling me that although she was raising frogs, she would not sell them to go way out in the ocean. She added that it would be a crime to let me take them to those faraway islands, that they would probably die after they got there, and I would not take care of them well enough to get them there alive. I suggested that if she gave me full instructions . . . I could deliver them safely but I could not vouch for their continued health after their arrival. Finally she decided to risk it, and the next day she sent me two dozen frogs in a large whiskey barrel with a gunny sack covering the top. . . .

"We made a fine trip of thirteen days and delivered all the frogs but one—a sacrifice to a large Newfoundland dog on board. His constant watch on the tempting barrel was rewarded by one frog, who put his nose through the gunny sack one day and promptly got eaten for his curiosity. After landing the remaining twenty-three frogs, they were distributed in stagnant pools around Hilo. [Johnson did not specify the date of the shipment, but he commanded the *Santiago* only from late 1894 to 1897.]

"Their former owner needed to have had no fear, for they did thrive, multiplying very rapidly. There was one place that seemed especially suitable for them, on the Wailoa River. I would give a native boy or girl a gunny sack and a lantern, and for a reward of ten cents he would fill up the bag with frogs. . . .

"In 1902, when I arrived in San Francisco on the S.S. *Rosecrans,* among the various items in the cargo were twenty-four hundred dozen frogs. This was Saturday and on Sunday morning the papers had a front page item on my unusual cargo, with the number of frogs given as twenty-four thousand dozen. Monday morning on my way down to the ship, I stopped to buy some candy at a little store at the foot of Market Street. The young lady in the store seemed quite excited . . . and said her aunt had been in that morning looking for me. . . . I found that it was from this aunt that I had bought my frogs a few years before. . . .

"So we continued the shipping of frogs to the different leading restaurants and also to Paladini, the dean of the fish market. But we flooded the market and the price went down until there was no more profit in it for the Hilo shippers—from two dollars a dozen to thirty-five cents a dozen.

"The frog industry became almost extinct later, for the government filled up all the stagnant pools in the Hilo district. Today they are a luxury in the islands."

Pacific Ocean shipping changed rapidly at the turn of the century. The Spanish-American War and annexation of Hawaii recolored political maps and shifted lines of commerce. The Oceanic Steamship Company's joint operation with Union of New Zealand ended, since the New Zealand vessels no longer could run on the Hawaii–California route, even though Union's 3,000-ton *Moana* had provided the only civilian steamer service between those points during the war under a temporary suspension of regulations.

Union substituted Vancouver, British Columbia, for San Francisco as a northern terminal and began an active campaign with Canadian railroads and British ships on the Atlantic for the home-to-Britain trade from the Antipodes. Oceanic lost its mail contract but finally received another from the U.S. government by ordering three new, 6,000-ton, 17-knot steamers, the *Ventura, Sierra,* and *Sonoma,* which took over the Australia run in 1900–1901. The older *Mariposa* and *Alameda* were shifted to the San Francisco–Hawaii route and a new, subsidized service from San Francisco to Tahiti. The *Australia* and *Zealandia,* older and slower still, were retired. The *Australia* was chartered to the imperial Russian government as a troop transport in 1905 during the Russo-Japanese War and promptly was captured by the Japanese, who scrapped her at Osaka in 1912, without so much as a by-your-leave to the owners. The *Zealandia,* sold to a New York firm and converted to a freighter, survived German attacks during World War I but grounded on Mersey Bar, Liverpool, in 1917, and broke in half.

In six winter months of 1900–1901, Matson sent six ships down to Hilo, including the *Santiago* with thirty-three Portuguese to work in a sugar mill. The captain "fitted up a house on deck for their accommodation." Competition, however, was growing rapidly. During 1900, Hilo logged in 576 vessels from mainland or foreign ports: 203 steamers, 373 sailing ships. Included were 406 American bottoms (including those formerly registered as Hawaiian), 107 English, 24 Japanese, 14 German, 8 Norwegian, 3 French, 3 Italian, and 1 Chilean. Nationalities of the other 10 were not recorded, or someone counted wrongly.

Matson had three paramount needs: new and bigger ships, preferably steamers; a firm organization to handle them; and a steady source of funds to replace hit-or-miss financing for individual ships or single voyages.

An unsupported story is related in a biography of San Francisco banker William H. Crocker:

"As this story has been handed down, the veteran master mariner, Captain William Matson, wanted to start his own shipping company and needed more money than he possessed to do so. Accordingly, he came to the Crocker-Woolworth National Bank and stated his case. Will Crocker listened, asked some searching questions, then arose and requested his caller to come with him. Walking downstairs, he swung open the heavy doors to the gold vault and, pointing within, said, 'Well, Captain, there it is. Take what you need.' "

Whether anything this dramatic ever happened is debatable, but Crocker did begin to share in Matson financing at about this time. When the company was incorporated in 1901, directors were A. B.

Spreckels, N. Ohlandt, and J. A. Buck, partners in a San Francisco company (Buck being the same man who figured in the *Falls of Clyde* affair); Walter D. K. Gibson; C. H. Daly; Henry St. Goar, a partner in E. Pollitz & Company brokerage firm in San Francisco; and attorney A. F. Morrison. Contemporary newspaper accounts in Hawaii listed capitalization at $1.5 million, but company or official records which could confirm the figure were lost in the San Francisco fire.

Captain Matson, reasonably, was president. Crocker was not mentioned then but was listed as one of twenty stockholders in 1910, when the company also acknowledged a debt of $60,000 owed to the Crocker bank.

For all their advantages, corporations tend to color individuals in monochrome so that the inventor of a camera, the pathfinding airplane pilot, or the intrepid seaman becomes indistinguishable from the bankers, attorneys, and accountants allied with him. This fate, however, never even threatened William Matson. The most casual examination of company literature—reports to stockholders, correspondence, memoirs of employees—reveals the imprint of the man on the company rather than the reverse.

Quotations tell the story: "The best-dressed captain I ever saw"; "He always drove a fine horse"; "I never saw him without a carnation in his buttonhole"; "He could see farther than any man I ever met and I admired him tremendously for it"; "always paid his men five dollars a month more than any other ship on the Pacific Coast"; "In return for good treatment he expected a full day's work. . . . the food on the *Lurline* was better than any other ship on the Pacific"; "On the ships, we always said the seven stars in the Matson flag meant 'work seven days a week.' "

Captain John Diggs, speaking of a later period, described what likely was a continuing situation: "It was Captain Matson, the owner; he ran everything. There was just a tiny office. You know, Captain Matson was not very careful in his language. He'd be dictating a letter to a man . . . he'd call him an S.O.B. and everything else . . . but he had a secretary who would just type the important part and make it a real polished letter. He [the captain] would never read it, just sign.''

Many a waterfront tale tends to dry up and blow away if examined too closely, but there is some supporting evidence for the theory that Matson did not bother to read his own letters. One fascinating surviving letter dated October 11, 1901, is addressed to ''W. Griffith, Esq.,'' Honolulu, and reads:

I sent on the *Annie Johnson* two cases of wine, one case of claret and one case of white wine. Please accept same with my compliments. Very sorry I did not have a chance to see you while you were up here but I was so busy I did not have time to get around. Hope you are well and the trip will benefit you.

We are having a picnic here in the oil business. I do not know how it will turn out but there is a chance we will enter the oil carrying business.

Yours very truly,
Wm. Matson

There is only one trouble with the letter, as explained in another sent a month later. The first had been intended for Walter M. Giffard, with whom Matson had been well acquainted for years; but it had been returned for improper addressee's name. To the captain's credit, his explanation and apology indicted no one else for the mistake in names. Nothing was said then or later about what became of the two cases of wine.

The ''picnic in the oil business'' definitely was under way, coincidentally with the acquisition of new ships. In 1901 Matson realized his dream of owning a steamer by purchasing the 2,675-ton, coal-fired *St. George* (built in England in 1882 as the *Ehrenfels*) and renaming her the *Enterprise.*

He did not spell out his reasons for converting her to the Pacific's first oil-burning steamer, but he did so after talking with Captain John Barneson, a Scottish clipper ship captain and natural proselytist. Barneson had sailed the South Pacific and had come ashore to drool over the California supplies of fuel oil that had been known since Indians used the crude in basketry. The state production in 1900 was

about 9,000 barrels a year. As skipper of the transport *Arizona* and superintendent of transports for the U.S. government at San Francisco during the Spanish-American War, Barneson had tried unsuccessfully to convince both the U.S. Navy and civilian shipowners of the advantages of oil for fuel at sea. His theory: ''Three and a half barrels of petroleum can do the work of one ton of coal. You can buy oil from thirty to sixty cents a barrel while coal costs an average of seven dollars a ton. It is high time to make a change.''

Matson agreed. Fuel tanks and oil burners under the boilers were simple to install and created invaluable advantages in deadweight, space, cleanliness, and reduced manpower needs. The *Enterprise,* used on a Panama–California run before joining the Hilo-bound fleet, trailed oil fumes instead of coal smoke; and a new age in Pacific shipping had begun. Official recognition of the revolution, however, was slow to come. The *Enterprise* had to make three trips to the islands before Matson could obtain a change in government requirements that every steamship must have a crew of coal passers. During those trips the coal passers rode but had no coal to pass.

Matson also realized that oil could be a boon to Hawaiian plantations and sugar mills then using imported coal, wood, or locally grown cane fiber as industrial fuel. To this end, he constructed oil storage tanks at Honolulu and began converting his sailing ships from general cargo vessels to tankers—the *Santiago, Roderick Dhu, Falls of Clyde, Marion Chilcott,* and *Monterey,* now reduced to a barge. The steamer *Rosecrans,* built in 1883 as the *Methven Castle* for passenger service between England and South Africa and later used as the military transport *Columbia,* was purchased and also converted to an oil tanker.

Captain Peter Johnson, who had managed the neat trick of getting an unrestricted license to operate any ship in any ocean without ever having been to sea in a steamer, took the *Rosecrans* to Alaska and through 600 miles of ice floes to Nome with a cargo of fuel oil, kerosene, black powder, and dynamite, and was as happy as a boy with a new bicycle.

"The *Rosecrans*," he said, "had been built for a passenger steamer . . . the conversion left us ample room for my family, besides four spare staterooms which we managed to fill up with guests, for Captain Matson never objected to my taking friends on the trips."

In 1902 and 1903, the *Rosecrans* made two more Alaskan trips, sandwiching runs from Alameda Point to Honolulu between the subarctic adventures. Meanwhile, the sailing tankers were running steadily to the islands, stopping at Hilo and sometimes at Honolulu. Captain Charles Brocas remembered: "They'd pump those vessels full until their decks were awash. The waists were full of water all the way down. They really cracked on [sail]. You couldn't *buy* a job on those ships. There were a few old-timers left in sail and they liked the jobs. Nothing to do, you know, just set the sails and go."

If sailing with a ship full of bunker oil was simple, the rest of the oil business provided all necessary contrasts. Captain Matson is credited by several writers as having said, "If you use fuel oil in large quantities you must control the source." Certainly he proceeded on that basis, involving himself, his friends, and his shipping company in enough complications to satisfy the most devious modern builder of conglomerates.

His first recorded shoreside oil operations were with partners Crocker, Irwin, and Buck in a corporate frame known as the Western Union Oil Company, which in 1901 built a forty-five-mile pipeline from the pioneer Santa Maria oil field near the California town of that name to Alcatraz Landing at Gaviota, where most of the Matson oil-carrying ships loaded. The captain himself commuted to the oil field and was accustomed to riding horseback on inspections.

Mrs. Roth, born in 1891, was her father's confidante from an early age and shared his interests. Horses, she said, "were his big love. All the Swedish captains were crazy about horses. I always thought it a little strange until I went back to see where my father was born. Most of the places those Swedish captains had lived, or were born, were a little bit in the interior, inland say ten miles, because the seacoast is so rough. That's all agriculture, of course, and they all had horses in their youth. We were always horse poor. Father used to park horses with all the sea captains because we always had too many and mother didn't think we should—so the captains always got a horse to park in their back yards. My father used to drive them in trotting races, amateur races with a sulky. . . . It got so that my mother wouldn't let me go to an auction with him because I baited him and we always came home with a couple of horses we didn't need. . . .

"He was determined. He used to go down to the oil fields; and the man who owned all the land, a Spanish gentleman, said to him this day, 'Captain Matson, I wouldn't get on my horse today. You ride this other horse.'

"My father said, 'Why not?' and the man said, 'Well, if you do ride him, get on from the porch.'

"My father never had gotten on a horse from a porch in his life, so he got on from the ground. The horse threw him right over and broke his arm, but he wasn't going to be told to get on a horse from a porch. Nobody could tell him what to do."

The captain had other problems with horses. Mrs. Roth continued: "Father was very strong, like cast iron. He was in an accident with Mr. Irwin and two others, directors, sugar people. In those days they had to go around the islands [Oahu or Hawaii] in a horse-drawn carriage. This time the horses ran away and everyone was thrown out. The whole carriage ran right over my father's chest, cut his clothes right off but never broke a bone. . . . I think Mr. Irwin gave each of the men on that trip a gold watch as a memento of the accident.

"I think [my father] probably wanted a son and I turned out to be a girl which was a great disappointment to him. But he always treated me like a boy. He always thought that anything he could do I could do. Once, he took me up in the rigging of one of the ships. I couldn't have been very old, maybe about eight, or I wouldn't have gone. But I went with him. That was a treat for me. We slid out to the end of the yard. . . . I guess I was a sailor's daughter, all right, but a terrible sailor, like my mother.''

By 1904 the oil business included new names: Pacific Oil Transportation Company and National Oil & Transportation Company, while Matson was promoting a third, Coalinga Oil Transportation Company, with headquarters at San Francisco. This was incorporated with $750,000 capital, primarily to build a 112-mile pipeline from Coalinga, in the newer and more promising Wheeler Ridge–Elk Hills –Lost Hills oil fields, to the port of Monterey, California. Writing about it, Matson said: ''This company is composed of members of the Pacific and National Oil companies, with a few of their friends. These friends are interested in oil production in the Coalinga field. This amalgamation of interests absolutely insures future business for the line.''

Names on the company's letterhead were familiar: Matson (president), Buck, Irwin, Ohlandt, the Captain Barneson from whom Matson had learned much about using oil at sea, plus newcomers Frank Pauson, Louis Rosenfeld, and George T. Cameron. Notably absent was William H. Crocker, whose strong interest in the Southern Pacific Railroad (generally unenthusiastic about pipeline competition) could have been the reason. Matson also invited some outside participation, especially from Walter M. Giffard and the Hackfeld interests in Hawaii. He wrote to Giffard: ''I have my list out for subscriptions and will send it down to Honolulu and let you see what you can do for me. I do not want you to peddle it, but take in a few of your people who want to get in first. It is a big thing and I want to give you a chance to get in. We will have a million barrels of oil to put through the line every year.''

Simultaneously, Matson was fighting for oil customers in the islands, mainly against the Union Oil Company, with Standard Oil an unfriendly

presence in the wings. Captain Barneson's $0.30 to $0.60 oil quickly became history, but the competitors still could deliver in the islands at about $1.30 a barrel.

Matson had problems to spare. One G. E. H. Baker had been hired as his oil representative in Honolulu but was much more efficient in running up expenses than in making reports. Matson cut off his credit but was not quick enough in firing him. After a slow trip, the *Marion Chilcott* arrived in Honolulu when all shore tanks were full. Matson wrote: ''We were at a loss to know how much oil they had on hand as Mr. Baker did not write us. . . . The ship will have to lay in the stream and discharge some of her crew, waiting for a chance to discharge cargo. . . . [Baker] has acted so badly that I do not want to have any more to do with him [but] he can come up on the *Chilcott*. I hope he does not get any chance to draw too much money on us.''

The captain also had problems with territorial regulations, especially a proposal to specify that bunker fuel should have a flash test at 110 degrees. Matson wrote: ''An oil that flashes at 110 degrees contains considerable gaseous matter, and if you should touch a match to such oil, it would take fire immediately. . . . We are in a position to furnish the same kind of oil as the Union Oil Company and can buy it cheaply, but I will not do so as long as we can get a safe oil that will better satisfy the interests of the people. . . . Mr. Baker [by now in the employ of the Union Oil Company] must have made quite an impression . . . trying to advocate a one hundred and ten flash test in a country having a temperature of one hundred degrees. . . . I realized the Standard Oil Company are working hard to do us up there, as in other places. We feel satisfied we can hold our own for a while at any rate, and when they are tired of us, I presume they will come around and adjust matters.''

The Dillingham family at this time owned docks and sheds on the Honolulu waterfront as well as both the Hilo and Oahu railroads. Although Emma Dillingham was a Matson stockholder, her son

Walter added little to Captain Matson's tranquillity. Matson wrote to Giffard in January 1905: "I am in receipt of your letter, with full explanation of the Oahu railroad contract. [The railroad had signed with Union for its oil supply.] I realized there was little chance for us to get the business unless there was an even break. Mr. Dillingham is a slippery fellow. He owes the Matson Navigation Company 9,000 tons short shipped freight and he should have had you fix up the contract . . . but since he has gone the way he did we have turned the matter over to Attorney R. W. Breckons."

In June of that year, however, a Matson letter to Walter Dillingham was friendly: "There is nothing new to write about except that I have done as I told you I was going to do, and I am ordering the steamer. You can tell your mother her stock is good for $1.00 a month for years to come."

In four years from 1901, Matson put together his tangle of oil companies, ran the shipline, became president of the Honolulu Sugar Plantation Company, invested in another plantation, challenged his old friend J. D. Spreckels in sugar refining, and gave some aid to the Spreckels-owned Oceanic Steamship Company. Now and then, he took time out for personal trips to the islands. On one such voyage to Hilo, Mrs. Roth remembers watching her mother sew seven stars (presumably representing the seven ships being operated at the time of incorporation in 1901) on a blank banner to create the company's first house flag.

"I gather," said C. C. Kennedy in a quoted interview, "that it riled Captain Matson to see the Oceanic Company's flag on his ships [as it had been from the first operations in 1882]. . . . I also recall that just about the time that the Matson house flag came into being Captain Matson came to Hilo and they gave a dinner in his honor at the Hilo Hotel.

"J. T. Stacker of the old Hilo Herald printed the menu and on the cover he had his idea of the Matson house flag; the only trouble was that he used red ink and black ink instead of blue ink and the captain gave him hell for not putting the right picture of his house flag on the menu."

For a time, the shipline appeared to be the easiest of the Matson activities. The *Falls of Clyde, Roderick Dhu, Santiago, Annie Johnson,* and *Marion Chilcott* kept up their steady, almost monotonous service to Hilo; the *Enterprise* sometimes challenged steamers of the Oceanic and American-Hawaiian lines for Honolulu passengers and cargo, and the *Rosecrans* alternately served Hawaii and western Alaska with oil cargoes. Only occasionally were there signs of strain. Matson's letter of complaint to Giffard in June 1904 said: "Regarding the *Santiago* and other ships of this company: Whenever your people have no more work for them, all we can do is to take them off the run but I do think that as long as you have room for the '*Helene*' you should have room for the *Santiago* or *Annie Johnson* inasmuch as we are entitled to the preference over outside vessels. . . . Last summer the *Helene* left here without taking a boiler that should have gone on her and I had to send the *Rosecrans* in there and we lost about $3,000 on that trip."

In December 1904, he wrote again: "There has been some talk about the *Enterprise* calling at Honolulu for a cargo of sample sugar. . . . the directors of the Honolulu Plantation do not want to ship any of this sugar on the Oceanic vessels and they have agreed with this [Matson] company to have us carry that freight."

In January, however, Walter A. K. Gibson wrote to Giffard: "I am very glad to advise you that, after considerable dickering, we have arranged to carry at least one cargo of the Honolulu Plantation Company's product. This is largely due to Captain Matson's influence. . . . The California and Hawaii steamers were bidders for the business and were 'moving Heaven and Earth' to get it. However, we won out, at least for the time being." His letter was written on Oceanic's letterhead. It's a little hard to tell, more than seven decades later, who really was on first.

Confrontation with Spreckels over refining came early in 1904. Matson wrote on April 14: "I had a talk with Mr. J. D. Spreckels yesterday. He seemed to be up in arms on account of the Honolulu Sugar Company talking about making white sugar. He said he was going to fight us to a finish and I feel somewhat upset. I do not want to fight with our own people, but at the same time we cannot lay down, and I don't know what the outcome will be. I told Mr. J. D. if he could pay us a reasonable price for the sugar we would not make white sugar but if he cannot, something has to be done so we can get a better price. He seemed to be very confident that he could beat us out and I suppose he can."

The Honolulu Sugar Company did proceed to make white sugar, at least during 1905, but there are no records of the eventual outcome of this particular struggle.

In that year, however, almost the whole shipping and oil picture changed. U. S. Porter, William Mulholland, Bernard Bienenfeld, and A. F. L. Bell early in the year induced forty-five independent oil producers to join them in establishing the Associated Oil Company. On June 15 the new company bought from Matson and his partners 2,680 shares of stock in the Pacific Oil Transportation Company, 6,280 shares in the Coalinga Company, and 20,000 shares of National Oil stock, along with real property at Alcatraz Landing and certain pipelines. The steamer *Rosecrans* and the sailing ships *Roderick Dhu, Santiago, Falls of Clyde,* and *Marion Chilcott* also were sold to the new company in separate transactions. Actual transfer of the real property or ships was incomplete, however, by April 18, 1906, the date of the San Francisco earthquake.

Peter Johnson, bringing the *Rosecrans* in from Hawaiian and Alaskan trips in October 1905, had been dispatched to the East Coast to oversee the rebuilding of one more aged vessel, the Spanish steamer *Gagitano*. Damaged and abandoned by her owners, the twenty-five-year-old ship could be registered under the U.S. flag if sufficiently rebuilt.

"She was dirty and rusty," Johnson wrote. "Fitting up a tramp like that was a new experience for me and it took some time to figure out where I should begin." He did push the work, however, fitting out the 3,000-ton ship with accommodations for forty passengers, a cold storage plant and gear to handle general cargo, as well as wireless apparatus,

not then in use by any other merchant ship in the Pacific. Picking up a cargo in New York, Johnson headed the ship, now named the *Hilonian,* through the Strait of Magellan and north to San Francisco, arriving on April 20, 1906.

He wrote: "After coming to anchor, I stood stunned for a few minutes, watching the city burn. I then turned my papers over to the first officer, for I had a wife and children in San Francisco to find." Johnson found his family safe and returned to the ship to oversee unloading the cargo, including 3,000 cases of malted milk, much needed by the emergency food centers.

Captain Matson and his family also were safe. He wrote to Giffard in Honolulu: "The *Chilcott* will have a load of the Union Oil Company's oil as our pipes have been busted in so many places and it will take about ten days to repair same. . . . Everybody is doing their level best to keep everything supplied. . . . This calamity has been something awful and a sight I never want to see again. . . . We are going to open an office in Seattle for the time being where our ships will load: from there they go to Hilo via Honolulu."

The *Hilonian* did go to Seattle and loaded mostly foodstuffs, for which merchants scrambled when she reached the islands.

Minutes of the June 22, 1906, meeting of the Matson Navigation Company directors read:

The president then stated that all records of the company had been destroyed in the conflagration . . . and that he had with him in his pocket at the time of the conflagration a copy of a statement made to the board of directors on March 21st, which showed the assets and liabilities of the company on that date, that this was the only record the company had and that the secretary, from this record, had made a trial balance as of May 31, 1906. . . .

The directors declared a monthly dividend of seventy-five cents a share, payable immediately.

President reported that in the purchase of stock of the Paauhau Sugar Plantation Company he had borrowed the sum of . . . $401,250 from Daniel Meyer and had given his personal note bearing interest at the rate of five percent per annum. . . . the company had paid the interest thereon and had also paid . . . $193,138.34 on account of the principal of that note, of which sum, however, $40,000 was advanced by William Matson. He further stated . . . on November 23, 1905, he had advanced another $31,000 for purchase of other shares in the plantation.

Four months after the earthquake, the Hawaiian islands still were short of fuel oil. The *Enterprise* had to wait several days in Honolulu for propulsion oil; the Oahu plantation had to shut down its irrigation pumps for two days, and the Honolulu Sugar Company threatened to cancel its Matson contract. All this occurred while the Union Oil Company had full tanks in Honolulu but refused to deliver any of it to Matson, despite a previous agreement to do so, unless specific orders came from its San Francisco office by a cable signed by one man. The man? None other than G. E. H. Baker, once fired by Matson.

Matson wrote to Giffard: "I found the Union Oil Company played us the 'Double Cross.' We took care of them to the extent of 210,000 barrels of oil [when] their Portland tanks were blown up . . . they made a written agreement to deliver 25,000 barrels a month to us in Honolulu. Suddenly, they sent us notice that all arrangements were off, and they fixed the Red Stack towboats so they would not do any towing for us. I worked the *Enterprise* Saturday night, Sunday and Labor Day in order to take the *Monterey* in tow; but the *Rosecrans* came in from the north . . . she can get [to Honolulu] a little faster than the *Enterprise.*

"I could not get a Spreckels towboat, but they did all they could to get the Red Stack to help us, but Baker of the Union had them 'fixed.' "

So Baker had his revenge, doubled in spades. Matson's letter must be assumed to have been edited by his secretary, perhaps never read by the author. The original language could have been diverting.

Matson's ability to inspire confidence and loyalty was repeatedly demonstrated. Investors risked their money with him time and again, no matter how

wild his proposals sounded. They did make money, and hard-nosed tycoons became happy rubber stamps on his boards of directors. Sea captains stayed with him for decades, accepting tongue-lashings along with bonuses. Seamen liked the pay and the food, as well as the fact that the captain personally watched as much of his companies' operations as he could.

One captain said: "Everybody respected him. He was friendly with the sailors and if they ever had any gripes, he'd say, 'What the hell do you fellows want?' They'd say, 'We worked so-and-so and we didn't get overtime.' He'd look at the mate and say, 'Did these men work that overtime?' The mate would say yes and the captain would answer, 'Then pay them! What the hell's the matter with *you?* ' "

David K. Richards, the onetime borrowed cabin boy, did not see Matson for eleven years after that initial experience. Matson and his brother-in-law, James Low, then invited Richards, by this time a boilermaker, to bid on the job of erecting some oil tanks at Honolulu. When Richards finished the job in less than half the agreed time, Matson wrote him a letter of thanks and "a note informing Henry F. Wichman [a jeweler] to give me a watch I would select, and another note to Mr. McInerny to give me the best Panama hat they had." Five years after that, Matson gave Richards and his wife passage to California and arranged weeks of free treatment for his rheumatism at a spa owned by John A. Buck.

The captain did not inspire universal approval, however, even among those who knew him best. Early in 1906, the wealthy William G. Irwin (the same who had been in the runaway carriage with Matson) wrote to Giffard: "The above covers, as near as I can see, the whole situation. It is no use discussing the business ethics with which Matson, Buck, et al., conduct their affairs. It would have no effect on them if we did try to discuss it with them. The only question is, what are we willing to do the business for?"

Irwin was not the only one unimpressed. The Castle and Cooke history said:

"Captain Matson, a barrel-chested man with a

sea-weathered face,* a black thatch of hair and a heavy moustache, was walking down the street not far from Honolulu's waterfront one day in June, 1907. He soon encountered one of the Castles . . . George Parmele Castle.

"Matson was scouting for an agent to drum up more business for his freighters. Might Castle and Cooke be interested?

" 'Why don't you talk it over with Ed Tenney?', Castle suggested.

"So the captain turned into the Stangenwald Building on Merchant Street where Castle & Cooke had its offices. Ed [Edward D.] Tenney was at his roll-top desk with its stuffed gooney bird brooding on top. When Tenney recognized his visitor and learned of his mission, he adjusted his pince-nez spectacles and hitched forward in his chair.

"Captain Matson always had liked Hilo, and he had made money and found plenty of financial backing there. Only when his fleet and his plans outgrew Hawaii's second seaport did he decide to make Honolulu his main mid-Pacific terminus.

*The "sea-weathered" description possibly was imaginative. Matson had not made a passage as anything but owner/passenger for seventeen years.

"For half of 1907, [his] *Hilonian* steamer had been putting into Honolulu harbor. His agents there, W. G. Irwin & Company, also were agents for his competition, the Oceanic Steamship Company, and Matson felt his affairs were getting secondary attention.

"Castle & Cooke had been in shipping for half a century, being part owners and agents for several schooners and barks, which interests they sold to buy into the Planters Line Shipping Company, for which they were currently the agents, handling island sugar and general cargoes for a fleet of ten sailing vessels. Matson believed the islands had to have even bigger ships and more of them, operating on regular and dependable schedules with better service all around. He proposed to supply that service.

"After Ed Tenney heard Matson's proposal that Castle & Cooke become his agent, the outspoken manager bellowed, 'No! Why in Hell should we?' "

Throughout his business life, such a response from Edward D. Tenney usually was sufficient to stop any proposal cold. The explanation of why it did not do so in this instance requires complicated backgrounding—as do many odd events in Hawaiian business history.

CHAPTER FOUR

AGENTS, INVESTORS, AND NEW SHIPS
(1907–1912)

The confrontation in the Castle & Cooke offices came close to the classic meeting of irresistible force and immovable object, with improbable contestants. If the tale of runaway Swedish deckboy William Matson clawing his way to shipline ownership and importance to Hawaii was an unlikely true story, so the presence of Edward D. Tenney at the rolltop desk with the stuffed gooney bird on top represented another just as curious.

This began with sisters Angeline and Mary Tenney, in Oberlin, Ohio, and the American Board of Commissioners for Foreign Missions. These careful gentlemen wanted their missionaries to be above reproach. Translated, "above reproach" could mean insulated against South Seas sin, and that meant married. Hence, young Samuel N. Castle and Amos Starr Cooke, bachelor candidates for the Hawaiian mission in the mid-1830s, could not go until they found mates the commissioners would approve.

Following a suggestion from the board, Cooke proceeded to Massachusetts and there convinced Juliette Montague to skip down to Connecticut for a marriage quick enough to allow them to catch the bark *Mary Fraser* on December 14, 1836. Castle, also following suggestions, headed for Oberlin to check out a reputedly pious young lady, Angeline Tenney. He reported to the mission board: "We talked for an hour and the matter was arranged. I

have found a suitable female." They also sailed on the *Mary Fraser*.

The Cookes became schoolteachers in Honolulu, and Castle was appointed assistant manager of a mission warehouse. The Cookes started a family that eventually included J. Platt, Martha, Juliette, and Charles, most of whom inherited what a contemporary writer called their mother's "straight nose and prim, firm mouth."

Angeline Castle had one daughter but died only four years after arriving in the islands. With the child, Castle returned to the East Coast on a miserable 138-day voyage and then spent months on a 6,000-mile speaking tour. A year and a half after Angeline's death, he married her sister, Mary Tenney, in Oberlin, although the mission board had hesitated before concluding that she really was pious enough. Samuel and Mary Castle returned to Honolulu and eventually produced ten children.

Cooke and Castle parted from the mission in 1851 to become partners as merchants and commission agents. Joseph B. Atherton, arriving from New England, became a forty-dollar-a-month clerk for the partners and later married Juliette Cooke. Probably encouraged by his aunt, Mary Tenney Castle, Edward D. Tenney traveled to the islands from his home in New Jersey in 1877, spent three years as a sugar plantation foreman near Hilo, contracted rheumatism, moved to Honolulu, and went to work for Castle & Cooke as a laborer, but soon stepped up to more rewarding jobs.

Thus, a succession. Castle had become sole head of the company when Amos Cooke died in 1871. When Castle died in 1894 the partnership became a corporation, with Atherton as president and general manager. Upon Atherton's death in 1903, George Parmele Castle, Mary's second son, was elected president but had no taste for the day-to-day decisions required of a general manager.

Cousin Ed Tenney was ready and willing. By now he had been involved in most of the company's diversified activities, which included merchandising, plantation representation and operations, shipping, and interests in island railroads. By 1907 Tenney's control of the company was nearly complete. George Castle usually was willing to let him have his way, and there were challenges from no one else.*

The Castle & Cooke history outlined the one great exception, which began with Tenney's flat refusal of Captain Matson's proposal that the company become his agent:

"Captain Matson is reported to have bellowed right back, emphasizing where he stood in the shipping business and where he intended to go . . . 'and by God it isn't to Hell, either, Mr. Tenney!'

"After this heated exchange, it's no wonder that the captain was astonished, later in the day, when Ed Tenney hurried down to the wharf and proclaimed that Castle & Cooke, indeed, would like to serve as his agents.

"What had happened to change the scene so quickly? Well, incredible as it may seem, the usual-

ly soft-voiced George Parmele Castle howled when he heard of Tenney's curt turndown.

"Said Castle, 'You find Matson and make a deal with him before he gets together with one of the other agencies, and don't waste any time doing it!'

"This bold statement must surely [have been] the high point of Castle's thirteen-year presidency.

"Amazed—and amazingly—Tenney rushed to the docks, where the skipper and Tenney shook hands, and the deal was closed. Thus the long association between Castle & Cooke and Matson began without the scratch of a pen. . . .

"That first year, Castle & Cooke hustled enough cargo for Matson ships' three homeward-bound trips to double the profits and make a net gain of $23,000 for Matson in the last six months of 1907 and commissions of $2,529 for Castle & Cooke. Reviewing the year with a certain insouciance, Tenney noted a general decrease in the business of the sailing vessels and added, 'Consequently it is well that we secured the agency for this line of steamers if we wish to continue in the factoring and shipping business in these islands.'

"In line with this, Castle & Cooke divested itself of its 731 shares in the Planters Line in a swap for 429 shares in Matson, besides investing $100,000 in Matson stock, to be used in the construction of a new steamer. For half a century Castle & Cooke became virtually synonymous with Matson in the islands."

The Hawaiian archipelago has produced or attracted its full share of odd ducks: kings with delusions of grandeur; missionaries turned prosperous merchants or such scoundrels as to get themselves unfrocked; adventurers advising native royalty and introducing German band music; a personage important enough to get mentioned in newspapers but only as "Preserved Fish" Wilcox; and one delightful, handicapped soul who, as a company official, limped around Big Island sugar plantations where cane was floated down to the mills in flumes. His particular fancy was to disconnect his wooden leg, send it down the flume as a warning to mill workers below, then to hop aboard a bundle of cane

---

*A persistent story, impossible to verify, is that James Castle, Mary's fourth son and the man who secretly had obtained options enough for control of Spreckels' Hawaiian Commercial and Sugar Company in 1898, first offered them to Atherton for a one-third interest in Castle & Cooke, but was rebuffed when Tenney advised Atherton against the move, which would have made Castle & Cooke the dominant presence in the sugar industry.

The man who accepted Castle's proposition on behalf of Alexander & Baldwin was J. Platt Cooke (the second of that name), who was Atherton's nephew. So went business in Hawaii in the palmy days.

and float down to the mill himself, yelling and hanging on to his hat.

Tenney fitted well into this galaxy. The Castle & Cooke history notes:

"Ed Tenney was typical of the times and although you might not approve of his one-man oligarchy you couldn't help but admire secretly his rough, gruff style. He was a jealous dictator of all that happened in his company. He represented a philosophy in business in those days: that what Castle & Cooke did was nobody's damn business.

"Tenney prided himself on being the only Castle & Cooke executive who was 'neither preacher, school teacher or deacon.' One of his favorite descriptions of himself was, 'I'm not one of those missionaries who came around the Horn, brought it with him and has been tooting it ever since. . . .'

"Hail-fellow-well-met, booming, domineering, he loved to go to directors' meetings and steam-roller them with his exuberant personality and iron will. . . . One friend recalls that Tenney never 'pounded the table as some reported but he did tap it with a finger or two until it bounced. At that point you would vote the way he wanted or he would adjourn the meeting. . . .'

"His 'Good Mornings' about the office were bustling affairs. . . . [He would bring] rough stories, straight off the docks, especially for the more solemn of his 'missionary' associates. . . . he was forever pinching the behinds of company secretaries. . . . he kept track of everyone in the office and their families. . . .

"Tenney provided recognition for all his employees, 'and that made Castle & Cooke a nice place to work,' a retired bookkeeper recalls. . . .

"Tenney usually wore a light grey suit and a straw hat atop his bald head. . . . boat day was always a gala event. . . . at the blast of the Hawaiian Electric Company's whistle, Tenney invariably grabbed his Panama hat; and the entire staff of Castle & Cooke, along with most of Honolulu, raced to the dock to bid the new arrivals welcome."

Had the shipowner with the carnation in his buttonhole and the autocrat with the Panama hat continued their few hours of open hostility in 1907, the struggles could have been titanic and perhaps ruinous. The peace between them gave Captain Matson the strongest possible island ally for a decade, and very little happened in the Matson Navigation Company for the next twenty-seven years that Ed Tenney did not initiate or approve.

The Oceanic Steamship Company ran out of luck in the first decade of the new century. With the liner *Mariposa* committed to a San Francisco–Tahiti route, and the three new ships, *Sonoma, Ventura,* and *Sierra,* on the San Francisco–Honolulu–Pago Pago–Auckland–Sydney route, only the *Alameda* was left for the profitable San Francisco–Honolulu shuttle. The South Pacific ships did carry a few passengers to Honolulu, but the service could be offered only once every three weeks. Matson, rapidly increasing its steamer fleet and schedule, claimed more and more of the Hawaiian business.

To add to Oceanic's woes, all three new ships had basic design faults: engine foundations were weak; blowers were ineffective; and the handsome short double stacks failed to produce enough draft for the coal-fired boilers. In sequence, each ship went back to the yards for lengthening of the stacks and other expensive alterations. Meanwhile, New Zealand's Union Steamship Company vessels continued tough competition, using the Vancouver northern terminal. Expected freight business to Tahiti failed to develop. Even with subsidies, Oceanic's South Pacific services lost $2 million by 1907.

In 1906 Walter D. K. Gibson had suggested:

"It may take some time to get back some of the customers lost. . . . I still believe a combination of interests with the Matson Navigation Company would save the day; and with Captain Matson as general superintendent of the newly organized company and no other 'cooks' to dabble in the broth, this combination of freight and other interests would pay well. . . . But to do this, O.S.S. Co. must be willing to pass to Profit and Loss a large sum representing the loss caused by the Australian service. As matters now stand, you have allowed

Matson to get a foothold in the Honolulu, as well as the Hilo trade, in addition to that of the Hawaiian-American S.S. Co.; and mark my words, if Matson continues putting on more steamers, the final result (unless you combine) will be that the O.S.S. Co. will be knocked out of the competition unless radical improvements are made and the steamers are properly managed.''

His advice was not accepted—then. In October 1907 the U.S. government terminated Oceanic's mail contract for the South Pacific. The company canceled that service, laying up the *Ventura* and *Sonoma* and placing the *Sierra* on the Honolulu shuttle. The aging *Alameda* lay idle until 1910, when she was sold to the Alaska Steamship Company, converted to oil, and placed on a Seattle–Alaska route. For four years from 1908, the Australia–New Zealand route from San Francisco was left to foreign ships.

The new Matson steamer *Lurline* was launched late in 1907. The company never has used numerals to differentiate between ships of the same name; but this was the second *Lurline,* not counting the company launch in Hilo. The 6,571-ton vessel cost $655,000 and could carry fifty-one passengers as well as 8,000 tons of cargo, more than double the capacity of either steamer the company already had. She cruised at twelve knots and immediately was chartered by the government to lift a cargo of ''ordnance and ordnance stores'' to Honolulu.

Matson was not yet finished with sailing vessels, however. At the end of 1907, the captain was negotiating for full control of the Planters Line with R. P. Rithet, a Victoria, B.C., financier with San Francisco and Hawaii interests, representing both C. Brewer & Company, Honolulu, and Welch & Company, San Francisco.*

*Among many activities, Rithet had been mayor of Victoria, had built the first of its big ocean piers, and had served in the provincial legislature. In 1893 he was chairman of the British Pacific Railway, which planned a rail line from the east through British Columbia's Yellowhead Pass to Bute Inlet and crossing Seymour Narrows by a bridge that would use infamous Ripple

Involved in the negotiations were the barks *George Curtis, St. Katherine, Mohican, R. P. Rithet, Gerard C. Tobey, Hawaiian Isles, Amy Turner,* and *Andrew Welch,* plus the four-masted ship *Fort George* and the five-masted schooner *W. H. Marston,* all built between 1877 and 1901. Matson traded 2,994 shares of stock, with a book value of $299,400, for the vessels and some freight contracts that may have been more important. Records indicate that the Castle & Cooke shares were included in this transaction. The point of the purchase of course was to eliminate cheap competition for the steamers Matson had or expected to get. The company quickly sold the *George Curtis* and *St. Katherine* to Alaska salmon cannery firms, which, needing vessels for only one trip north and one trip south each year, could use the old sailing craft, too slow or decrepit for sustained ocean trade.

The remaining windjammers mostly were laid up and sold later, at prices from $5,875 for the wooden barkentine *S. G. Wilder* (not a Planters Line ship) to $70,000 for the *Hawaiian Isles.*

The four-masted *Fort George,* 1,756 tons, made one trip for Matson between Honolulu and San Francisco, then went around the Horn to New

Rock as a pier. Had the scheme succeeded, Victoria might have become a great ocean freight terminal. Instead, surveyors got into trouble with mainland Indians, who killed some of them. The others were in no hurry to go back into Indian country to complete the survey.

Ripple Rock was one of the most dangerous menaces to navigation on the Inside Passage to Alaska. Open-mouthed Indians watched from the shore as Captain George Vancouver negotiated the treacherous western channel through Seymour without harm to his awkward sailing vessel in 1792. But the double-domed spire, reaching to within ten feet of the surface in a narrow channel otherwise 300 feet deep, sank or damaged 25 ships and more than 100 smaller craft between the first recorded wreck, that of the paddle-wheel steamer U.S.S. *Saranac* in 1875, and the holing of the U.S. Survey Vessel *William J. Stewart* in 1946. In all, 114 people are known to have died in the turbulent, twelve-knot currents.

In 1958 Canadian engineers drove a shaft 570 feet down from Maude Island and tunneled 2,400 feet to the base of the rock and another 300 feet vertically up into it. Using 3 million pounds of Niramex-2-H, they then set off the world's largest nonnuclear explosion, blowing off the top forty-five feet. The last dream of a rail connection to Vancouver Island blew up with it.

York. Leaving that port on July 26, 1908, she headed for the South Atlantic and disappeared without a trace. Not even the names of her crewmen survived.

By 1912, when the *W. H. Marston* met "with a sudden accident which left her in water-logged condition and abandoned at sea," Captain Matson was able to tell his directors that a satisfactory insurance settlement had been made and that "This schooner is now in Martinez and we have made no repairs on her yet, hoping to sell her . . . as we are out of that business now." It was not quite the last of the sailing ships, but the end was not far away.

Late in 1908 Captain Matson reported that Castle & Cooke wished to buy another 1,000 shares of stock; C. Brewer wanted 1,276 to add to those it received in the Planters Line trade; and Alexander & Baldwin asked for 2,000. Thus, the investment in Matson by its largest customers increased. Growing complexity of the company's financial affairs was indicated when Matson not only gave Associated Oil more time on a $78,000 payment due on the properties sold to it three years earlier but lent the struggling oil firm another $96,000, apparently because Associated could not get it from banks but Matson could. Most of the oil properties were pledged as collateral.

Matson chartered the *Hyades,* a 3,753-ton steamer, for a year, running it part of the time from the Pacific Northwest to the islands, and then bought it for $225,000 in 1910. The company had to go to the banks for that money and once again —for much more—to pay for the new, 452-foot, 6,974-ton (gross) steamer *Wilhelmina,* by far the fanciest piece of marine hardware that had ever been seen in the Pacific. With room for 146 passengers, eleven bathrooms, modern oil-burning engines, wireless equipment, and tanks for 720,000 gallons of fuel oil (enough to give her a cruising radius of 8,820 miles at fifteen knots), she appeared to be a risky gamble on a Hawaiian passenger trade not yet visible. Launched in 1909, she was named for the daughter of Ed Tenney. Father and daughter attended the launching.

"We were to leave Washington [for Newport News] in the evening of the second day," Captain Peter Johnson, skipper of the new ship, reported, "and that evening when we went down to the dining room for dinner Mr. Tenney called the waiter over and . . . placed a dollar, fifty cents, twenty-five cents and a dime on the table. 'George,' he said to the colored man, 'I don't know which one of these pieces of money you will earn but we want the best dinner you've got, so bring it in.' After dinner, Mr. Tenney shoved all the money together and told George to take it."

John Diggs was a foreman on the rigging gang at the shipyard building the *Wilhelmina.* "I asked him [Peter Johnson] for a bos'n's job," he said. "He was an ugly, mean man to sail with, meanest in the world; but if you stayed with him for one voyage, you were fixed. He'd take care of you. I never appreciated it until I became a captain. . . . He was talking to this man with a red carnation in his buttonhole. Of course, Captain Johnson would never introduce you to anybody, but that was my first meeting with Captain Matson. Johnson said, 'I'll give you a quartermaster's job'; I was only about nineteen. Matson was aboard every day [in the shipyard], friendly and talked to me.

"On the trip out [some 13,000 miles around the Horn in forty-two days], some of the crewmen told me, 'You'll have to leave when you get out to the Coast because if you're not a Swede in this company you don't get any place.' "*

Although the *Wilhelmina* with her bathrooms attracted the luxury trade, a few travelers preferred the older ways. In 1911 the bark *Andrew Welch* still was offering passage to Honolulu for forty dollars, compared with the sixty-five-dollar fare by steamer. Palm Langdon, writing in the publication *Forest & Stream* on January 12, 1913, described a trip with fifteen crewmen and eight passengers. Baths, he

*The Virginia-born Diggs, with Matson until 1928, commanded half a dozen of the line's newer steamers, then retired to become a San Francisco bar pilot until he was seventy and a bay pilot for another decade. His personal log shows he had handled 8,000 ships.

said, were refreshing: a bucket of sea water was hauled aboard in the morning and poured over the head. For entertainment, passengers played cards, watched the stars, (no nasty engine pounding, just the wind in the rigging and the sea slapping the hull) and, at least once, danced the Virginia reel to the music of a phonograph the skipper brought out of his cabin. The entire fourteen-day trip from San Francisco was made without tacking, the only course changes being made by hauling the ship.

The following year, however, Captain Kelly of the *Andrew Welch* had a thirty-day westbound trip of a different sort. "There was no way of running away from the storm," a Honolulu newspaper reported. "Fourteen days after leaving San Francisco, they were not far south of that port. The seas were mountainous. The deck cargo suffered and some of the sails were blown away, but otherwise the ship came through all right. Drums of distillate were lifted out of their lashings by the water that poured over the . . . side as the ship wallowed in the swirling waves. Most of the drums of distillate went overboard of their own accord but others had to be jettisoned in order to save the ship. Altogether, 150 drums were lost . . . two topsails were torn right out of place by wind which must have reached ninety-five miles an hour, according to the calculations of the officers. The *Welch* had a mixed cargo . . . coal, bricks, pipe, matches, lamp chimneys and many other sundries."

If she had any passengers, they made no report. Perhaps they were in no condition to talk.

Matson sold the *Welch* in 1915 to a G. W. McNear. Sailing from the United States to Belgium in 1916, she was intercepted by a British warship, under suspicion of actually intending her cargo of beans for Germany. She later did drift to Germany, intentionally or otherwise. Sold to Swedish owners, she was renamed the *Olga,* then was sold to Norwegians and received at least three more names: *Sophus Magdalon, Canis,* and (in 1948) *Einvika.* By then she had auxiliary engines and sailed for another two years, running onto rocks off Raufarhofn, Iceland, in a gale on November 16, 1950. The Icelandic Life Saving Association rescued the crew, but the sixty-two-year-old vessel was lost.

CHAPTER FIVE

THE PREWAR YEARS
(1908–1917)

Captain Matson was appointed Swedish consul general for the western United States in 1908. While the position was partially honorary, considerable work was involved. For this, he hired Dr. F. Westerberg, a Swedish-born physician, so crippled in an accident that he could no longer practice. His command of Swedish, however, made him valuable to the consulate, even though he was confined to a wheelchair and considerably embittered. In a series of Swedish-language letters to relatives, he wrote:

"Consul Matson, or Captain as he prefers to be called, is a remarkable personality; a self-made man if anybody is. As a young man he left Sweden as a simple sailor and has now worked himself up to the rank of a millionaire. He hasn't any education. I don't think he can speak, write or read a word of Swedish, but he is a clever businessman and enjoys a high and well-deserved reputation in the business world.

"As Sweden pays very little for the work here, Matson is of the opinion that it is not worth much. . . . Matson of course has to pay a lot for the honor of being consul, but I don't think he would have let himself be persuaded to take the position if it had not been for another's ambition that had driven him to it. . . . Mrs. Matson wanted it for Lurline's sake. . . . It was a little odd in the beginning when I found out that Matson didn't even bother to introduce me to his family, but now I

know my 'captain' well enough to understand that he doesn't have time to think of anything else but to collect money [for his family]."

In another letter, he added:

"The articles in the papers about the 'Swedish boy who becomes a millionaire' are having a ridiculous effect in Sweden. I have a big pile of begging letters and they're not small requests. Although some are content with a few hundred kroner, others ask for twenty, thirty-five, forty and up to one hundred and fifty thousand—they have not managed well, they have been in poor health, etc., and since he is so rich he will not miss this. . . . I guess we are getting our one thousand kroner a year raised to four thousand so Matson will have to wait for his Order of the Vasa."

Another time, he was more unkind:

"As a business man, he [Matson] is real important on the coast, but while he was born in Sweden he doesn't know anything about Sweden or care about it. He has no breeding, Swedish or American, is abrupt, brusque, boorish. He is intractable and sometimes rather difficult to manage but whoever made the choice made the best decision and I have nothing to do with it. I am here only to assist him and everything rests on me. He signs his name and that's all he ever writes, whether it's English or Swedish."

When his son sent him some snapshots, Westerberg reported he had shown them around the office, then still at the Matson Navigation Company, and that Captain Matson had commented, "He takes good pictures, but there's no money in it."

There is no indication that any of this troubled Captain Matson in the least. Mrs. Roth remembers: "My father always regretted that he had not gone to school. He always told young people to be sure they had an education, because he had to educate himself. He didn't know a word of Swedish. . . . he'd forgotten all of it. . . . oh, he could say a few words, but he was too busy. . . . As far as Mother and I were concerned, his being consul meant that we had a steady stream of visitors from Sweden.

"I remember my mother saying, 'What I'm going to do is to turn the whole house over to Lurline. She's going to run it.'

"Well, I did. I ran the house. I was about sixteen. I paid all the bills, did everything. At the end of the month, my father said, 'It's fairly expensive.'

"I just said, 'Well, there they are. Pay them.' And he never said anything more to me about the bills. It made my mother very mad.

"I guess I knew my father best. He always went over all his projects with me. I knew everything they were going to do at the office. In fact, once in a while, they'd call me to say, 'Have you any idea what your father's going to do about this?' They knew I'd know. I always knew everything that went on but I think he probably was just thinking out loud and I was smart enough not to answer so he'd go on telling me everything."

Matson was busy, mixing oil with ships, if not with water. The mix was well illustrated in his report to directors for the year 1908, made on the following February 11, when the company president's salary was raised from $800 to $1,000 a month. The report said:

"In addition to enormous local business we have worked up in the last year, we have been favored with the bulk of the United States government's freighting from here [San Francisco] to Honolulu. This freight was secured by competitive bidding and

on two occasions when our figures were the same as those of our competitor, the government favored this company on account of the dispatch and satisfactory manner in which we carried out former contracts.

"At the present time we are transporting two twelve-inch disappearing guns weighing fifty-seven tons each. These are the heaviest single pieces ever handled in the island trade and aside from the $8,000 we will receive for the service, it directs attention to the company for its facilities in handling such lifts.

"The bark *Mohican* has been fitted so as to be used in connection with the lightering of material intended for the building of the naval dry dock at Pearl Harbor."

Matson also said contracts with oil suppliers at 50 cents a barrel would expire soon and no new ones were being offered at less than a dollar. He recommended that the shipline try to find oil lands of its own.

Records are slightly contradictory, but Matson personally may have been interested in the Buena Vista oil field in California's Central Valley by 1908. He informed his directors in February 1910 that he had invested $56,000 of the line's money in the Lakeview Oil Company of Midway. On April 10, 1910, the Honolulu Consolidated Oil Company was formed, absorbing Lakeview and several other firms. The Matson Navigation Company built up its interest to 331,000 shares of Honolulu Oil.*

One Matson history, without revealing its sources, said:

"He [Matson] invested over three million dollars of his money and that of his backers in this oil venture before anyone received a dollar in return. . . .

*The Castle & Cooke history notes: "In 1910, Matson founded the Honolulu Oil Company. . . . Castle & Cooke invested $140,000 as a friendly gesture. . . . By 1960, this gesture was paying $390,000 a year in dividends. When Honolulu Oil was liquidated [1961–68], Castle & Cooke stock brought $23,274,638.14 into the company's coffers."
Mrs. Frank Thompson of Honolulu, sister-in-law of Lurline Roth, remembered hearing that "Captain Matson told people investing in Honolulu Oil, 'You'll either go broke or get rich.'"

the first well blew wild for about two months from a depth of 1,608 feet. A second well went down 1,604 feet, but neither was a spectacular producer. Work returned to the first and it was deepened to 2,540 feet and completed as the first oil well in the Buena Vista hills, producing two to three thousand barrels of oil a day. Drilling was hampered in the area by heavy gas pressures and many a well went sky high. Although aggravating at the time, this proved to be an unexpected windfall. . . . Matson managed to capture the gas and entered into a contract to supply ten to thirty million cubic feet of gas per day through a pipeline to Los Angeles.''

The new company was strictly a producer, selling its product at the wellhead and leaving transportation to others. For Hawaii, that meant Matson Navigation Company ships. The Honolulu Consolidated Oil Company never operated in or near Honolulu. The name served mainly to confuse generations of journalists. One *San Francisco News* writer, reporting with some relish that an L. A. Crandall had sued Captain Matson for $400,000 over a stock transaction, identified Crandall as ''original owner of big tracts of oil lands in Hawaii''—considerable news to islanders who to this day have located no oil whatever in their volcanic soils.

In the court action, filed in 1914, Crandall sought payment for a block of Honolulu Oil stock pledged to Matson several years earlier as security for loans of $10,000, $41,000, and ''other amounts.''

Matson told a reporter: ''The bill of sale is in my possession. Crandall came to me and said he had to have money and wanted me to buy the stock outright. I did so for my company, and the sale was witnessed by a notary. I do not remember the price. It was before oil came. Now, of course, the stock is worth much more.''

A state court returned an odd verdict: $40,000 for the claim of $400,000. Many years later, an attorney involved admitted some extremely fancy footwork for the defense. The lawyers waited until the statute of limitations had run out, then informed the state court it never had enjoyed jurisdiction: Matson, as consul general for Sweden, could be sued only in a federal court. The state court reluctantly agreed, so the legal action was ended. Even more curiously, the attorney said, Matson's counsel then advised him to pay Crandall $40,000, for reasons unstated. This he did.

Matson Navigation Company in 1910 reported $542,634 income and net profit of $199,887. All revenue except a $35,750 dividend from the Paauhau sugar plantation came from the vessels, listed as the steamers *Enterprise, Hilonian, Hyades, Lurline,* and *Wilhelmina;* the tug *Intrepid;* the barge *Mohican;* and the barkentines *Irmgard* and *S. G. Wilder.* Several other sailing vessels still were in the fleet but went unmentioned in the financial report. The company had $911,864 surplus at year end. Stockholders listed were William Alexander; Alexander & Baldwin, Inc.; C. Brewer & Company; E. F. Bishop; William H. Crocker; Charles M. Cooke; Castle & Cooke, Ltd.; Emma L. Dillingham; William G. Irwin; Captain Peter Johnson; William H. Marston Company; William Matson; Miss M. D. Oxnard; Estate of Alice Oxnard; R. P. Rithet; R. H. Sprague; A. B. Spreckels; E. D. Tenney; I. E. Thayer; A. S., G. W., and S. W. Wilcox.

Matson's shipping profits in this period were earned against multiple competition. The American-Hawaiian Steamship Company provided most of it, with several vessels in the Hawaii trade. Oceanic kept the passenger liner *Sierra* on the same shuttle and in 1912 brought the *Sonoma* and *Ventura* out of retirement, gave each new oil burners and boilers, removed one ugly smokestack and shortened the other (oil did not require as much draft as had the coal-burning equipment), and sent them out on the Australia run under a new mail contract. Honolulu was a stopover in each direction, and the ships welcomed Honolulu–San Francisco passengers and freight when they had room. So did vessels of the old Pacific Mail Line, running to the Orient with stops at Hawaii.

Against them, Matson kept careful schedules, even with ships disinclined to sail in a straight line. ''The *Hilonian* was a narrow-gutted thing and hard to steer,'' Captain Diggs remembered. ''When she'd get a load of sugar, coming home, she'd be all over the place. Once when I was steering, Captain Peter Johnson came up on the bridge, took a look at the wake, and the wake was kind of like a snake. He said, ''Vot's de matter wit' you? You go along like a snake. I don't mind you write your name, but don't go back and rub it out.' ''

Matson's principal answer to competition, as always, was to improve his ships and acquire larger ones. In 1911, after telling his directors that the Honolulu Oil stock now could be sold for several times its cost, the captain obtained approval to install molasses tanks in both the *Hilonian* and the *Hyades*.

To Hawaiian sugar producers, molasses for many years was more of a problem than a product. Early mills were discouraged from the obvious use—distilling rum—by missionary opposition and its influence on some Hawaiian royalty. There was no practical method of shipping the sticky stuff, so mills either dumped it into the sea or, where they could, down apparently bottomless fissures in the lava flows. Only when oil became an important import to the islands could shipowners afford to install bulk tanks to carry oil to the islands, and molasses, for rum, cattle food, or chemicals, back to the mainland. The steam cleaning of those tanks at either end of the runs had to be done by sailors going down into them until the invention of the Butterworth system of mechanical spraying and flushing with seawater. That equipment was made obsolescent, finally, by various legal prohibitions of dumping either molasses or oil-bearing flushing water overside. Modern vessels carry separate tanks for each product.

Production of rum, incidentally, never was important in the islands until World War II. Memories of that curious wartime product still provide nightmares for the survivors. Much more sophisticated production was attempted in the 1960s when a distillery was built on Maui and its product marketed under the Leilani label. This distillery had a daily capacity of 2,500 wine gallons, all of which was carried in stainless steel tank containers on Mat-

son ships to the Pacific Coast for aging. Although the rum was satisfactory, the distillery was shut down in 1967 and the last bulk shipment made in 1975. Despite the concoctions of Trader Vic and his competitors, rum does not sell well in the United States, and low-wage competition from the Caribbean and elsewhere rules out the world market for Hawaiian producers. So cattle still get most of the islands' molasses, mixed into their ensilage.

The 6,800-ton steamer *Manoa,* accommodating eighty-five passengers, joined the Matson fleet in 1913, adding 7,500 tons of cargo capacity. Matson paid her builders $815,000. The twin-screw, sixteen-knot *Matsonia,* first of the company's million-dollar ships (actual cost $1,350,000) arrived in January 1914. Fastest and largest of the fleet, she could carry 10,000 tons of cargo and 250 passengers. Each of the new ships, like the *Wilhelmina,* had deep tanks for delivering excess bunker fuel to Hawaii or to provide long cruising range. That range was not needed in the Hawaii trade but turned out to have great importance elsewhere.

The senior captain in the fleet, Peter Johnson, had taken command of the *Matsonia* at the builder's yard in Newport News, Virginia, and brought her around South America, celebrating New Year's of 1914 at Punta Arenas, Chile, southernmost city in the world. At San Francisco, however, as he wrote in his *Memoirs,* ''I had some words with Captain Matson and he took the command of the *Matsonia* away from me. He was perfectly in the right, but he had listened to some of the crew, which was the poorest set of men I ever saw aboard a ship. I was thoroughly disgusted when I left the ship. . . . I was home ten days when Captain Matson sent for me and put me in command of the *Wilhelmina* again. He gave me a good fatherly talk, which no doubt I needed.'' Matson then was sixty-four, Johnson fifty-one.

On January 24 Captain Matson gave a party aboard the *Matsonia* for 207 dinner guests. A San Francisco newspaper account read:

''Captain Matson told with relish of the time,

back in 1882, when he took the freight schooner *Emma Claudina,* with a total cargo capacity of only 300 tons, from this port to Honolulu [*sic*] and entered into such brisk competition with the old established lines that he earned the title of 'pirate.' . . .

"The handsome vessel, the scene of last night's banquet, will . . . cater to the best tourist trade, for it was built on a scale which must satisfy the most fastidious. Nothing like it has ever entered this port. . . .

"An indication of the sumptuousness of the *Matsonia* is furnished by the fact that it has twenty-six staterooms with private bath, fitted with rare tapestries and furnished with costly woods."

Oceanic Steamship Company's San Francisco–Tahiti route never had been a paying proposition and was abandoned in 1912 when a mail subsidy was withdrawn. The old *Mariposa,* like the *Alameda,* was sold to the Alaska Steamship Company, renovated, and converted to an oil burner; but she gave her new owners nothing but trouble. On October 15, 1915, she struck rocks off Pointer Island, near Bella Bella, B.C., and was beached. The crew and seventy-nine passengers managed to get ashore. Refloated, repaired, and returned to service, the ship lasted only two years, this time striking the Straits Island reef in Sumner Strait. The crew and 265 passengers were rescued; but high winds battered the ship, which slipped off the reef and sank.

On its Australian run, Oceanic did better. The outbreak of World War I and maneuvering of the German raider *Dresden* in the Pacific disrupted British flag services and created more call for American cargo and passenger space than the *Ventura* and *Sonoma* could provide. Oceanic refitted the *Sierra,* shifting her from the Honolulu shuttle to the Australian service, which now was so demanding that virtually nothing could be carried by these ships between San Francisco and Hawaii.

The Pacific Mail Line, controlled by the Southern Pacific Railroad, had comfortable ships and always had operated them with Asian crews, mainly Chinese. For years American seagoing unions had been attempting to get rid of the Chinese competition, and the La Follette Seaman's Law provided the method. In effect, the law said any seaman on an American ship must understand the language of the master. Pacific Mail officers were mainly American, so this meant English and eliminated most of the Chinese.

Discouraged by thin profits on the Orient run, competition from Eastern Seaboard ships coming through the newly opened Panama Canal and the prospect of having to pay U.S. wages to all hands, Pacific Mail literally gave up the ships, selling its five largest to the Atlantic Transport Company. The corporation itself was also sold, and Matson's second competitor in the Hawaiian trade thus vanished, leaving only American-Hawaiian in the contest.

Matson's response was predictable: the steamer *Maui,* 9,801 gross tons, with room for 240 passengers, was ordered at a cost of $1,750,000. The price, unthinkable a decade before, did not even start a tear among the directors: the ships were making money and both the Paauhau sugar plantation and Honolulu Oil stocks were paying dividends. The oil company stock would continue to do so, in increasing amounts, for a half century.

With the *Wilhelmina* offering eleven bathrooms and the *Manoa* and *Matsonia* even more wonders, passenger enthusiasm for the ripe old *Hilonian* and *Enterprise* declined, even though the latter was modernized in 1913. These and the *Lurline* (no. 2) carried mostly steerage passengers or none.

Captain Diggs described one trip on the *Hilonian:*

"We ran into a northeast gale. By heck [the storm] caved in the skylight over the dining room. She didn't carry passengers at that time, so we loaded sugar in the dining saloon, the staterooms, everywhere. Peterson [the captain] shouldn't have done that, loading the ship so heavily. She didn't founder but came terribly close. The sugar was full of water. Oh, boy! We got a tarpaulin and by hook and crook got that hole covered up but a winch

Matson's *Enterprise* was the first oil-burning ship in the Pacific, 1902. (Courtesy of the National Maritime Museum, San Francisco)

The Matson steamer *Manulani* was said to be the largest freighter under the American flag in the early 1920s. (Courtesy of the National Maritime Museum, San Francisco)

Above: Wreck of the *Roderick Dhu,* off Monterey, 1909.

Left: The ill-fated *Fort George,* shown here at Sydney in 1904, disappeared with all hands in the South Atlantic in 1908. (Courtesy of the National Maritime Museum, San Francisco)

The tanker *Rosecrans* ashore at Gaviota, California. She was eventually got off, only to perish in 1913 with loss of 33 lives in a stranding at the mouth of the Columbia River. (Courtesy of the National Maritime Museum, San Francisco)

R. P. Rithet, equipped with auxiliary diesel engines, burned and sank in the North Pacific in 1917. (Courtesy of the National Maritime Museum, San Francisco)

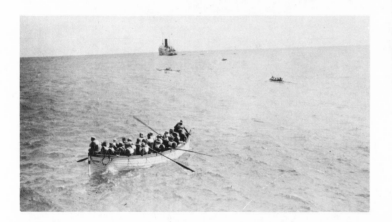

Oceanic's *Ventura*, near Samoa in August 1930, picked up an SOS from the New Zealand liner *Tahiti*, 750 miles away and sinking. *Ventura* arrived and took off all passengers and crew minutes before *Tahiti* upended and sank.

driver was washed overboard. He hung onto the sheet and we got him back on board again. . . . that was Con Hubbenette, who later skippered several Matson vessels [he was widely known for taking a pet mynah bird along on most trips] and finally was a bar pilot.''

The wartime shipping boom that Pacific Mail missed enabled Matson to find a buyer for the thirty-six-year-old *Hilonian* in 1916. She was sunk by a submarine off the Irish coast on May 16, 1917.

Charter rates around the world quickly ballooned, creating a needed opportunity for the American-Hawaiian line, which long had been represented in Hawaii by Hackfeld & Company, started by a German sailor and still operated by German nationals. This company owned the Ehlers Department Store, an insurance company, and interests in sugar and pineapple lands. Even before American entry into World War I, the shipline's contracts with these Germans became an embarrassment in the climate of sympathy for the Allies. When chances for profitable charters multiplied, the company quickly abandoned the Hawaii trade for distant waters. So Matson alone maintained Hawaii's lifeline.

Gordian knots have connected major Hawaiian businesses from their beginnings, family relationships forming the most complicated. Thus, the history of Matson Navigation Company could not be complete without reference to the vastly different personal histories of Edward Tenney, Alexander Budge—or Samuel Roth.

Samuel Roth arrived in Honolulu from Bremen in 1861, invested in sugar, and married a widow with six children. The marriage produced four more children, including William P., born in Honolulu. William attended the University of California and later Stanford, where he captained a championship tennis team in 1900. He returned to Honolulu when his father died, worked in a bank, and later had his own stock brokerage firm. He met Lurline Matson in 1912 during one of her visits to the islands.

Captain Matson's daughter remembers her father

as strict: "I couldn't go out with anybody he didn't know. I had to be in by midnight. If I had callers and they stayed five minutes after twelve, he'd drop his shoes upstairs or bang on the ceiling. The caller would say, 'Well, I hear your father up there. Time to go.' And that would be that.''

Mrs. Frank Thompson, née Roth, remembers the captain's opposition to Lurline's proposed marriage to William on the basis that she was too young, at twenty-three, and that he offered to give Lurline ''the best horse in the world'' if she would forget about the marriage. The gift horse being declined, Matson proposed a compromise: the marriage would be approved, but Roth should give up his Honolulu business, move to San Francisco, and go to work for Matson Navigation. Roth finally agreed, with a reservation of his own: the couple would live in a small apartment and on his salary.

Lurline Matson and William P. Roth were married on May 27, 1914, the twenty-fifth anniversary of her parents' wedding. Roth became a clerk in the Matson offices.

James Low, brother to Lillian Low Matson, had managed sugar plantations, served the Hawaiian provisional government, and organized the Kohala Ditch Company to bring irrigation water from the mountains of the island of Hawaii to the Kohala Peninsula through a spectacular system piercing lava dikes and producing 31 million gallons a day for the water-starved plantations. Later he was sent to Russia on a business project and there married a Scottish girl.

Low died shortly after the marriage, however, and Barbara Low, his widow, pregnant and alone, came to San Francisco to meet her husband's relatives for the first time, and to have her child.

"They stayed with us a while," Mrs. Roth remembers, "because I don't think James had left her any money." The child, Richard, had the run of the Swedish consulate almost as soon as he was able to walk and "could do whatever he wanted with the captain and by the way was well liked by everyone," according to Dr. Westerberg.

In 1915, however, Mrs. Low took Richard to Australia where he, too, died suddenly. Westerberg reported that Captain Matson "took it very hard."

The captain's activities, however, did not slacken. President of several companies besides the shipline and oil corporations, he found time to head the San Francisco Chamber of Commerce as well as the consulate. It's understandable that there are no records of any extended vacations. His report to Matson Navigation Company stockholders for 1916 read:

Net earnings . . . amount to $1,630,667.92. . . . it is deemed advisable to increase the capital stock by giving each stockholder a share of bonus stock for every share of the capital stock held. . . .*

We have during the past year fitted out sailing vessels *Annie Johnson* and *R. P. Rithet* with twin-screw Bolinder's engines, giving to each a speed of approximately seven knots under power alone, thus insuring four or five more trips per year for each, even though the winds are not favorable.

Our new steamer *Maui,* building at the Union Iron Works, San Francisco, . . . is now nearing completion. We expect to have her on the run between San Francisco and Honolulu in the early days of April, and look forward to considerable economy of fuel in her operations, due to her geared turbine propelling machinery. She will have accommodations for ten more passengers than the *Matsonia* and this increase is in the highly finished special staterooms, with some ten bathrooms additional. She will be able to make somewhat greater speed than the *Matsonia* . . . and it is my intention to operate her as the twin vessel with the *Matsonia* on the same schedule.

We have purchased a corner lot . . . fronting on Market and Main streets [San Francisco] at the price of $325,000. It is our intention, when prices on building materials decline to a reasonable level, to erect a ten-story building on this lot and use the second floor for offices of the company, leasing the balance to stores and offices. . . .

We have made arrangements to acquire under a

*The company's annual report listed 35,472 outstanding shares of common stock, with book value of $3,547,200. Total assets were $6,002,544.14, including vessels valued at $4,655,697, a $300,000 investment in the Paauhau Sugar Plantation Company, and shares in the Honolulu Consolidated Oil Company valued at $204,284.

twenty-five-year franchise a wharf 900 feet long, in fine location at Crockett . . . and have purchased ten acres . . . for tank sites. This is being graded down . . . for two 55,000-barrel oil tanks. . . . This will give us a very fine station for receiving oil in large quantities and fueling our ships at any time. . . .

We had serious strikes of the longshoremen during the months of June and July, at San Francisco, and in October at Honolulu, which handicapped us materially and caused a great congestion of freight, particularly at San Francisco. The difficulties, however, were overcome and congestion relieved and the situation is now normal. The increase in down [westbound] freight was sixty percent and the pineapple up freight showed an increase of 100 percent over that of the preceeding year.

William Matson

A few weeks later Captain Matson suffered a severe stroke. Mrs. Roth says of it:

"I remember when . . . the doctor came to have a look at him when he was lying in bed. My father said, 'When will I be able to get down to the office?' The doctor said, 'Well, Captain Matson, I think if you take it easy you'll be back in about six weeks.'

"My father started laughing so hard that they thought he was going to have another stroke. And I want to tell you, in two weeks he was down [at the office]. He had this kind of a disposition: we had a trained nurse. The nurse and Mother and I would be downstairs for luncheon and we'd hear a noise upstairs. That would be my father falling because he'd get up out of bed to go to the bathroom. He wanted to do that himself. He'd try it. He'd fall and get up. He was absolutely determined.

"I remember when he first went down to the pier. Here he'd had a stroke and had been so sick. I remember going down with him the very first day. You know, he had no feeling about standing on the edge of something. Here he was, right on the edge of the pier. I said to a policeman, 'You stand near my father so you can grab him if he gets shaky. He's just out of bed.' "

Shortly afterward Westerberg wrote, "I now have

to go through four doors to see Matson and so see very little of him. He has been in rather poor health . . . lumbago, limping. . . .''

Nevertheless, the captain was a passenger on the first trip of the *Maui* to Hawaii beginning on April 7, 1917, one day after the United States declared war on Germany. After a day or two in port at Honolulu, the *Maui* sailed for the island of the same name. Alexander G. Budge, a boiler salesman later to be president of Castle & Cooke, recalled the trip: "Because they had a lot of notables going along, Peter Johnson, the captain, said, 'We'll go an hour later than usual.'

"They had to get into that port of Kahului and the result was that we all but went ashore. Captain Matson was aboard and Mr. Tenney and Faxon Bishop and I guess, Lawrence Alexander. I didn't know all of them; I was just a bystander. I do remember all of them getting around the old captain, trying to divert his attention from the fact that it was nip and tuck whether we would go aground. That was quite a stirring moment for all of us. We didn't hit but we plowed a hell of a lot of the bottom before we stopped.''

War did not affect operation of the Matson fleet immediately. The *Maui* made nine round trips with civilian cargoes and passengers during the early months. Only the old bark *R. P. Rithet,* now equipped with the Bolinder engines as auxiliaries, had trouble.

K. W. Lindberg was a well-known sailing ship captain, especially noted for record-breaking runs between the coal docks at Ladysmith, B.C., and San Francisco. "He was quite a clever gentleman,'' according to Captain Diggs. "He would go up and load coal and sail his ship out of the harbor without help, make a round trip—and the other vessels in there would still be weatherbound. He wrote the most beautiful script I've ever seen. He used to tell me (he had a beautiful great moustache), 'I go down and look in the mirror and take a shot out of the bottle and say, "Lindberg, put more sail on this son of a bitch." ' ''

But on the *Rithet* his skills did little good on the morning of July 24, 1917, while two fifths of the way between Mahukona, island of Hawaii, and San Francisco, with 1,900 tons of sugar, then worth $266,000, and a crew of sixteen or eighteen (accounts differ).

As might be expected, it was the newfangled Bolinder engines that did him in. These pioneer diesels were known as hot-bulb types that could be started only after the combustion chamber was heated with a blowtorch. Various possibilities, all bad, were obvious. A Honolulu newspaper said:

"Unassumingly thankful that they had been saved from a watery grave, Captain K. Lindberg, officers and crew of the *R. P. Rithet* told today of the fire which destroyed their ship at sea and a ten-day voyage of nearly 900 miles to land and safety at Port Allen, Kauai.*

"Flooding of the engine cylinder head with oil from a feed pipe broken by the vibration of the vessel is held responsible for the fire. It was discovered by H. A. Houston, the first engineer, at about 3:30 a.m. . . . When the blaze flamed up, he grabbed a fire extinguisher and attempted to stop the fire. Unable to do so, he rushed up to the officers' sleeping quarters and called the chief engineer. . . . they discovered the blaze had made such headway that it was impossible to curb it. . . .

"So rapid was the progress of the fire that a few minutes later it would have been impossible for the officers to have made their way forward along a narrow passageway. Fearing that an explosion would result when the oil tanks were reached by the fire, the captain gave orders to launch the lifeboats.

*Normal courses for sailing ships from the island of Hawaii to San Francisco lay well to the north of a direct route, sometimes carrying them beyond the fortieth parallel to take the trade winds from the most advantageous quarter. A lifeboat seeking land, however, reasonably would run almost straight down the line of the trades. Lindberg's landfall, some 250 miles northwest of his port of departure, may not have been the nearest land, but was the easiest to reach. It was touchy. If he had been more than ten miles off to port, he could have sailed right through the Hawaiian chain.

[Lindberg: "The only one not in flames was the long boat aft on the starboard side."] As the steering wheel was aft among the flames, the ship could not be brought about and it was necessary to launch the boat on the weather side. . . .

". . . they pulled away from the ship about 200 yards and lay to, waiting for daylight. Sometime before daylight, a great amount of smoke and flames shot up from the ship and it was thought the expected explosion had occurred. As the danger did not seem great [at daybreak], the captain ordered a part of the crew placed aboard the vessel to attempt to obtain additional provisions and water and to fight the fire. Then an all-day but hopeless fight began. With two lines of hose . . . streams of water were turned on the fire but with little avail. Two big holes in the stern of the ship had been burned . . . and the *Rithet* began to sink, slowly, stern first. Nevertheless the fight . . . was not given up until . . . the hot decks began to buckle, great seams appearing . . . in the deck, beneath which the fire was burning halfway to the main hatch."

The newspaper said a scarcity of containers and the capacity of the single lifeboat made carrying large quantities of water or food impossible. Captain Lindberg, in another interview, added: "We spent some time rigging up a canvas bulkhead to keep the water out when the boat rolled. Then I decided . . . [to steer] . . . a course for the islands. I did not have time to grab my sextant or chronometer . . . and all we had was a boat compass.

"The weather was clear and fine but the rollers were high and it was a job keeping her from yawing so that she would upset. . . . Sixteen of us took the boat down so low that there was scarcely half a foot of freeboard.

"By the time we made the Kauai landfall we were pretty well all in. Some of the men, called from watch below, had on only their thin underclothes. They suffered terribly from sunburn during the day and cold at night. We had a fair wind and rigged something of a sail from the canvas of the boat cover and a couple of 'oilies.' "

The Honolulu newspaper said also that Lindberg, using only a small map of the islands torn from a memorandum, an improvised "circle" compass rose, and a canvas towed overboard periodically to determine his speed, calculated his landfall with only a fifty-mile error (fortunately, in the right direction).

Amid all the uproar of war, sea disasters, and the frenzied expansion of the company, the ailing Captain Matson attempted to continue his lifelong work habits and did continue to dream. The possibilities for a family succession in the businesses were enhanced by the birth of a grandson, William Matson Roth, on September 3, 1916.

For the captain, however, iron will was no longer enough. After-effects of his stroke intensified. As the work of the Swedish consulate increased (it now had to look after Austrian interests in the western United States as well as those of neutral Sweden), Matson appeared less and less often; and Dr. Westerberg's letters mentioned that his health was failing. It is not clear whether Matson officially resigned his position as consul general when the possibility arose that Sweden might join the Central Powers, but certainly Westerberg did most of the work. (Sweden eventually awarded Westerberg a pension for his efforts, even though he was a naturalized American citizen.)

Close associates feared that Matson could not live long, and he did not. Captain William Matson died on October 11, 1917, just a week short of his sixty-seventh birthday. The *San Francisco Chronicle* estimated his fortune at more than $3 million.

CHAPTER SIX

WORLD WAR I, ODD SHIPS, AND SKIPPERS (1917–1919)

All American flag vessels over 2,500 gross tons were requisitioned for war service in November 1917. The *Maui*, *Matsonia*, and *Wilhelmina*, all built with oversized fuel tanks and heavy decking to permit their conversion to auxiliary cruisers in case of war, actually were put into service as armed troop transports. The *Wilhelmina*, for example, received four 6-inch guns; two one-pounders; two Colt automatic machine guns; and four depth bombs. If these did not make her exactly a fearsome fighting machine, perhaps they inspired confidence in the 23,312 military passengers she was to carry in hastily enlarged accommodations.

The *Manoa* and *Lurline* (no. 2) also were taken but were returned to Matson control, for service to the Philippines rather than to Hawaii. Peter Johnson pointed out that the freight rate to the Philippines soon became $60 a ton and that *Lurline*, carrying 8,000 tons, made more money on one trip than her building costs. Since Matson was operating the ship for the War Shipping Board, however, the company received only a small commission (the size not specified by Johnson), with the rest going to the government.

Very little cargo space was left for Hawaii. During the first months of the war Matson continued to carry sugar from the islands at a contractual $2.75 a ton, although it represented a considerable loss. Shipping rates everywhere else were skyrocketing, however, and Hawaiian shippers consented to one raise while Matson still was in control. When the War Shipping Board took charge, rates went up another 100 percent.

The Oceanic Line fared somewhat better than the Hawaiian service. The *Sonoma* and *Ventura* continued in the Antipodes run, under some control by the War Shipping Board. The *Sierra* was chartered first by the army, then went into navy service in the Atlantic in 1918.

Captain Johnson, now ashore, reported:

"The government was building ships of both iron and wood so fast that it looked as though they were turning them out overnight. In the Spring of 1918, the Matson company was manager and agent for eighty-four ships belonging to the government. These were mostly wooden ships, some small interned German vessels. The wooden ships were built in a hurry and very poorly constructed. Quite a number which we loaded in San Francisco for the Hawaiian islands and South America never made the round trip. Nearly all of them were leaking and quite a number came back to San Francisco with twisted rudder stocks. Our docks, piers thirty and thirty-two, were full of ships being repaired. . . . After segregating the fleet, we found we had a sufficient number to carry merchandise to Hawaii and the sugar back to San Francisco."

The *Maui* and *Matsonia* each could carry 3,500

troops at a time. The *Maui* made thirteen trips from the East Coast to France, carrying 37,444 troops in all, the *Matsonia* fourteen voyages with 38,974 troops. Both carried enough oil to permit them to refuel other ships—mostly destroyers—at sea, along with lifting gear allowing them to load or unload guns and other heavy equipment without using shoreside facilities.

The record of the *Wilhelmina*'s service, however, is the most detailed. Under government control, the ship sailed from San Francisco to Iquique, Chile, on December 2, 1917, loaded 5,000 tons of nitrate, made her first trip through the Panama Canal (she had come around the Horn on her delivery trip in 1910), and reached New York on January 22, 1918. There she was officially commissioned as a navy ship and put under command of her former civilian skipper, Joe E. Jory, who had become a navy lieutenant commander. She sailed for France in heavy seas and fog three days later, unloading at Brest with her own gear and French men and women stevedores, and returning in convoy. The only excitement occurred when this convoy and a British convoy running in the opposite direction met head-on in the dark. There was confusion but no collision.

The *Wilhelmina*'s conversion to carry troops was completed in May, providing bunks for 1,703 troops and stateroom accommodations for 113 officers (lucky fellows). Commander William Tennant, U.S. Navy, took command of the crew of 32 officers and 281 enlisted men.

The *Wilhelmina* then began her six eastbound troop-carrying trips, carrying 2,085 on her heaviest passenger list, 1,260 on the lightest. On the initial trip, her first attempt to fuel a destroyer at sea (possibly the first ever) was made with the destroyer *Conners* steaming abreast and fifty yards off the *Wilhelmina*. "The attempt was unsuccessful," says the ship's record, "and the idea abandoned. This method was considered too dangerous." Subsequently, fueling was tried again, this time with the *Wilhelmina* towing the destroyer *Stevens* on a buoy line at five knots while feeding it oil through a parallel hose. After one more slightly botched attempt,

this method was adopted and used throughout the war.

Although the ship's crew spotted many suspicious wakes, floating barrels that could have been mines and objects that could have been whale fins or periscopes, only one torpedo wake was identified positively, although several ships with which the *Wilhelmina* was in convoy were sunk by submarines later.

Her one tragic trip began on September 21, 1918, when influenza broke out among the troops while the ship still was at dock. Within four and a half hours, forty-one cases had been reported. Thirty-three men were removed to an army base, but the ship was ordered to sail the following morning. By the twenty-fourth, doctors reported fifteen cases of influenza in the ship's crew.

Daily, the list increased: 85 (influenza and/or pneumonia) on September 25; 128, including 8 cases of mumps, the next day. The epidemic worked through the convoy, and the destroyer *Rathbone*, lacking medical help for her sick, turned back to the United States. *Wilhelmina*'s list showed 168 cases of influenza or mumps by the twenty-seventh and 155 serious and 200 under treatment the next day, when the epidemic peaked. The first death occurred on October 1, a few hours after another vessel in the convoy had conducted a burial at sea. Two more men died October 2, and 4 the following day. By October 6, when the *Wilhelmina* docked at Saint-Nazaire, France, 18 men had died on board, all but one, soldiers. In the convoy, there had been 1,300 virulent cases of influenza/pneumonia and 49 deaths.

A board of investigation reported, in part: "Service records of the men indicated that the majority of them have been in service less than three months . . . and factors considered to be of special significance [include] lack of rest at Camp Merritt; the cutting short of hair done at Camp Merritt just prior to departure, and the delay in damp weather at the ferry boat landing. No evidence could be found that the troops had been exposed . . . to any epidemic of influenza."

Except for a few wounded passengers, the *Wilhelmina* made her first five westbound trips of the war empty. She was in Brest on November 11, 1918, dressed ship in celebration of the Armistice and sailed that afternoon with wounded and sick soldiers aboard and running lights showing for the first time in months. Thereafter, eastbound trips were mostly without passengers, although some cargo still moved in that direction. Westbound trips beginning in January 1919 from Bordeaux, Brest, and Saint-Nazaire were jammed. She docked at Hoboken on her final government run on July 3, 1919.

All three Matson ships received government plaques for meritorious service. If the nickname "Battling Willie" was a mite exaggerated, certainly the *Wilhelmina,* as well as the others, demonstrated reliability and the usefulness of her design. Peter Johnson went to New York to get the *Wilhelmina.* "My wife was with me," he wrote, ". . . and she cried when she saw the condition it was in. I expected it and did not mind as much as she did, but the filth and dirt and the unsanitary conditions were too much for me." He loaded coal at Norfolk for San Francisco, where the ship went to yards for general repairs. The *Maui* and *Matsonia* followed soon afterward.

Matson gained considerable loyalty in Hawaii for managing to serve the islands with relics and junkers during the nearly two years when its best ships were scattered from Manila to Saint Nazaire. Rightly or wrongly, islanders blamed the American-Hawaiian Line for not doing so, and knowledge of this feeling may have influenced that line's decision not to try for the island business again. Also important was the fact that it had lost its valuable agency, Hackfeld & Company, and would have difficulty finding another as useful.

Hackfeld & Company was seized as enemy property and never returned to its former German owners, although they eventually did receive some compensation after court actions that dragged on until 1943. Assets of the old corporation were sold in 1918 to the self-styled American Factors, Ltd.,

actually a consortium in which Alexander & Baldwin, C. Brewer & Company, H. P. Baldwin, Ltd., Castle & Cooke, Matson Navigation Company, and Welch & Company each had 2,300 shares. This new company then bought out German interests in three Hawaiian plantations. The city of Honolulu eliminated "Hackfeld" from its street names, and the subsidiary Ehlers Department Store was renamed Liberty House.

All this ensured that while the new company would continue with department stores, pineapple and sugar investments, and its insurance business, it most certainly was not going to operate as a general agency in competition with Castle & Cooke nor ship merchandise on vessels in competition with Matson. The formidable Edward Tenney, now president both of Castle & Cooke, Inc., and Matson Navigation Company, could be trusted to take care of that. He did so.

Thus, for the moment, Matson had things nicely in hand: a lock on much of the island-bound cargo through American Factors and other consignees more or less controlled by Castle & Cooke, plus what amounted to a monopoly on eastbound sugar shipments through the same agency. Connections between large Hawaiian businesses in this period included interlocking directorates, mutual interests between producers and agencies, mutual dependence on the same suppliers of capital. Not always obvious or simple, almost always they were there.

Of course, sweetness and light could not be expected to continue and did not. Islanders thought freight rates should go back to prewar levels; Matson thought not. There also were new sharks in the waters: by name, the Los Angeles Steamship Company.

Two slim passenger ships, the *Yale* and the *Harvard,* were launched at Chester, Pennsylvania, in 1906 for the New York to Boston coastal trade. In 1908, however, they were chartered to the Pacific Navigation Company and sailed around Cape Horn to set up a similar overnight service between Los Angeles and San Francisco. There they acquired a reputation for clocklike regularity, interrupted only when they were leased to the Alaska Navigation Company for use on the Inside Passage. When the Alaska and Pacific companies merged, the Chester ships were returned to the California coastal run, making four round trips a week.

The U.S. Navy bought both ships in 1917 for $1 million each and promptly converted them from oil to coal burners, a reverse switch if there ever was one. The *Harvard* was renamed the *Charles,* and both ships went in service between Southampton and Le Havre, where their twenty-three-knot speed reduced the danger from submarines and made the rough English Channel crossings bearable if not happy.

At war's end, the ships were sold back to the Pacific coast. A loose confederation of buyers became the Los Angeles Steamship Company in 1920. Officers were Fred L. Baker, president; General M. H. Sherman, vice-president; Earle M. Leafe, secretary; and M. H. Whittier, treasurer. Directors included Harry Chandler, the legendary head of the *Los Angeles Times* and several other companies; his nephew, Ralph J. Chandler, sometime motorcycle enthusiast and executive of a family-owned shipyard; and Frank R. Seaver. A. J. Frey was general manager, but Ralph Chandler was the prime mover.

The two ships returned to the coastal run after both were reconverted to oil burners and the *Harvard* was given back its original name. They were reliable but the high speed and narrow beams tested the stomachs of the unwary. "They'd go up and down this coast like corkscrews," says one account, "and [people] said if you could live through a trip in any kind of stormy weather you had a cast iron stomach."

Ralph Chandler was not satisfied with a two-vessel shipline, however, and persuaded other members of his family to put into the company enough additional capital to buy ships for a Los Angeles–Honolulu route.

The timing was right. The U.S. government had a variety of ships for sale, including former German vessels taken as war prizes. The Los Angeles Steam-ship Company (LASSCO) purchased the former *Friederich der Grosse,* built in 1896, and the *Grosser Kurfurst,* built in 1900. Under different names, they had been used as U.S. troop transports during the war. Old as they were, the 12,000-ton ships had good passenger accommodations and competitive speed.

The *Friederich,* renamed the *City of Honolulu,* began the new service and nearly ended it. East-bound after her first call at Honolulu, she was 700 miles out on October 12, 1922, when a passenger taking his morning stroll on deck smelled smoke. He spoke to some sailors scrubbing the deck, but was told, "Aw, you're crazy."

He is reported to have said, "You open that door there and see. This ship is on fire." They did, and it was. The crew managed to keep the fire down until the army transport *Thomas,* coming up from Manila, arrived and took off all passengers and crew; but the ship was lost.*

The setback did not stop the LASSCO operation. The company secured the steamer *President Harrison* for one trip, starting only eleven days after the fire, then bought the army transport *Sherman,* renamed it the *Calawaii,* and sent it out to Honolulu with passengers on February 10, 1923. The *Grosser Kurfurst* was renamed the *City of Los Angeles.* In 1926 the company bought another German veteran, the liner *Kiautschou,* launched in 1900 and subsequently operated as the *Princess Alice, Princess Matoika,* and *President Arthur.* She now became the second *City of Honolulu* and assisted the other LASSCO ships in snaring enough passenger and freight business to make Matson management uncomfortable.

Matson also had other worries. The passenger-freight ships *Wilhelmina, Manoa, Matsonia,* and *Maui* for the time being were sufficient for the trunk-line runs from San Francisco to Honolulu, with occasional stops at Hilo; but the freighter fleet

*The *Thomas* had been headed for San Francisco but the company applied enough political pressure to have it diverted at the last minute to Los Angeles for the convenience of the rescued civilians. Army personnel with families waiting on the dock at San Francisco were not overjoyed.

was another matter. Only the *Annie Johnson,* burbling along with her sails and auxiliary engines, the thirty-year-old *Enterprise,* the also elderly *Hyades* and the *Lurline* (no. 2) were left to serve the outports and load their sugar. All were slow and the total capacity was insufficient. Matson scrambled to buy three "Lakers," cranky vessels built in Great Lakes shipyards for the government. These 2,500-ton ships were used mainly to pick up sugar in the doghole ports—Kauai's Port Allen was one where, according to Captain Charles Brocas, "We used to go in and drop an anchor on ninety fathoms of chain, then swing around and drop a port anchor, then a stern line." Thus anchored in the stream with the stern attached to buoys, there was nothing further to be done except to hope the wind didn't blow too hard. For Brocas on one voyage, it was not enough. With stevedores aboard, the wind rose. "Fortunately," he said, "we had those ninety fathoms of chain. So we just picked up everything and went out, taking the stevedores around to Wiliwili [probably a sailor's term for Nawiliwili] on the lee side of the island."

Other ports served by the Lakers included East Maui's lonesome Hana, Hawaii's Mahukona, Kawaihae, and wonderfully named Kukuihaele, barely a dent in the shoreline. The ships had euphonious names—*Mahukona, Makaweli, Makena*—and were called other names by captains and crews attempting to operate the flat-bottomed vessels in high winds or seas.

Matson also bought a new freighter, the *Manukai,* 7,409 tons, in 1921. The *Manulani,* 9,556 tons, was built in 1922; the *Mauna Ala,* 6,805 tons, and the *Makiki,* 6,095 tons, were bought from the government in 1923. There was an increasing call for service between Hawaii and the U.S. East Coast immediately after the war. To meet it, Matson leased from the War Shipping Board two "state"-class liners, the *Hawkeye State* and *Buckeye State,* each equipped with problems the company didn't need.

John Fischbeck, of a Stonington, Connecticut, seagoing family, first worked for Matson as a freight clerk on the San Francisco docks.

"When I first went to sea," he said, "I had one stripe [as a purser] and I thought I was commodore of the fleet. . . . it was the old *Lurline* [no. 2] and we had something like fifteen Filipino passengers and seventy-five mules on deck. I asked my mother to come down and see me sail in my new uniform . . . with my aunt, whose husband was a captain for one of the oil companies. We put those mules in stalls on both sides of the deck with their tails outboard. . . . Those poor donkeys [*sic*] had to stand up for seven days and seven nights. . . . If they ever got down we'd never get them up. . . . there wasn't enough room. . . . our office was aft and you couldn't see the bridge for the hay stacked up. . . . we also had cows on the forward deck. They used to call her the Matson Ark.

"So here are my mother and my aunt down there at the end of the dock, seeing their son and nephew going to sea for the first time, keeping up the old family tradition.

"We had to back out of the slip, so my mother didn't see me at all. The only thing she saw was thirty-seven mule behinds on the starboard side going by, just an array of mule back ends."

Of the "state" ships (also known as "535s"), he said:

"Those were the damndest ships I've ever seen. They had Yarrow triangular boilers, designed for destroyers and cruisers so they could get up steam in a hurry. . . . They were always blowing the boiler tubes. When we'd get to New York, we'd go over to the Erie Basin and lie there for a month, getting new tubes. By the time we'd get to San Francisco, we'd come in with a couple of boilers out.

"Somebody had designed these ships in such a way that if you were to go to the john and flush it you were likely to get an upside down, hot water shower. The electric power would go off. . . . there was something every day. One night out of Havanna, we had a pretty good crowd of passengers. This woman was ironing her dress or something and left the iron on the ironing board and forgot to turn it off before she went down to dinner. Everybody's having dinner and all of a sudden the damn ship's on fire. . . . smoke got in the ventilating system and came out the other side. We were all looking for the fire where the smoke was, and it was on the other side of the ship. We had two or three feet of water in the passageway down below before we finally got it out.

"The ship would go from New York to Baltimore to Havana, through the canal, and if we could make Los Angeles we would. If not, we'd stop some place to take on more fresh water for the boilers. We were short of water one trip and went into Salina Cruz [west coast of Mexico]. There's a great big drawbridge at the entrance to the harbor. We got in all right, early in the morning, and were there all day, pumping water. I think we were using it up about as fast as they could pump it in through a regular fire hose. We also loaded quite a few tons of coffee.

"When we were backing out, they hadn't raised the drawbridge high enough, or something slipped. The wing of the ship's bridge got fouled up with that great high drawbridge. I could hear this screech, howl, bang! Poor old Johanson was the chief officer. He told me later, 'I wasn't worrying too much except I'm wondering how the hell am I going to get that bridge off the deck of the ship.'

"Captain Diggs warned the harbor pilot to get off in his boat in a hurry, 'because when we get out, I'm going to go out of here as fast as I can.' And he did. Later on, another Matson ship went in there and the shore people lowered the draw and wouldn't open it until the company paid for the damages."

Many of the early Matson ship captains indeed were Swedish, like their employer. There was Charles Rock (original name Sandberg), who twice ran away from a well-to-do family and spent much of his life on the scow schooners and in the Sandwich islands trade without serious accident, only to break his eighty-three-year-old neck in a fall in 1924. Arthur Matson, forever explaining he was not a relative of the line's president, was among the first, as was Peter Johnson, who spent most of his forty years at sea in Matson vessels. Konrad Hubbenette, famous for his mynah bird companion as well as for winning a 1909 marathon running championship, followed, as did Charles A. Berndtson,

eventually commodore of the company's fleet, plus coveys of Rasmussens, Johansons, and others with like names.

In the years immediately after World War I, however, the roster became more multinational. Jonny P. Bruns, born in Hamburg, Germany, went over the side of the German steamship *Harcourt* at San Francisco just before the war and signed on with Matson in 1921. Hans O. Matthiesen, also a German, arrived in San Francisco aboard the full-rigged German sailing ship *Tamara XII,* eighty-two days out of China, in 1922.

"We were in Chinese ballast—sand," he said. "We had to throw all that ballast over the side and clean the hold. Then the cargo of barley started to come alongside in barges. We saw these workers, all Spanish speaking. Some of our men could speak Spanish and one of them said, 'You know what those fellows are getting? Ninety dollars a month and food. We don't make that much in a year. The captain doesn't get that much.' "

A shipmate agreed to look after his sea chest on the way home; and Matthiesen followed Bruns' over-the-side route, worked three months on a farm, turned himself in to the U.S. Immigration Service, paid an $8.08 head tax, and was on his way to American citizenship and eventual Matson employment. When he retired in 1970, he, too, was fleet commodore.

The most unusual import, however, was Mely Julius Gordenev, who held a Russian Imperial Navy commission equivalent to that of an American commander. Among other exploits, he had been with a Siberian scientific expedition that turned up a mastodon frozen in a glacier, and reputedly chipped out some of the flesh and ate it.

As the Czarist government was disintegrating, he arrived at a Russian port for assignment. As Gordenev told it, the port captain pointed to a ship in the harbor and said, "I'm going to give you command of that ship." Gordenev's reply: "No, thanks. The sailors on that ship killed all their officers yesterday."

Whether or not this is precise history, Gordenev

definitely did get his family to Archangel on the White Sea, and aboard one of the last ships to sail before the port was closed. He himself made his way separately to New York, picked up a fisheries patrol vessel, and started back to Russia with it. The crew mutinied off Nova Scotia, and Gordenev and his first officer swam ashore.

Meanwhile, the ship escaping Archangel had followed a sea track to be made infamous a quarter century later as the Murmansk run. Westbound, the vessel stayed well out in the Atlantic. Gordenev's family saw no land except the grim coast of Iceland until they were approaching New York and reunion.

Like other Russians abroad, Gordenev attempted to work with rapidly changing governments. He was again in New York when Alexander Kerensky fell and Admiral Kolchak established his short-lived "All Russian Government" at Omsk on November 18, 1918. Gordenev was ordered to take a coal-burning steamer to Vladivostok. This he attempted, with his family aboard, and reached San Francisco but received no further orders. So he coaled his ship and started backing out of the coaling wharf for the trans-Pacific voyage. His engineers missed a signal to stop, however, and the Russian vessel backed into a U.S. destroyer.

That ended the odyssey. The Russian ship was towed to an East Bay dock and rusted there. The Gordenev family went ashore in San Francisco and stayed there. Gordenev sailed on Matson ships as an unlicensed seaman until 1924, when he became a U.S. citizen and second officer on the venerable *Annie Johnson*. His first assignment as master of a Matson ship, the *Mala,* came in 1930.

The old sugar port of Kukuihaele on the exposed northern coast of the island of Hawaii would have been an easy winner in an unpopularity contest if Matson skippers did the voting. Waipio Bay is no more than a dimple, the shoreline a high cliff. Only small ships called there, and they called only because the plantations and mills there had no way to move their product overland to a decent harbor. To load sugar, a ship moored 200 yards offshore, parallel to the cliffs, with two bow anchors down

and stern lines to a fixed buoy, picking up the end of a seawire running up to and over the cliff to a donkey engine. This wire was secured over the deck with a quick-release Pelican hook. A block in the loop of an endless loading wire then was sent down and secured, and sugar arrived aboard in slings suspended from a traveler. All this was controlled by a lookout on the cliff edge, since the donkeyman could not see the ship. The operation required skilled and virtually fearless longshoremen brought from Hilo who, as needed, "rode the wire" up or down, clinging to sugar bags. At least one was killed doing it.

For ship captains and mill managers alike, it was a nervous business. Aware that the sea bottom was well seeded with lost anchors, captains tended to pace the decks, consult watches, and run for sea room the minute the wind started to blow, which was frequently. Sometimes they took all the cargo offered, but often they chose not to wait.

Quite early, mill managers decided that some small inducement to captains to hang around for a full load would be a good investment. Hence, one of the first bags over the cliff usually contained a small envelope for the skipper as well as sacks of sugar.

One veteran remembers it well: "There was always a present for the skipper crazy enough to bring his ship in there. When I was a pilot . . . there was always a hundred dollars. If I didn't get it, I wouldn't bring the next ship in. It was fine until Mely Gordenev came in once. I guess nobody had told him. When the envelope came down, he not only sent it back but reported to San Francisco that 'There was some money they sent down the wire to me and I don't know what for. It didn't belong to me so I sent it back.'

"He nearly ruined the whole industry."

(Anatole Gordenev followed his father into the Matson fleet in 1930. Mely retired in 1949 and Anatole got his first command in 1951, keeping the family name on the list of Matson captains for two more decades.)

CHAPTER SEVEN

NEW ROUTES, GRANDEUR ASHORE AND AFLOAT
(1919–1927)

Matson management was two-headed from the time of the captain's death in 1917. William P. Roth, vice-president and general manager, directed company activities from San Francisco. Edward Tenney was president but spent most of his time in Honolulu, handling the company's serious affairs in the islands but also finding time to check applications for eastbound passenger accommodations when space sometimes was short. He and Faxon Bishop, the head of C. Brewer & Company and also opinionated, placed checkmarks beside the names of people they liked. Everybody else had to wait for another ship.

When he himself went to San Francisco, Tenney did so in style, taking along not only his Lincoln automobile but also his personal chauffeur. At company headquarters, Tenney and Roth shared a large office, with desks at opposite ends. A company official said, "They sat facing each other all the time, kind of an odd arrangement . . . sort of listening to each other."

Odd the arrangement may have been, but the completely different men got things done. In 1919 Matson vessels for the first time carried the entire Hawaiian sugar crop to the Pacific Coast. The next year, nearly 1 million tons of cargo crossed the Honolulu docks, three fourths moving in Matson bottoms. Four years after that, Matson carried 95

percent of the cargo handled by Castle & Cooke —690,000 tons—plus freight for others.

Interisland shipping also increased rapidly in the early 1920s, the movement of fresh pineapple from Maui and Lanai to Honolulu for canning accounting for much of it. In 1924 Matson bought a tug and barge especially for this cargo but so upset directors of the Inter-Island Steam Navigation Company, Ltd., that Inter-Island offered to sell out to the larger company. In the end, Matson bought $1.5 million worth of Inter-Island stock and turned over its tug and barge, then sold part of its holding to Castle & Cooke and four of its executives. Thus, one more link was forged in the chain connecting Hawaiian industries.

Another link was also in the making. At World War I's end, management of the Oceanic Steamship Company believed the *Ventura* and *Sonoma* could handle the South Pacific business. So when the *Sierra* was returned to the company after war service, it was sold, ending up on an Atlantic route for the Polish-American Navigation Company under a new name: *Gdansk*.

By 1922, however, Oceanic had a new U.S. mail contract paying $3 per mile for the outbound voyages to Australia; and passenger business was better. Oceanic therefore repurchased the tired old vessel, reconditioned and named it *Sierra* once more, then put it back in service with the other two sister ships.

Good times in the trade were short-lived. Four British lines, all with subsidies of some sort, came into the Australian picture: New Zealand's Union Steamship Company, Ltd., operating 8,075-ton *Makura* and the slightly smaller *Tahiti* between Australia, New Zealand, Tahiti, and San Francisco; the Canadian Australian Royal Mail Steamship Company, with the 13,500-ton *Niagara* and the new, 17,500-ton motorship *Aorangi* running between the Antipodes and British Columbia; plus the Peninsula & Orient Steamship Company, Ltd., running the 20,000-ton ships *Mooltan* and *Maloya,* and the Orient Steam Navigation Company, with the 16,000-tonners *Chitral, Comoin,* and *Cathay.* The last two companies operated to Europe via the Suez Canal.

Oceanic's ships, by contrast, were outdated relics, and the company was operating at a deficit. Adolph Spreckels had died, and his brother John was more than seventy and very tired. On April 24, 1926, The Oceanic Steamship Company (a new firm, although only the word "The" was added to the old name) was organized with paid-in capital of $1.5 million, all provided by Matson. The new firm acquired the ships, the mail contract, and the goodwill, if any, of the old.

At the year's end Matson was operating seventeen ships under its own house flag, with three more in the Oceanic company, now a subsidiary. The annual report showed $2,320,608 earnings, $1,622,291 from the ships and the rest from Honolulu Oil Company and sugar stocks. Much greater changes than the Inter-Island and Oceanic investments were coming.

Two decades earlier, Captain Matson had recognized the value of a complete commodity-handling system: oil wells, ships to carry oil, tanks to store it in the islands. Now, Tenney and Roth needed another new system to handle a new commodity: tourists-with-money. For the time being, the hyphenated term was descriptive. Florida and California salesmen for real estate under water or invisi-

ble among desert dunes were reaping harvests from schoolteachers and farmers with only enough money for a down payment or perhaps a vacation in a tent. The wildest Hawaii enthusiasts, however, could not imagine a time when thousands of people barely able to save or borrow a month's salary would swarm to the islands. The commodity of the day was the tourist who could afford about what he wanted. For him, there must be great ships and great hotels.

Honolulu then had the downtown hotels Alexander Young and Blaisdell, neither luxurious, and the twenty-three-year-old Moana and the even older Seaside Bungalows at Waikiki. The beach hotels were owned by the Territorial Hotel Company, Ltd.

In 1924, Castle & Cooke subscribed $200,000 toward a new hotel. Early in the next year, Roth told a Honolulu audience that a new company, incorporating the Territorial Hotel Company properties, would spend $2 million for such a project. Tenney was president of the new company, Atherton Richards treasurer, and Alexander G. Budge secretary. T. H. Petrie and F. C. Atherton, both Castle & Cooke officials, were directors. A few weeks later the company announced signing of a fifty-year lease from the Bishop Estate, owner of most of the Waikiki real estate, for 15.21 shorefront acres, once a royal playground. Four hundred acres of the Waialae Ranch beyond Diamond Head were bought for a golf course. Organization of the new company, capitalized at $2.5 million, was complete by August 1925, and the name Royal Hawaiian had been chosen for the hotel. There had been a hotel of that name during the monarchy, but it had been sold in 1917 to the Army-Navy YMCA. By October plans were drawn by Warren & Wetmore, New York hotel architects, and the expected cost was up to $3.5 million. Landscape architect R. T. Stevens was hired to convert twelve acres of the hotel grounds to tropical gardens, and Seth Raynor was designing an eighteen-hole golf course for the ranch.

Tenney and Roth agreed about the hotel they wanted: nothing but the best. To make sure they got it, they chose a rather unusual agent, Alexander Budge. This red-haired farmboy from North Dakota, with the inevitable nickname of "Pinky," an engineering education, and experience in selling boilers, had joined Castle & Cooke in 1920, assisted in the planning of a downtown headquarters, then had been named to manage all that company's relations with Matson. Budge promptly corrected, among other things, the Tenney–Faxon Bishop practice of deciding who could get shipboard reservations and who could not. "That," he said later, "was when I used to call a ship a boat and things like that."

His preparation for dealing with resort hotels? "I'd never been in one in my whole life."

This inexperience he undertook to correct immediately, setting out with Arthur Benaglia to learn about fine hotels and their inner workings. The Italian-born Benaglia, who had lost a hand in a Canadian train wreck and was a graduate of the Canadian Pacific resort hotel chain, had been chosen to manage the new Royal when it should be completed. He began Budge's education at the famous Vancouver Hotel. "We had," said Budge, "four rooms at the front. One of them had a card table just loaded with every kind of liquor you could imagine."

It was unlike North Dakota.

The education continued at Lake Louise, at Banff ("We were having dinner and I looked out to a pond, where a moose was having his dinner"), and at New York City's St. Regis Hotel.

"Benaglia was a remarkable guy," Budge said. "On those trains he'd manage to get ahead of me going from one car to another and even with only one arm would open the doors so I could come along. . . . once in New York I mentioned that I liked a certain wine when I was in France . . . and when I got back to my room about 3:00 A.M., here were two bottles of that wine on my bed."

Budge was less impressed by the architect, Wetmore, who drew plans for the Royal without visiting the islands. Much of Waikiki was a swamp prior to the digging of the Ala Wai Canal, and the remains

of it have plagued builders ever since: old coral reefs, solidified sandstone, and primordial mud-ponds seemingly without bottoms.

Wetmore's plans called for an odd-shaped building with one wing parallel to the beach. Hawaiians, none too happy about a hotel on the old monarchial gathering place, warned that the site was unsuitable for a heavy building. Agreeing, Budge protested to the architects but was ignored.

"I was the only one in any of these companies with engineering experience," he said. "Wetmore was a fathead. He was a skilled architect in many respects but he couldn't take advice. I had a hell of a time, because he wouldn't listen. We knew we were building on top of a stream, a sort of quicksand. We finally did get him alarmed to the extent that when he put in the footings, those columns, he left pockets in the columns so that if it settled he could jack it up.

"It was hard to talk to Wetmore because I was very much a junior at the time. Mr. Tenney would say, 'You don't know a damn thing about it.' Well, I didn't, but I'd say, 'It's very hard to put a steam pipe through a plate-glass window. . . .' "

The waterfront side of the hotel rested firmly on an ancient compacted sandstone ridge parallel to the beach; but the remainder of the building started to sink even before it was completed, and it kept on sinking. Wetmore's jacks were much too small. Builders finally had to dig under the partly finished structure, put in huge bridge-type girders, then operate jacks between the girders and the sinking columns. Concrete blocks inserted after years of frequent jacking can still be seen in the hotel basement.

Despite such problems, the pink stucco palace did get finished in sixteen months. The 35,000 barrels of cement, 75 miles of wire and cable, and 9,000 gallons of paint and stain no longer sound impressive in a day of high rises; but nothing of this size had been done before in the Pacific area. The style was Moorish, Mission, Spanish, or late Rudolph Valentino, depending on the acidity of the critic; but there was no question of its opulence. Public rooms were huge, and a theater ballroom was decorated with representations of barges floating down the Nile. An art gallery was "French in spirit and treatment," according to a contemporary report, and art lovers trod on a Czechoslovakian rug. Other carpets came from Tunisia; Persia; Holland; and Trenton, New Jersey; and Italian cherubs gazed down from the frescoes. An outdoor dining space and bar (not very profitable in those Prohibition days) was protected by a decorative fiber cover that was more handsome than sturdy. A photographer's model taking a walk out on it from an upper-level room fell through, landing unhurt beside a Matson executive entertaining guests at dinner.

The 400 guest rooms also were large and handsomely furnished, many with lanais, all with louvered hall doors and monel screens. Lanai furniture was bronze. Three men worked full-time just trimming the 800 palms on the property and lopping off coconuts likely to drop on the heads of unwary strollers.

Twelve hundred guests attended the gala opening on February 1, 1927. Only one thing was lacking: the *Malolo* wasn't there.

This was the first unit of the seagoing magnificence that was to match the lushness of the hotel, and she required all the superlatives advertising copywriters had left over. The ship was 582 feet long, with seven decks, a Pompeian-Etruscan swimming pool, electric baths (whatever they were), as well as a veranda cafe, a ballroom lounge, two theaters, a gymnasium, and room for 650 first-class passengers in 480 Simmons beds, each with a telephone beside it, and 170 Pullman berths.* No ship afloat could match the *Malolo*'s one hundred complete private baths and fifty private showers with toilets. Hot and cold fresh- and saltwater taps were in each bathroom, and a ventilating system changed the air in the staterooms every three minutes.

Each anchor weighed seven tons, the rudder twenty-six. With 25,000 horsepower, she could

cruise at twenty-one knots and cross from San Francisco to Honolulu in four and one half days. She also was safe, perhaps the first vessel able to prove it. If she had a tendency to roll a bit despite her eighty-three-foot beam, well, you can't have everything.

The *Malolo* was acquired through one of the complicated deals that abound in the shipping business. The American-Hawaiian Steamship Company obtained a large settlement from the government for vessels lost or damaged during World War I, but the settlement required that the money be used to build a new ship. It did not specify what the company should do with it after it was built. Having no wish to return to the Hawaiian trade, American-Hawaiian simply built the *Malolo* to Matson specifications and sold it to that company while it still was on the ways at Philadelphia's Cramp shipyard.

Construction of the ship was slow; a fire damaged some of the vessel's plates while it still was on the ways; and tugs managed to ground it on a mudbank after launching. Omens were not good when sea trials began in April 1927.

Peter Johnson, by now commodore of the Matson fleet and nearly ready to retire, was sent to Philadelphia to take command of the completed ship and rode along on the sea trial as a passenger. He described the experience in his *Memoirs*.

"It was a fine morning with light fog. The ship was in command of a shipyard captain and pilot. After leaving the dock, I naturally started to go up on the bridge but before getting to the top of the ladder I saw that the bridge was full of people, who or what they were I did not know. But I knew it was no place for me so I retraced my steps and at the foot of the ladder I met Captain C. Saunders, operating manager for the Matson company. He could see something was wrong and I told him to go on the bridge and look for himself. He came back saying just what I thought: 'No place for us, Pete.' . . .

"Captain Saunders realized at a glance at the bridge that things were not being carried out ship-

* By contrast, other Matson liners appeared small. *Wilhelmina* was 460 feet and carried 150 passengers. *Matsonia*, at 503 feet, and *Maui*, at 505 feet, each carried 275 passengers.

shape but told me we could not interfere. We continued down the river with fine weather and light fogs. We entered the Atlantic and continued up the coast. . . . after we passed New York the fog set in heavier and they slowed the speed down to about fourteen [miles an hour].

"I went up on deck at daylight and we were going through dense banks of fog . . . and we continued at the same speed through the forenoon."

Johnson said that after lunch, he was playing bridge in the smoking room with William P. Roth, Matson director Wallace M. Alexander, and a guest from New York when they heard a terrific smash and the ship began to tremble.

He continued: "We went out on deck on the port side . . . and saw a steamer with about fifteen feet of her bow crushed in. . . . I got up on the bridge where all was excitement and finally discovered that the steamer had hit us and crashed a big hole in our side. In the boiler room compartments the water was rushing in and the *Malolo* settled by the head.

"By quick action of the crew, all watertight compartment doors were closed [confining] the water to two rooms. I was looking for the ship to list over to either side but fortunately she kept an even keel. I then realized that if the bulkheads would hold we had a chance of saving the ship. We spent a very anxious four or five hours. . . . The anchor was dropped in about twenty-five fathoms. . . . We were about twenty-two miles south of the Nantucket lightship. A fishing trawler came alongside and offered to give us all the food we wanted, and when they found we had no means of cooking them [the fish] they also cooked them for us. . . . we found charcoal broilers in the kitchen and by ripping some of the woodwork from the lifeboats we managed to get enough wood to operate them. . . . at four o'clock in the morning the cooks started making flapjacks and prepared some coffee in a homemade coffee boiler. . . .

"The *Malolo* was rammed in the most vital spot, flooding the two engine rooms with over five thousand tons of water. It's no exaggeration to say that

no ship afloat at that time, outside of the *Malolo*, could have survived under those circumstances. . . . the ship cost eight million dollars to build and was at the time the most expensive and fastest merchant ship ever built in the United States. . . . The Norwegian ship [*Jacob Christensen*] that rammed the *Malolo* was valued at three hundred and fifty thousand dollars, and the estimated cost of repairing the *Malolo* was one million, five hundred thousand."

Wrangling between shipyard, Matson, and insurance company officials continued while the repair work dragged out. Captain Johnson and a Matson crew took the ship on a successful sea trial October 22, 1927, and five days later sailed for San Francisco with 300 Matson guests.

The ship easily maintained her design speed, but the trip was not fast. At Havana, all those VIPs hurried ashore, waving dollars, while Johnson kept his crew sober by denying any shore leave and fending off bumboats by turning firehoses on them. He could do nothing about the passengers, however, and those worthies soon returned with their purchases.

"It was about $6,000 worth of liquor," Budge remembers. "Going down through the canal, the crew spent the time putting it all in crates and marking them 'machinery.' . . . a lot of champagne was put in a spare boiler in the engine room. . . . Saunders was in Los Angeles saying everything was all right; but as we got closer some of the company people got colder feet and colder feet, and finally they dumped the whole damn business [the "machinery" crates] overboard the night before we got to Los Angeles."

The ship delayed there for a reception and luncheon, and again at San Francisco at an open house that drew 30,000 people during a long weekend.

"After we left San Francisco," Budge said, "the people who owned that champagne down in the spare boiler were buying it back from the crew for five or six dollars a bottle."

At Honolulu, all other welcomes for the new ship were put to shame. Johnson described the event:

"I had orders to anchor off the harbor at ten o'clock and there we were met by a couple of dozen canoes, all manned by Hawaiian chiefs, royalty and warriors. The first canoe that came alongside had two old Hawaiian chiefs carrying a koa platter on which they had a roasted pig. . . . This was taken to the after 'A' deck where the principal guests and officials were gathered. The second canoe which came alongside carried about twenty warriors, all in full regalia. . . . On the forward part of the ship we had built a platform large enough to take care of all these warriors and their equipment. The third boat alongside was filled with pretty Hawaiian hula girls. After they came aboard, the pig bearers came aft, to the accompaniment of the singing and dancing of the girls, bowed before me and presented me with the pig.

". . . After thanking the giver of the pig, I had the boy carry it to a table . . . and there I cut off pieces of the pig for distinguished guests. . . . We entered [the port] very slowly and in mid-channel met a large number of canoes manned by different chiefs of all the islands. The canoes lined up in front of the *Malolo,* half on each side. . . . we then threw long flower leis to each canoe. . . . this ceremony represented old times when the canoes had towed the ships to the dock. . . .

"The *Malolo* stayed in Honolulu two days and then left for Hilo, where we were given another royal welcome. Upon our return to Honolulu, a grand banquet was given at the Royal Hawaiian Hotel."

The hotel indeed was ready. It had been waiting ten months but now, at the tail end of 1927, the complete commodity-handling system could start working.

CHAPTER EIGHT

FLEETS MODERNIZED,
THE MILLIONAIRES' CRUISE
(1927–1929)

Edward Tenney had dominated Castle & Cooke almost without challenge from the day in 1907 when he had informed company directors that he disapproved of the $1,000 a year each of them was being paid, whereupon they meekly canceled their salaries and agreed to accept $5 payment for attending each meeting. Harold Castle, a grandson of the firm's cofounder, recalled the situation in a 1967 interview:

"Heads of firms such as ours were absolute dictators. They fought each other like cats and dogs, trying to outslicker the others in any business deal but they were good friends otherwise. They wrote the ticket for all business in the islands and everybody knew it. What Tenney said in Castle & Cooke was *law*. He used to bellow, 'Don't argue with me. Do as you're damn well told and do it now!'

"He was as arbitrary as he could be, but none of us really objected since he knew more about the business than all the rest of us put together. He managed to keep it that way. At board meetings he had everything cut and dried. He told us exactly how he wanted us to vote. Most of us didn't even know what we were voting on. The minutes could just as well have been written beforehand."

Tenney never exercised any comparable power during his decade as president of Matson (the Roths, Crockers, Rithet, Bucks, and other mainland investors were a bit formidable for bulldozing); but he did enjoy the ships and hotels and left his mark

on the company. (When the Honolulu Chamber of Commerce wished to make a gift to the new liner *Malolo,* Tenney suggested it would be very nice if the chamber paid for either of two paintings, one very good at $3,500 or another at $2,000 if they wanted things on the cheap. There is no record that he deigned to reply to a counterproposal that the chamber buy a nice bell that could be used to summon passengers for deck sports.)

By 1927, however, even Tenney recognized he was spread too thin for a man in his seventies. Almost simultaneously, he resigned as general manager of Castle & Cooke, although retaining its presidency, and moved to chairman of the board of directors of Matson, leaving the presidency of that company to William P. Roth.

Roth was something of a scholar and an outdoorsman whose idea of a splendid Sunday was a duck hunt in the San Francisco Bay marshes. No bellower, he had spent thirteen years rising through the Matson ranks and learning to deal with personalities such as Captain Matson and Tenney, as well as stevedores, ship captains, and prickly company directors. If the company presidency did not entirely delight him, neither did it offer any terrors.

Modernization of the freighter fleet had been under way for some time. The *Maunalei* and *Maunawili* had been added in 1925; the *Maliko* in 1926; and the smaller *Mana, Malama,* and *Mapele* a year later. All were used ships but improvements over what Matson had. The twenty-five-year-old *Hyades* and the *Lurline* (no. 2) went to Matson's favorite outlet for tired ships, the Alaska salmon-packing industry. The *Hyades* lasted only a decade before going to Japanese shipbreakers; but the *Lurline,* renamed *Chirikof* and finally the Yugoslav *Radnik,* continued to sail until 1953.

Now in full charge, Roth also moved to improve the company's passenger-carrying capabilities. The *Maui, Matsonia, Manoa,* and *Wilhelmina* all had face-lifts, including more bathrooms, improved galleys, and enough other amenities to soothe passengers who could not ride the *Malolo.* This million-dollar program was a stopgap but helped to keep passengers away from the old but comfortable liners of the Los Angeles Steamship Company.

In Honolulu, Matson did a complete renovation of the old Moana Hotel, which had been purchased for $1.6 million in 1928; while Inter-Island Steam Navigation Company, in which Matson still had an interest, acquired two new ships, the *Waialeale* and *Hualalai,* and built the Kona Inn on the island of Hawaii, to give tourists one more place to go.

Matson always served Hawaii without government subsidy and still does so. Subsidies were important, however, to the new Oceanic subsidiary, as they always had been to any line operating to Australia. Early in Roth's presidency, the U.S. Shipping Board offered to turn over to Matson and the American-Hawaiian Steamship Company the ships and routes of the American-Australia Orient Line, then government owned.

The two companies accepted the offer by forming, as a joint venture, the Oceanic & Oriental Navigation Company, with Matson to operate eleven freighters throughout the South Pacific, and American-Hawaiian taking ten ships for Pacific Coast–Orient services. Matson received a $380,000 annual subsidy for its portion of the service.

As this service began, Matson also was negotiating with the government for improvement of South Pacific passenger operations. On September 6, 1928,

Oceanic signed with the U.S. postmaster general a new mail contract calling for increased government payments in consideration for the building of larger and faster ships. On October 29, 1929, the company ordered two new liners. The *Matsonia* was 582 feet long, 17,323 gross tons; the *Mariposa,* 631.5 feet, 18,017 tons. A third ship, the newest *Lurline,* ordered slightly later, also was 631.5 feet, at 18,163 gross tons. Each of the three could carry approximately 695 passengers in two classes. Price tags were $8.3 million each.

On the Hawaiian run, the *Malolo* quickly proved to be a very popular ship for the ordinarily well-to-do and celebrities, including, in the first winter, a member of Egyptian royalty; Newton D. Baker, former secretary of war; Richard Barthelmess, Laura La Plante, Colleen Moore, Dorothy Mackaill, and a passel of other movie stars, ascending and descending. Very soon, however, certain truths about the Hawaiian tourist business became evident: it still was a seasonal thing, filling ships and hotels in mid-winter and late summer, not so good the rest of the time. So the *Malolo* was made available for special tours during the off seasons. Pacific Northwest chambers of commerce loaded her on a voyage out of Portland, Oregon, for Honolulu; the Shriners took every berth for a run from Los Angeles to Hilo and Honolulu.

But the fanciest trip by far was a 22,509-mile cruise around the Pacific, organized by the San Francisco Chamber of Commerce with a 325-passenger limit, and promptly dubbed the "millionaires' cruise" by journalists. This began in the autumn of 1929 and included Honolulu, Yokohama, Kobe, Miyajima, Chinwangtao, Shanghai, Hong Kong, Manila, Saigon, Bangkok, Singapore, Batavia, Freemantle, Melbourne, Sydney, Auckland, Suva, Pago Pago, and Hilo.

Charles Moore of the San Francisco group originally suggested limiting the passengers to 300 but was pressured to let another 25 in on the fun. Joyce Jones was not included. (The name is invented. The events were not.) Her story definitely belongs to Jack Fischbeck, no longer concerned with the care and feeding of seagoing mules. Fischbeck, by then the *Malolo*'s chief purser, related it:

"She was a dilly . . . a rather attractive girl who had been around San Francisco as an actress. She played the part of Tondelayo in a play called *White Cargo*. There was something about this girl. She never could do anything right. . . . when she was in the play, she created quite a furor because something went wrong in the middle of the play before a packed house and she started raising Cain and backing everybody else off the stage. Then she quit and walked off.

"That finished her as an actress. That's all the introduction I can give you to Joyce Jones.

"Now, we're going to sea on a very important cruise. Captain Charles A. Berndtson was the skipper, high man on the totem pole; and I was handling the business thing.

"To my knowledge, nobody in Matson had ever been to all these ports. We had to get papers to enter and clear all these places, and I had to write to all of them. I gathered papers for nineteen ports. It was a hell of a job. So I was up at the office of Castle & Cooke right after the ship docked at Honolulu. I was there all day, and Captain Berndtson was doing the same sort of business. We were in adjoining rooms, so we could hear each other talking. We were scheduled to sail at four in the afternoon and I was up in this office until about twenty minutes of four. Then Berndtson and I were driven down to the ship. He went right up on the bridge, and I didn't even get into my office to change into my uniform. The Harold Rice family from Maui was on board. I used to spend my vacations on their ranch whenever I could. So I went right up on deck to see them because they were going to sit at my table. When the ship pulled away from the dock, I was standing right there with them.

"So the ship gets out to sea and the next morning—it must have been half past five or six o'clock—Girvin Wait, the executive officer, comes into my cabin, shakes me and says, 'Get up. Get up!'

"I said, 'What's the matter with you? Are you drunk? You'd better have your coffee.'

"He said, 'We've got a stowaway.'

"I said, 'So you've got a stowaway. You know what to do with him. I'll see you in the morning. I'll get all the records and things we need from the guy; but he's your problem, not mine.'

"He said, 'This is a woman.'

"I thought, well, we never had any of this before. So I got my clothes on and went up to this dame. They had found her away up on A deck when they were cleaning up about six o'clock. So we bring this gal into the skipper's office and asked all the questions, 'Who are you?' 'How'd you get here?'

"She claimed she had been drugged, that she tried to get off the ship but passed out. Now, the gangway had been down on D deck, and how the hell she got up on A deck to get off the ship—but that wasn't the worst. That was when she said she'd been in Fischbeck's cabin to have a farewell drink with him. She said, 'There must have been something in the drink. . .'

"So you can see why I said so much about where I'd been all day.

"Well, we didn't want to be too rough on her, so we put her in a stateroom. The thing was, how are we going to get rid of this dame? Captain Berndtson sent a wireless to some ship of the Dollar Line that was coming in from Japan. That captain said yes, he'd take her off our hands.

"We sighted him after a while and he did stop. But when they got this Jones woman down at the side port to put her in a boat, she started raising Cain, waving and screaming.

"The skipper could see some of it, looking over the wing of the bridge; and he knew something was screwy. When you ask another captain to stop his ship, you do whatever you have to do quickly. He's doing you a favor and you let him get on his way.

"Wait and I went up on the bridge and we all decided we'd better not take any chances. This dame was likely to jump overboard from the boat.

She might not want to be rescued and we could be in a lot of trouble. So let's bring her back. The Old Man signaled the other ship to go ahead.

"So we still had her. She started going all around the ship, telling people she'd been drugged and shanghaied, brought aboard against her will. Then these people would come to me or the captain, saying, 'What are you doing? What the hell kind of a ship are we on?'

"We thought, we've got to put this dame away. So we locked the door of her stateroom and had a stewardess sitting by all the time. Then she starts writing notes on the stationery, shoving them under the door at night. Somebody would be walking along the passage at night and he'd see this note and say, 'Here's this poor woman . . . now they've got her in prison.'

"So we took all the paper out of her stateroom. Whenever Wait or I had to deal with this woman, we'd make it a point to go together. So, with no writing paper, she started writing notes on toilet paper. I tell you, she was smart as a whip. After that, we never left her enough toilet paper for notes. We put her in an inside cabin, away from the main passage. Then she said she had to have a hairbrush. And damned if she doesn't bang herself with that, on her breast and her legs, and start yelling and screaming. Even after we got to Yokohama she showed people these black-and-blue spots and claimed that either I or Wait and I together had beaten her up.

"You have a stowaway, you have to report it to the port authorities before you can put anybody ashore. So we spoke to the Japanese authorities; but no dice, so sorry. The United States consul was sent for; but he said, 'I can't help you. She has no money, no passport. The Japanese won't let her land here.'

"The *Taiyo Maru* was in port, about to head for San Francisco. We got our agent to buy a ticket for her. We couldn't send her over by herself; so Wait got one arm and I the other, and down the gangplank we go. From the abuse we got from the passengers, we couldn't be sure where their sympathies were.

"We walked her over to the *Taiyo* and into her stateroom. She's rational for a change; and she said she wanted a drink. Well, we thought, it's all over. This ship's going to get out of here in half or three quarters of an hour, so what's the harm in buying her a drink? So we called the steward and both had a drink with her.

"It was a stupid mistake. Immediately, she starts acting up again, very irrational and loud. The Japanese purser came by, and she gets crazy as hell then. So he brings down the ship's doctor.

"He took one look and bing! 'No way! You've got to take her off. She's insane. She needs hospital help. Take her off!'

"So off we go. Wait has one arm, I the other. Across two or three docks, up our gangway and back to her inside stateroom again. We were in Yokohama three or four days, but Wait and I don't see much. We were just nursemaids.

"At Kobe, we tried again to get rid of her but there were no ships leaving. We'd taken away the hairbrush and practically everything else except her nightgown; but every few minutes one of the crew would be up, saying, 'Come quick!' Joyce was a very active gal.

"We were a day and a half at Miyajima, then seven or eight days at Chinwangtao, while most of the passengers took land trips. Not Wait and me. This nutty dame still has to be fed, bathed, everything. We didn't forget her because she wouldn't let you forget her.

"Finally we get to Shanghai. A Dollar Line ship, the *President Pierce* [the same cantankerous vessel Matson once had operated as the *Hawkeye State*] was about to leave for Seattle. We bought Joyce a second-class ticket but she was having none of that. She said, 'If you think you're going to get me away down here and send me back second-class, you're crazy. I just won't go.'

"We bought her a first-class ticket. We'd have bought her a ticket to heaven to get rid of her. This time we stayed with her on the *Pierce* until they were ready to pull up the gangway but we didn't buy any drinks.

"We got back to the *Malolo* in time to see the *Pierce* pull out, and lo and behold, Joyce was right up there on deck. So we gave her the old sailor's farewell: 'Good-bye and God bless you.'

"By the time we got to Hong Kong, word about the affair had gotten out. The wire services had broadcast it all over. I was interviewed and interviewed. I was kind of kingpin, I guess, in the shanghaiing department . . . I was almost afraid to go back to Honolulu, ever. I thought old E. D. Tenney would be down at the end of the dock with a big blue envelope: 'You're fired!' "

Fischbeck was not fired but Joyce Jones did eventually bring suit for damages in the federal court at Honolulu, acting as her own attorney and changing her testimony in midcareer: it was not Fischbeck who had given her a drugged drink, but his assistant. The case was dismissed.

The millionaires' cruise produced no further drama of this sort but continued to stir interest wherever the ship docked. A Bangkok newspaper reported:

"There are many ladies on board and they are the first contingent of travelers to arrive here exhibiting the bare back and bare leg of fashion. We may be old-fashioned but we prefer a nice leg clothed in a New York silk stocking, but that is only a personal preference. Siamese women for a generation have been evolving costumes to replace the *pahom* [a long wraparound skirt] and clothe the legs. The prevailing mode of the young women from abroad is not therefore likely to be copied in Siam."

In several ports, Captain Berndtson predicted that Matson soon would be in the trans-Pacific trade. He did not indicate whether he spoke for the company.

Australian reporters interviewed Chief Chef H. E. Weidendorfer, reporting that he bossed sixty-seven kitchen hands, exclusive of stewards, and cooked 1,900 meals a day at a cost of $1,300. The story was headlined: "What Do American Millionaires and Near-Millionaires Eat?"

A Melbourne newspaper reported that Robert Newton Lynch, vice-president and manager of the San Francisco Chamber of Commerce, had brought along "some goldfish, of gorgeous hue and irreproachable pedigree, worth $500. [They were] installed in his cabin. In spite of the fact that it was a $5,000 cabin, the goldfish died. They were buried at sea." It added: "It is melancholy to report, from the picturesque point of view, that the ship's company is almost devoid of the horn-rimmed glasses or any other of the comic strip artist's standbys for treating Americans pictorially."

One Sydney reporter found Charles H. Hyde of Tacoma, Washington, to be the oldest passenger, at eighty-two, but could not identify the richest, so referred to all the passengers as "the big dollar brigade."

Another said there were "at least twelve millionaires" and added about the cruise: " 'Wonderful,' breathed every one of the fifty-seven widows."

The *Sydney Sun* noted that there was mixed bathing in the ship's pool with "no beach censors here." Fischbeck was reported to have "looked after more money in the last nine weeks than most people would care to count on a hot day."

So went the cruise of the *Malolo*. There would be others, but none more grand.

CHAPTER NINE

EARLY 1930s:
SEA RESCUE, HOTELMEN,
A MONKEY IN THE
BAGGAGE
(1930–1935)

If ships have minds—and any sailor who has wrestled to keep a cranky *Hilonian* on course or nursed the sick boilers of a *Hawkeye State* will swear they not only have minds but malevolence to spare—then the creaking old *Ventura* must have gone smiling to the ironmongers. Inexpertly designed, repeatedly repaired, remodeled, and patched up, she plowed the South Pacific for thirty years with her sisters, *Sierra* and *Sonoma*, at first the best in the business; at the last sad, outmoded, outspeeded, and mostly ignored by shippers and passengers alike. The big *Niagara* and bigger *Aorangi* whipped past her on their way from Australia to Canada; New Zealand's *Makura* and *Tahiti* added insult by carrying most of the passengers and freight from the same South Pacific ports to San Francisco, where *Ventura* eventually would arrive. Even her Matson owners were deserting her: keels for big ships to replace her and her sisters already were laid.

On an August morning in 1930, however, it was *Ventura*, between Tin Can Island and Samoa, that intercepted a call for assistance from the 7,998-ton *Tahiti*. Captain William Meyer headed for the stricken ship, 750 miles away to the southeast. He remembered:

"The *Tahiti* had broken one of her two shafts and it threw out. Water rushed into the shaft alley about two o'clock in the morning. At the end of the alley there is always a bulkhead and a door.

They started to close that door but something got stuck so they couldn't get it down." (Another source says the crew had left loose duckboards in the shaft alley and these, floating on the rushing water, created a jam that prevented the closing.)

Meyer continued: "There was a sea state six or seven at the time, fairly rough weather. . . . the engine room flooded and on that ship the dynamo was on the lower platform. The water reached that and threw her in darkness.

"But the next day one of the engineers dove down in the engine room and cleared the wood that was blocking the jammed hatch; but the shaft tunnel still was leaking and when they got the hatch shut the after hold started filling. Even the bulkhead between the engine room and the cargo holds was porous. Water was banging up against it, and almost any minute they were afraid it would give away and she'd go down.

"They finally were able to pump the engine room and get the dynamo back into operation, but she was leaking a little faster than they could pump. She gradually was settling and they were sending frantic messages all the time to please hurry, because they were going to take to the boats.

"We could make seventeen knots, full out, but it took two days to reach them. Fortunately the weather had moderated to about sea state four. While they were pumping they also hoisted water manually in drums and poured it over the side, keeping her afloat a little longer. When we got there, they still were able to put the people in boats and bring them over. I think it was about 130 passengers and 130 crew but I've forgotten the figures. . . . the *Tahiti* went down while we were standing by.

"We didn't have many passengers, so the extras weren't too much of a problem for the two days they were aboard. We took them to Pago Pago, and another Union Line ship came over from western Samoa and took them to New Zealand."

The *Ventura* never had a millionaires' cruise; and she was laid up two years later—but she had her one great day.

In retrospect, it could be argued that Matson chose the worst of times for its greatest prewar expansion; and certainly 1930 must have given management some sleepless nights. The company then was committed for three new passenger vessels, which were on the ways and would cost in excess of $8 million each. A government loan of $11,711,000, given to aid construction of the first two, was outstanding. Mail contracts for the South Seas route (the main reason for building two of the new ships) had been canceled after a congressional investigation and were not yet renegotiated.

A $280,000 annual subsidy for operation of the Oceanic & Oriental freighters was failing to meet their deficits, and Australian and New Zealand legislation favoring British Commonwealth goods was hurting southbound shipments from the United States. In Hawaii, Walter F. Dillingham, a director of American Factors, Ltd., and a backer of the Los Angeles Steamship Company, was attacking the American Factors freighting contracts with Matson, while James D. Dole was trying to arrange a contract between the Hawaiian Pineapple Company, largest shipper of that product, and Isthmian Steamship Company for eastbound cargoes. LASSCO vessels were carrying about half of all passengers to and from Hawaii.

Other competition came from five of the old "535"-model passenger ships, two of which Matson once had leased from the U.S. Shipping Board and briefly operated between the Atlantic Coast and Hawaii as the *Hawkeye State* and *Buckeye State*. In the early 1920s all five were leased by the reorganized Pacific Mail Steamship Company, which gave them the names of presidents—*Pierce, Taft,* and so on—and put them on Orient runs, with stopovers at Hawaii. This shipping line went out of business for the second and last time in 1925, but the Dollar Line paid $5,625,000 cash for the five vessels (compared with the $8 million Matson had spent on the *Malolo* alone) and used them in the same trade. A third company, American President Lines, took over from Dollar, but the service was unchanged. Ships of this line continued to stop at Hawaii until World War II and resumed service for several postwar years.

The Royal and Moana hotels, while popular, still were not showing profits in 1930; and Matson ships earned only $301,657 for the year, compared with $1,622,291 earned in 1926. The company's net profit in 1926 had been $2,320,608 and was $2,653,043 in 1929, but dropped in 1930 to $699,695 on assets of about $40 million.

(Realistic valuation of company assets was difficult. Its holding of 250,000 shares in Honolulu Oil Company stock was carried on the books for a third of a century at cost, $429,259, even though dividends in 1952 were $625,000 and the market value of the shares was $12,750,000.)

Although 1930 deserved some sort of prize for gloomy news, there were omens of better times. The threat to the profitable pineapple cargo business was removed in fairly typical island fashion. James Dole had built the Hawaiian Pineapple Company almost by himself and had survived various near-disasters, mostly by inventiveness in growing and packing the fruit and by aggressive salesmanship. He had been restive about Matson freight rates for a long time, feeling that much of the generosity about rates for outer-island sugar was coming from his pocket. Many shipping people agreed that a line not burdened by uneconomic outer-island sugar cargoes could carry pineapple from Honolulu at lower rates, and the Isthmian Line was willing to try.

Dole, however, had a major problem: he did not see the Great Depression coming, and he did not realize it had arrived by 1930. With 3 million cases of canned pineapple on hand and a quarter billion plants in the fields, Dole this time simply could not sell enough to stay solvent, even though he mounted an eventually successful campaign to induce people to drink canned pineapple juice, essentially a new product.

Owning much of the land Dole leased, Castle & Cooke rescued the firm—but at a price: Dole lost control and was shunted from president to chairman of the board. Neither E. D. Tenney nor Atherton Richards, his choice as president of the Hawaiian Pineapple Company, was interested in talking to Isthmian or any other Matson competitor. The reasons were unsubtle.

Dillingham's effort to break the American Factors freighting contract was defeated when an arbitrator decided it did not conflict with existing law.

Of far greater importance in the competitive situation, however, was a fire that badly damaged LASSCO's second liner, *City of Honolulu,* at a Honolulu dock. This accentuated that company's dilemma: its cheap old ships could compete against the four veterans Matson was running with the *Malolo* but hardly would be able to do so when the new *Monterey, Mariposa,* and *Lurline* (no. 3) came into the trade in 1931 and 1932.

While the Chandlers and other Los Angeles backers very likely could pay for new competitive ships, there were negative considerations. Matson was a strong company, for all its troubles, and controlled the only large tourist hotels in the islands. It also had a lock on most of the cargo to the islands through its multiple ownership and powerful agencies, and effectively was subsidizing the shipment of sugar from the outer islands.

Matson stockholders, or a powerful portion of them, would tolerate this last uneconomic operation for the sake of the quid pro quo: better sugar prof-

its. A steamship company whose stockholders did not have such ancillary interests would find this outer-island service hard to justify. Without giving it, however, no shipline would be likely to lure much business from the amorphous Big Five companies. LASSCO could count on Dillingham as an ally; there was a chance to get the Dole pineapple business; and the Los Angeles Steamship Company had demonstrated it could attract tourists—but it wasn't enough. The Chandlers were ready to talk merger.

From Matson's viewpoint, the merger was especially attractive because the acquisitions could be accomplished without cash outlay. So it was done. Los Angeles Company stockholders accepted Matson shares for their interest, and Ralph Chandler became Matson's regional vice-president for Southern California and a company director.

In San Francisco, Matson in 1924 built a new sixteen-story headquarters building to house its own staff and the offices of so many Hawaiian companies that the structure was widely known as "Little Hawaii." Three years later, the company added a Port Accessories Building, only a block from its piers, to house its commissary, laundry, upholstery, and furniture repair facilities—everything needed to turn the ships around quickly.

As Matson's new passenger ships came into service, Los Angeles was added to the Oceanic South Pacific service, which now included Honolulu, Pago Pago, Suva, Auckland, Sydney, and Melbourne, as well as the home port of San Francisco. On the Honolulu shuttle, the *Malolo* and the new *Lurline* (no. 3) sailed alternately from San Francisco and Los Angeles.*

---

*On May 30, 1931, only weeks after announcement of the merger of the companies, the proud old coastal steamer *Harvard* went aground on Point Arguello, near Santa Barbara, California, and was lost. Passengers and crew escaped.

The sister ship *Yale* continued the San Francisco–Los Angeles run, sometimes serving San Diego as well, and in November of the same year flew a sixty-foot pennant from her foretruck to celebrate her one thousandth trip between the two major cities. . . . Her day was ending, however, and she never resumed civilian service after the maritime strike of 1934. Sold three years

The new ships were nearly identical. A San Francisco reporter, hearing a Matson executive describe the new *Lurline,* wrote:

"When he started to tell about the interior decorative scheme of the main lounge, with opalescent walls, black floors and old rose furniture, one felt that the last word in maritime trimmings has been reached until someone puts a keel under the Louvre and floats it."

The customers apparently agreed. Prior to this, travel between the Antipodes and Great Britain by way of the United States had dropped to a trickle; but the *Mariposa* and *Monterey* sailed at four-week intervals and could carry 9,000 passengers a year in each direction, as well as more than 57,000 tons of freight. In 1936, they did carry 6,422 people, 58,000 tons of through freight, and 8,000 tons interport. Revenues for the first five years of service were $12.9 million for passengers and $4.5 million for freight. Eventual settlement of the mail contract dispute provided $975,000 a year in addition.

For the first time, Australians and New Zealanders regularly could enjoy ships with outdoor swimming pools, air-conditioned dining saloons, the American concept of stateroom comfort, and the quality and variety of American menus. Travel time to England was reduced by one third on a route offering both frequent stops and weather much more pleasant than anything in the Indian Ocean or Red Sea.

The Commonwealth lines were hurting, and a premier of Tasmania, the Honorable Albert Ogilvie, was reproached for failure to travel under the Union Jack. His reply, as quoted by *Fortune* magazine: "Damned if I will until they melt the icicles."

In five years after its opening, the Royal Hawaiian Hotel registered 14,000 guests, including such as Mary Pickford and Douglas Fairbanks, Sr.; Al Jolson and Ruby Keeler; Fords and Rockefellers. Mr. and Mrs. J. Paul Butler brought with them their ultramarine blue Rolls-Royce roadster, Henry H. Rogers his Hispano-Suiza phaeton with silver disk wheels. One account says he drove it at eighty-five miles an hour but doesn't explain where on Oahu he found a road to do it. Mrs. Lamont Du Pont spent the entire summer of 1931 at the Royal.

The Territorial Hotel Company, Ltd., which owned the Royal and Moana hotels and the Seaside Bungalows, the Waialae Ranch Company, and Territorial Properties, Ltd., were liquidated in 1934, their properties being turned over to Hawaiian Properties, Ltd., with some of the same partners. This company in turn was liquidated in 1941, when the hotels division of Matson assumed full control.

Jack Fischbeck knew a bit about how luxury was accomplished at sea by the time he was thirty-seven years old, but circa 1936 he began to learn about the mysteries of shoreside hotel keeping.

"I think," he said in a 1974 interview, "it was Bill Roth who said, 'We think you have a flair for this sort of thing. We're going to take you out of the steamship division and put you in the hotel division. We'd like you to go down to the Royal and start at the beginning. Don't get any inflated ideas. You're not going down to take Benaglia's job. We're not going to fire him and we don't think he's going to quit. [Benaglia was manager of the hotel division, including the Royal, the Moana, and the Waialae golf course.] But if anything like that does happen you could be in a position to take over.'

"I knew Benaglia. We were friends. Finally I went down on the *Lurline* as a passenger and reported to Benaglia. He said, 'Now, Jack, you know why you're here. . . . You're going to be very comfortable. I'm going to give you a nice room on the first floor . . . but you came in through the front door today. Tomorrow morning you come in the back door. I don't want to see you in the lobby for two years. At seven-thirty in the morning, you report to the purchasing agent. You learn all about purchasing. (We had big walk-in refrigerators, one for vegetables, one for meat, about ten of them.)

later, she was used briefly as a barracks ship for construction workers in southeast Alaska, then was commandeered by the navy, serving as a troop transport in Alaskan waters under the name of *Greyhound.* She was scrapped in 1949.

Wilhelmina served as a U.S. troop transport in World War I, finally sank as an empty British troopship in the second world war.

S.S. *Kahuku,* dubbed a ''pineapple clipper,'' one of fourteen Matson freighters lost in World War II. (Courtesy of the National Maritime Museum, San Francisco)

The third *Lurline* was the pride of Matson's pre-war fleet.

Unlovely in wartime gray, she served as a troop transport throughout World War II.

Artist's conception of *Monterey* rescuing troops and crew from the stricken *Santa Elena* in the Mediterranean. Actually, the rescue occurred at night, in World War II blackout conditions.

States-bound troops aboard *Matsonia* when the war was over.

MATSON SKIPPERS: A FEW OF THE HUNDREDS

Four skippers of Matson's famous "white ships" in 1960. Left to right: Captain Ray Russell, Captain Mervyn Stone, Commodore Harold R. Gillespie, and Captain Hans O. Matthiesen. Matthiesen later succeeded Gillespie as commodore of the Matson fleet.

Captain Malcolm Peters was a prisoner of the Japanese for four years.

Matson skippers at a Honolulu reunion in 1976. Left to right: Commodore C. C. Wright and retired captains Malcolm Peters, John Diggs (aged 87), and John A. Mackenzie.

Captain Konrad Hubbenette, one-time winch driver, traveled with a pet mynah bird.

1.   2.   3.   4.

5.   6.   7.

1. Captain J. H. Trask was later commodore.   2. Captain Eugen M. Olsen received a presidential citation for saving ship and lives at Rabaul, New Guinea, during a volcanic eruption. During World War II, he brought 28 survivors of a torpedoed ship through 11 days in the Indian Ocean.   3. Captain Charles Brocas survived the 1946 Hilo tidal wave, became a San Francisco pilot.   4. Captain C. A. Berndtson commanded *Malolo* on the Millionaires' Cruise.
5. Captain Lester Hansen, of the old liner *Maui* and freighter *Maunawili,* greets retired Commodore Peter Johnson in Hawaii.   6. Captain G. B. Wait, reserve captain on the Millionaires' Cruise, later took command of *Malolo*.
7. Captain W. R. Meyer, master of *Ventura* during *Tahiti* rescue.

MATSON PRESIDENTS

1. William Matson, *February 9, 1901 to October 11, 1917.* 2. Edward D. Tenney, *October 25, 1917 to May 13, 1927.* 3. William P. Roth, *May 13, 1927 to March 16, 1945.* 4. Frazer A. Bailey, *March 16, 1945 to April 4, 1947.* 5. John E. Cushing, *May 8, 1947 to June 30, 1950.* 6. Randolph Sevier, *June 30, 1950 to May 11, 1962.* 7. Stanley Powell, Jr., *May 11, 1962 to April 27, 1970.* 8. Allen C. Wilcox, Jr., *April 27, 1970 to May 28, 1970.* 9. Malcolm H. Blaisdell, *May 28, 1970 to April 18, 1973.* 10. Robert J. Pfeiffer, *April 18, 1973 to October 25, 1979.* 11. James P. Gray, *October 25, 1979 to present.*

Then you do the purchasing. The agent will watch but you do it. Then about ten o'clock the food will start coming in. . . . you go out on the receiving dock and watch. You'll be surprised how many times instead of twenty bags of potatoes you're going to get fifteen; you'll find out you ordered a certain kind of meat but it isn't that kind. You're going to see you should have so many dozen eggs but there won't be that many. You inspect everything. . . .

" 'Now when you finish with that you go into the kitchen with Edgar Kina.' Kina was a Belgian chef, one of the greatest I've ever seen. A very attractive man, immaculately clean . . . I never tasted such food before or later. 'You go in there, have lunch with him in his office,' Benaglia said. 'If you don't eat well in the chef's office, you never will.

"I did that and went all through the kitchen. That was a marvelous place. They just don't get pastry chefs like we had. I don't know how they ever kept it all together.

"I did those kinds of jobs for two years. Administration was the part I was learning. I got so I knew when I was being kidded and when I wasn't being kidded and how to handle both kinds of people, when to talk to a chef about something that wasn't right and when not to do it. There's a right time and a wrong time: you don't just go in and start giving the chef hell when he's serving 600 dinners. You'll get a pot over your head.

"Then I went into the housekeeping department, just browsing around, then down to the accounting department for a month or so, as a clerk behind the desk, then as a room clerk. Then the big day came: assistant manager. But you know, all they do is to give you a desk in the lobby and put a carnation in your buttonhole—but no authority. You go back to talk to the chef and he'll throw you out of the kitchen. You talk to the maitre d' and he'll tell you, 'You're crazy. Why don't you get back out front and let me run the dining room?' You talk to the chief engineer and he says, 'That's the funniest story I ever heard in my life. Good-bye, I have no time for you.'

"So after all, you're just out there, taking the complaints, doing what you can about them, and reporting them to the manager. Be nice to the guests, pull out a few chairs and things like that. . . . you're a flunky in a tuxedo.

"After about a year, I went over to the Moana as manager. I enjoyed it until about December. The Old Man [Benaglia] had gotten some money to renovate that hotel. They tore out the whole lobby, all the shops. You could look right through to the sea. . . . the Old Man came over and said, 'Well, Jack, it's all torn to pieces. Now I have to go to New York. You put it together.'

"I worked and worked. We had a very good chief engineer. Finally he came to me one day and said, 'You're pretty worried, aren't you?'

"I said, 'I'm scared to death. I'm worrying about whether this guy's doing his job right and I'm not so damn sure. . . .'

"He said, 'Let me tell you something: relax. Just take it easy. Get a drink and enjoy yourself at night. When the Old Man left here, he knew where every bloody nail was going to go in this hotel. He just wanted you to sweat it out for two or three weeks. These decisions you make: I go around twenty minutes later and countermand them.'

"The Old Man came back. He wanted the hotel open by New Year's Eve and we did it. We had turned on all the lights in the lobby; and I told the housekeeper, 'You go up on all the floors. Don't make it even, but flip on room lights . . . put one shade up, one down, leave one window open, close one. Go through the whole Kalakaua Avenue side of the hotel. . . .'

"About eight o'clock the Old Man came over to see how things were going. He said, 'How many people do you have in the house?'

"I said, 'We've just opened. We may have about twenty-five.'

" 'What about all those lights?'

"I said, 'Everybody's out on New Year's Eve. . . . doesn't it look better than to have people think we opened an empty hotel?'

"He said, 'Leave them on.' "

The *Malolo* and *Lurline* now crossed to Honolulu in four and one half days, still not really fast enough for a person with a two-week vacation but the best speed ever offered on that run. When these ships lacked passenger space, the Oceanic liners occasionally could squeeze a Hawaiian round trip between their longer scheduled voyages. Passenger business built slowly from the early depression lows. Well-heeled tourists still were its mainstay, with a sprinkling of military families, some adventurous schoolteachers taking summer courses at the University of Hawaii (which was more fun and somewhat less demanding than the old summer school stand-by, Southern California), and twice-a-year migration of the children of island families whisking off to mainland prep schools, Yale (definitely preferred for those who someday would head island businesses), and other Ivy League or Western universities.

Quite aware that many of their parents owned pieces of the shipline or owned companies that owned pieces of the line, these youngsters took care to make the most of their positions. Standard procedure was to attempt to eat through the entire menu at one sitting. Behavior on deck and at shipboard parties was designed to further their reputations as hell-raisers; and one who later was president of Matson remembers that some students displeased with a ship's band threw its instruments overboard, although he is careful to specify that he personally did no heaving. These young gentlemen and ladies could be expected in June and September, with a few adding to the pleasure of the ship crews by going home to the islands for Christmas.*

Public relations for ships and hotels included the care and feeding of many egos, not the least being those of large shippers. Whether steel mill owners, sugar producers, or merchant princes, these expected the very best treatment from the shipline carrying their cargoes and from its hotels. Captain's table guests aboard ship were not always chosen for their

sparkling wit; and one executive remembers that far-sighted managers in the free-and-easy days made a practice of posting temporary rate schedules in the rooms at the Royal Hawaiian so that each of several incoming shippers would be quite sure he was getting reduced rates or a free ride on the most expensive rooms in the house.

Matson employees also got special treatment. Generally, they and their families could ride the ships and stay in the hotels at one fourth of the minimum rate, while occupying the best of the unsold accommodations. Some kept close check on reservations, then scheduled their holidays when they knew the finest outside rooms on a ship or the best lanai suites at the Royal had not been booked. Luxury it was, at bargain prices.

Occasionally, others enjoyed Matson luxuriousness quite unexpectedly. One was Jane Hicks Markuson, who remembers:

"In November, 1935, the *Malolo* embarked on its regular run . . . to Hawaii. Aboard in cabin class was a young social worker . . . having the temerity to take a winter holiday in the depths of the depression. . . . The fare could have been $100 round trip, but I'm not sure. Borrowing from friends all their best clothes and a steamer trunk, she began the trip. . . . it started with fun and games and each day the sun was warmer and the evening breeze balmier . . . sunbathing in the day and bingo or dancing at night, with dinner at the purser's table.

"The night before docking was the big night. I went to the baggage room with a ship's boy to get an evening dress from my trunk, which opened out into a 'V' shape.

"As I was unlocking the trunk I noticed a monkey tied by a long cord. When I turned around . . . the monkey jumped down and came toward me at rather a lively bounce. I was hemmed into the 'V' shape of the trunk and there was no escape route. I backed off and the boy tugged at the rope . . . but the monkey made a determined lunge, climbing up my dress. The attendant pulled

*It should be acknowledged that there also were many well-behaved student passengers who weren't rich and did not throw their weight around. Some even read books en route.

SEA RESCUE, HOTELMEN, A MONKEY IN THE BAGGAGE [81]

the monkey off my dress but must have relaxed the cord, because the monkey took a good bite in my leg just above the ankle.

"I was put to bed with the leg elevated, and the medic came to cauterize it. No party for me that night. Next day we disembarked and my leg was swollen. I met my military uncle and his wife, whom I was to visit. My aunt was all concerned and consulted her lawyer. They all decided I was suffering from 'mental anguish' and also that part of the trip had been ruined. Before I left the ship, the purser had given me some nice presents: silk stockings and a thin red lacquer cigarette case. However, Auntie had her lawyer get in touch with the Matson officials to secure something more substantial.

"On shipboard after the incident, I had been required to make a written report . . . and on reading it the captain noted that it was rather detailed. I informed him I was a social worker and making detailed reports was part of my profession. He thought I had planted that monkey?

"The shipline came through with some cash which enabled me to buy nice presents for Auntie, my mother and everyone at home, . . . also, the line threw in first-class passage for return to the States.

"It was vastly disappointing traveling with the stuffy, older group who took first class passage. . . . On my trip to the bridge, the captain detained me in a corner to tell me all about a young woman who had been bitten by a monkey in their baggage room. I never told him it was I, or that that damn monkey was still down there with the baggage on the return trip. Also, some stuffy ladies made a point of telling me the purser was the father of five children stashed somewhere in the U.S."

CHAPTER TEN

WARS: LABOR, AVIATION, AND INTERNATIONAL (1933–1941)

Captain William Matson certainly was no union sympathizer, although he had a reputation for treating his men fairly and paying them well, and he did hold meetings with Andrew Furuseth of the Sailors Union and Michael Casey of the Teamsters as early as 1910. Nevertheless, union negotiations and strikes were part of the Matson picture from that time on. Matson and other shipowners broke a San Francisco longshore union in 1919 and replaced it with a company-dominated organization. This was complete with blacklist and a system wherein a stevedore had to have a "brass" (a sort of identification tag) and a blue book to get his pay but could acquire neither unless he had paid his dues to the company union and was not otherwise in its disfavor.

Jess Rose, later Matson's stevedoring superintendent, reported his experience as a longshoreman:

"A buddy and I decided to go to a union meeting to try to get some rules changed. We had about as much chance as a snowball in hell. The minute we started talking we were out of order. There was a long flight of steps that went straight down. We were just trying to argue sensibly, but they wouldn't listen at all. They decided at last that the sergeant at arms should throw us out. We were going to make a beef but were just smart enough to know that wouldn't work, so we backed off. That

was the last time we ever tried to change the blue book."

Some days, 1,200 men would gather on the Embarcadero between Mission and Market streets, waiting for the two shape-ups and perhaps 300 jobs on Matson docks. The independent union was not completely dead, however, and when Matson cooperated with the employers' union in 1933 by ordering out of a ship all the longshoremen who could not produce the little blue books, 150 men walked off the docks, tore up their little blue books, and made a bonfire of them. After an hour's delay Matson capitulated and put three gangs back to work without blue books. Two weeks later, however, the company fired four men for wearing International Longshoremen's Association buttons on the job. President Franklin D. Roosevelt never had approved a National Recovery Act code for the waterfront, so NRA officials in San Francisco said they could do nothing to help the fired men.

At this time, Harry Bridges was only the leader of the Albion Hall faction within the ILA union, but this faction controlled a throwaway newspaper, the *Waterfront Worker*. This publication called for rank-and-file support of the fired men, and Bridges's group took action.

"What we did," he said, "was very simple: we went down there one morning, lined up in the shape-up, and as the fellows started going to work, we stopped every one of them and said, 'Look, fellows, four guys have been fired for joining the union. Let's have a program where they hire these four fellows back or nobody goes to work.'

"So everybody stayed out. That affected the docks and the strike lasted for five days. The Matson Company and the Waterfront Employers Association went up to Skid Row [sic] and they hired a bunch of men from the employment halls. Of course, we spoke to those men and got most of them to quit."

Eventually, the NRA persuaded Matson to fire 150 strikebreakers and take back all strikers except the four button wearers, leaving the fate of the four to arbitration. On October 17, 1933, the arbitration board ordered Matson to rehire them, too. Bridges said later, "That reestablished the union on the waterfront."

So strengthened, in the spring of 1934 longshoremen attempted to negotiate a coastwide contract. Failing, they went on strike May 9, supported by the Marine Industrial Workers and, later, the AFL International Seamen's Union. Trouble began immediately as stevedoring and ship companies hired strikebreakers, housing them aboard an anchored Dollar liner and Matson's laid-up *City of Los Angeles* and *Wilhelmina*. The employers also stated their aims: the open shop, employer-operated hiring halls, elections in each port between the ILA and the blue-book union, and port-by-port bargaining.

The federal government sent out Edward M. McGrady as a mediator; Joseph Ryan, the International president, appeared for the ILA. By June 16, these two hammered out an agreement with employers and signed it. Ryan could not persuade other union representatives present to sign, however, and Harry Bridges had not been invited.*

---

*Years later, Randolph Sevier, who had no part in the affair and thoroughly disapproved of it, confirmed that the Waterfront Employers' Association, using money provided by a Matson officer, attempted to bribe Bridges. Bridges agreed that a bribe offer had been made. Sevier at the time was a Castle & Cooke official and later became president of Matson.

Longshoremen stayed on strike, ignoring their president's action. On June 26, President Roosevelt, recognizing that the agreement was meaningless, appointed a National Longshoremen's Board, naming McGrady, Archbishop Hanna of San Francisco, and Oscar K. Cushing as its members.

On July 3, under police protection, trucks opened the port. Strikebreaker Argonne Riley was killed in battles between police and longshoremen. The next day stevedores stopped a train with cargo intended for a Matson ship preparing to sail. On July 5—"bloody Thursday"—longshoremen and police fought pitched battles, with two men killed and hundreds injured. National guardsmen were ordered to the waterfront, and cargo moved during the next three days. Then 2,000 Teamsters joined the strike; and on July 16 most other unions in San Francisco joined in a three-day general strike that paralyzed the city. On July 31 the waterfront strike was ended when employers reluctantly agreed to submit all issues to binding arbitration.

The National Longshoremen's Board in October decreed jointly operated hiring halls with dispatchers provided by the union, a coastwide contract, establishment of grievance apparatus, and a thirty-hour work week. This last meant that gangs worked six hours daily at regular pay rates and two hours at overtime rates.

The 1934 strike was the most spectacular but only the beginning of prewar labor problems on the West Coast docks. More than 150 strikes or "job action" refusals to work occurred in the next seven months. In 1936 employers closed the port of San Francisco for a week, trying to force the union to remove Bridges, by then its local leader. On October 29 of that year, seven maritime unions began another strike, which lasted ninety-eight days. In 1937 all the West Coast longshoremen except locals at Tacoma, Anacortes, and Port Angeles in Washington voted to leave the American Federation of Labor. The International Longshoremen's and Warehousemen's Union was formed in the Congress of Industrial Organizations (CIO). In 1939 failure of negotiations between employers and the ship clerks' union, a branch of the ILWU, again shut down the port of San Francisco for a month.

There were, however, no serious attempts after 1934 to drive the Bridges union off the waterfront.

In January 1929 the Inter-Island Steam Navigation Company, Ltd., filed incorporation papers for Inter-Island Airways, Ltd., to buy and operate a couple of Sikorsky flying boats between Honolulu and some of the other Hawaiian islands. Matson shared in the studies leading to the incorporation. Most islanders agreed that the flying boats would be convenient, especially for the seasick prone to whom boisterous Molokai Channel was a recurrent horror in interisland travel. There was no indication that the event had any greater importance.

Six years later, however, trans-Pacific air travel appeared to be something more than a fanatic's dream. Both the Boeing and Martin companies were building huge flying boats, with enough range to reach Honolulu from California and even Australia and the mainland of Asia by way of islands—Midway, Wake, and Johnston among them—previously known mainly as seabird rookeries and cable relay stations.

Pan American Airways had pioneered overwater routes in the Caribbean and now looked for financial aid in starting a Pacific service. Matson and Inter-Island each invested $500,000 in the aviation company's stock. Pan American ordered its first Clipper flying boats and made surface surveys of the routes, simultaneously agreeing that the three companies later would form a corporation to provide a separate air service between Hawaii and the U.S. mainland. First clipper flights to Manila were made in 1935, with the steamship companies providing shore services at Honolulu. When air service to New Zealand via Honolulu was established in 1938, Matson was the airline's New Zealand agent.

The clippers provided comfortable service, with double-deck accommodations, bunks for sleeping, and meals served on white tablecloths; but they had little effect on travel to Hawaii. Takeoff and arrival times were somewhat uncertain; and travelers headed only for Hawaii had some difficulty in getting space on the through aircraft. People who wanted both reliability and luxury still took ships.

In 1938, the U.S. Congress passed the Civil Aeronautics Act, and the Inter-Island–Matson–Pan American agreements concerning Hawaii air service were submitted to the new Civil Aeronautics Authority for approval. No action was taken until just before the entry of the United States into World War II. With minimal explanation, the Civil Aeronautics Board (a new name for the reorganized CAA) then disapproved all the arrangements. Matson thereupon sold its Pan American stock and briefly ignored aviation.

Pacific Ocean shipping was affected by World War II from some indefinite date when the westbound passenger lists began to be filled more with construction workers than with honeymooning capitalists taking along their Duesenbergs. Freighter manifests ballooned with steel, concrete, and pipe destined for the government rather than for the traditional civilian customers.

In 1937 Matson peddled the aging liner *Matsonia,* once the pride of the fleet, to one of its favorite Alaska fish-packing customers but preserved the name by giving it to the newer *Malolo.* This did nothing to improve the stability of that vessel but did get away from the nickname "More Roll O," which it had acquired, largely through the sincere efforts of competitors. The *Matsonia* sale appeared to have nothing to do with war rumors but turned out to be only the first of a number of sales related to the threatened conflict. The *City of Los Angeles* and the *Enterprise,* both in the lay-up fleet, ended in Japanese shipbreaking yards.

Matson had placed the freighters of the Oceanic & Oriental line under its own flag when the O&O company lost its mail subsidy and was dissolved in 1936–1937. By 1939 these were carrying both South Pacific and Hawaiian cargoes, so Matson was able to sell six older and smaller ships—the *Makena, Mahukona, Corrales, Kalani, Kainalu,* and *Onomea*

—to a variety of brokers sensing upcoming ship price increases. Only the last three were in service. The old passenger ship *Wilhelmina* went to a British government agency and was refitted to carry troops but was torpedoed in the Atlantic before it had a chance to do so. "Battling Willie" had gone to war once too often.

Understandably, the Oceanic Steamship Company's cargoes and passenger loads multiplied after the outbreak of war in Europe in 1939. The service still had the mail subsidies arranged in 1936 but could have operated profitably without them for the first time. Other Matson operations spread rapidly in 1940–1941 when company ships were diverted to the Red Sea, South America, Manila, India, the Orient, the Persian Gulf, the St. Lawrence River, and the U.S. East Coast, carrying cargoes for the British Ministry of Transport, the U.S. Army and Navy, as well as traditional customers and contractors for new or strengthened military bases. Such preparations also swelled the cargo lists for Hawaii from 1939. In 1941 that cargo totalled 2,726,947 tons, more than double the total for any previous year. The company also sold more ships to the U.S. Maritime Commission. The old liner *Maui* was included, along with the freighters *Mana, Makawao, Hawaiian Shipper,* and *Hawaiian Planter.*

Passenger space on the ships bound for Hawaii was at a premium and the lists consisted largely of construction people. Eastbound, the ships had been running half empty, as tourist trade dwindled and government surveillance increased. This situation became critical on November 21, when the new *Matsonia* (ex-*Malolo*) was turned over to the Maritime Commission under a demise charter (i.e., for its life or a term of years to be set by the government) and converted to a troopship, scheduled to sail for Manila as soon as possible. Oceanic's *Monterey,* arriving from Sydney, was turned over twelve days later, partially converted and readied to sail for Manila and Sydney. Neither voyage was made.

The *Lurline* left Los Angeles on November 29 for Honolulu with more defense workers than regular passengers aboard. For radio operators Leslie Grogan and Rudy Asplund, nights of this westbound trip were crowded. Grogan's watch on November 30 was eight o'clock to midnight. "The Japs," he wrote in a journal, "are blasting away on the lower marine radio frequency. It is all in the Japanese code and continues for several hours. Some signals were loud and others weak, but in almost every case a repeat-back was acknowledged verbatim. It appears . . . Japanese-based stations have their transmitting keys all tied-in together and controlled from a common source, presumably Tokyo. . . .

"Many of the signals reaching us were good enough to get good radio detection finder bearings. We noted that the signals were being repeated, possibly for copying by craft with small antennas. The main body of signals came from a Northwest-by-West area, which . . . would be North and West of Honolulu. . . .

"If anyone should ask me, I would say it's the Japs' Mobilization Battle Order. . . . Who knows? . . . the Japs must be bunched up, biding time. . . . It's safe to say something is going to happen, and mighty soon."

At noon on Friday, December 5, the *Lurline* was at her Honolulu dock ready to sail for San Francisco but was delayed several hours, waiting for a last group of passengers, mostly families of servicemen. The Royal Hawaiian Band and accompanying singers and dancers went through the usual Aloha ceremonies.

Edward Collins, chief officer, described the departure:

"We had an excess-of-capacity passenger list, . . . about seventy passengers beyond sleeping accommodations . . . to meet this emergency . . . cots were set out in the cabin lounge, men and women on opposite sides, separated by a cloth partition.

"Off Waikiki . . . we were greeted by the usual number of outrigger canoes and small craft extending their Alohas . . . passing the Royal Hawaiian, Commodore Berndtson ordered the customary three blasts on the whistle and we settled down to the usual routine voyage . . . bucking the Northeast trades. . . . As we steamed, we were buzzed by various military planes . . . extending their Alohas to relatives or friends among our passengers . . . a division of United States Navy heavy cruisers, accompanied by destroyers, by coincidence met us off the Honolulu harbor entrance and paralleled our course to beyond Makapu.''

On Sunday at 9:12 A.M., ship's time, Grogan heard radio signals from the army freighter *Cynthia Olson*. The first signal indicated either that a submarine had been sighted or that the ship was being attacked. The *Olson* operator, transmitting ''with a very steady hand keying,'' gave the ship's position and confirmed that it was being attacked.

After that, there was nothing.

Officers of the *Lurline* first heard of the attack on Pearl Harbor from a commercial wireless station on Kaena Point, northwest Oahu, when operators there saw large numbers of planes overhead and lost telephone contact with Honolulu.

According to Grogan, passengers and crew got their first information from the ship's cooks, who had their own powerful receivers, normally used to keep popular music coming while potatoes were being peeled or dishes washed. Commodore Berndtson confirmed the reports at a 5:00 P.M. meeting of passengers; but for the rest of that day and the next, all aboard got their news from Chicago and New York radio stations that ''came booming through at night with all the Pacific Coast stations closed down for emergency drills.'' ''News'' included an alleged eyewitness report of Japanese planes over San Francisco, last seen ''being chased southwesterly, presumably in the direction of their carrier . . . and where the *Lurline* is supposed to be trying to sneak up the Coast.''

Having zigzagged virtually at flank speed of twenty-two knots, the blacked-out *Lurline* did sneak into San Francisco on the night of December 9, finally docking at 3:27 A.M. the next day. Four days later, most of her conversion to a troopship completed, she sailed under a demise charter to the navy but with her own officers and crew; 3,292

troops; and a very heavy cargo of bombs, ammunition, and other military supplies. Honolulu was the destination of the convoy, which included the *Monterey* and *Matsonia,* similarly loaded. The three ships landed nearly 10,000 troops and returned to the Coast with overloads of military casualties and dependents, plus civilian evacuees.

Outbreak of war had found the *Mariposa,* fourth of the big passenger liners, in Sydney, Australia. She was given a quick coat of military gray paint, set out alone on December 16, averaged 20.42 knots on a circuitous course, and arrived at San Francisco unannounced on December 30. The following day, she, too, was delivered to the Maritime Commission for conversion.

The federal government took over all U.S. merchant shipping at the outbreak of war, along with foreign vessels it could reach if they were registered in nations under enemy control. Thus, Norwegian, Danish, Dutch, and French ships served U.S. purposes. Steamship lines served as government agents to operate their own and other assigned vessels. At the wartime peak, Matson was operating 143 vessels of all sizes and shapes in the Pacific. Its own vessels assigned elsewhere remained Matson crewed but were loaded and husbanded by other companies as subagents.

Ships, men, and shore facilities became cogs in the war machine. In contrast to World War I, shipping in this conflict was the only form of transportation wholly nationalized, the first to have its equipment requisitioned, and the last to have it released.

(Railroads operated throughout the war under their own auspices, although with some government controls. Domestic airlines flew their own planes but with government priorities. Pan American World Airways, principal U.S. international carrier, also flew its own planes and could sell tickets, but under navy restrictions.)

The Matson organization commandeered was a complete transportation system including thirty-eight freighters totalling 349,829 deadweight tons; the four large passenger liners; 3,100 seagoing and

900 shoreside personnel; terminals and stevedoring organizations in each of the principal Pacific Coast ports; a mainland ship construction and repair facility, designed to handle only Matson's own vessels but soon expanded to do construction and repair work on 1,850 fighting and merchant vessels during the war; staffs and port organizations in the mid-Pacific and South Pacific, and the two major Waikiki hotels.

Only the Moana Hotel, of all Matson's public facilities, continued to operate as in peacetime, but immediately was swamped by would-be guests and diners. It so remained for four years.

CHAPTER ELEVEN

TWELVE SHIPS DOWN
(1941–1943)

Throughout Matson's Pacific Northwest operations, the annual shipment of Christmas trees to Hawaii has been the most publicized cargo and one of the most troublesome. In earlier days, preserving the trees in any decent condition was a problem; and always, delivery dates and market fluctuations have been headaches for shippers, carrier, and consignees. "Sometimes when we got off schedule," says one Matson freight specialist, "some of the fast buck boys would come aboard as soon as the ship docked and yank the freight tags off all the bundles of trees they could reach. So Matson would end up with a lot of trees it didn't know what to do with, and consignees would only pay for short shipments. There are other headaches in that business, but who can fight Santa Claus?"

So, as usual, the company put out press releases when the freighter *Mauna Ala* left Portland for Honolulu with a cargo of Christmas trees and general merchandise in the first week of December 1941. There was no Santa Claus figure on the smokestack, but she was a Christmas ship nonetheless. At sea on December 7, she was ordered to return to the Columbia River. She reached the mouth of the river at night on December 10, attempted to find the bar crossing without lights or other navigational aids, but ran aground near the coast artillery batteries at Fort Stevens. The crew

escaped but the ship was lost; and beaches for miles were littered with Christmas trees.

In the 5,645-ton (gross), twenty-one-year-old freighter *Lahaina,* Captain Hans Matthiesen (who had gone over the side from the German grainship *Tamara XII* in 1922) left Ahukini, Kauai, for San Francisco on December 3, 1941, on a course some 300 miles north of Honolulu. He judged from his position on December 7 that Japanese bombers headed for Pearl Harbor probably passed directly over the ship but were unseen in very heavy weather. As soon as the attack news came, the ship's crew of thirty-four men mixed all the paint in the lockers together to get a dull gray and began repainting the ship from the stack down. Matthiesen put a sack of raw potatoes in each lifeboat. Continuing eastward, the *Lahaina* was some 700 miles northeast of Oahu when the first shot was fired at her.

"They hit us about 1:00 P.M.," Matthiesen said. "He [the submarine] came up on our starboard quarter right out of the sun, where you don't look or try not to look because it hurts your eyes. He fired a shot. I saw it hit, then another. . . .

"That was a strange feeling—when somebody shoots at you and you can't shoot back. He didn't give us any time to get into the lifeboats. The first shell went right through the starboard lifeboat.

"I ordered 'Abandon ship,' so everybody was

there by the port lifeboat. Then I went back to my quarters. I'd forgotten a bag with my instruments. I also figured I might as well get some cigarettes. I dropped the bag and my cigarettes to somebody in the boat and was just getting over the rail to go down myself when here came another shell, right into my quarters where I'd just been. That set the forward house afire. We got down into the water, and the two men who had lowered the boat slid down the falls. We were no sooner under the port quarter, sitting there, when a shell came right through the ship, cut half the falls, landed about fifty yards away in the sea, and then exploded.

"I thought, Man alive, isn't this something! That could have been absolute disaster. We hung there under the quarter. That was desperation but the best place because he couldn't see us. Then the sub came around across the bow. I could see them on deck, watching like hawks. I said, 'Everybody down. Sit and be quiet. Don't make a move of any kind. The first guy who makes any kind of a movement or turns around gets brained.' I had the officers placed so they could help me if necessary.

"So we just sat. The sub backed toward the ship, oh, maybe to within forty or fifty yards. Then the deck gun—I could see the whole thing—shot right into the engine room. One shell was short, one high, but the third hit right on the margin where the deck and the side of the ship join. They saw that was the crucial spot, and that the engine room would fill with water.

"Some of them yelled, 'Banzai!' The ship was afire from stem to stern and the engine room flooded. She would go down when the rest of the holds filled. When they had accomplished that, they steamed away.

"One lousy lifeboat, big enough for seventeen, and thirty-four men in it! I thought, This is a fine situation. Now what to do? The ship drifted all night, burning, the whole sky red from the flames, which might have been a hundred feet high.

"We drifted with it. About dawn, we realized the engineer's house wasn't burning yet and the ladder there was still intact, so we could get back aboard. I climbed up as best I could, with the third engineer and the bos'n to help me. We got the water breaker from the other useless lifeboat. That saved our lives, that one little thing, the water breaker.

"I was lucky enough to reach a case of eggs in the storeroom, a few bananas, a couple of oranges and some jars of marmalade. I shoved this stuff up the slanting deck, and the others passed it down to the boat. We had a hell of a time with that case of eggs, but we did it. The ship was listing and burning. It was high time to get off, and we did. Just about ten o'clock in the morning she finally rose by the stern a little bit, turned on her side, and slid into the sea. We got out of there in a hurry because a lot of debris was popping up.

"We lost four men. One died of shock, just plain fear, the second day in the boat. Another fellow, named Larson I think, had been a Swedish navy man and he just couldn't take it—no food after a day or so, 150 ccs of water per man per day, which is only a couple of swallows. He jumped overboard. He said, 'Now, let anybody try to stop me,' and jumped over backwards. He went right down, never came up. We could see him, going down like a dead weight.

"We had a little sail and set a course for Maui. A third man had been ill and taking medication. When he ran out of it, he was suffering so much that he tried to hang himself from the lifeboat mast. He lasted most of the ten days but died just before we sighted land. We brought his body in to Maui and buried it there.

"Most of the time, the weather was lousy. There was a howling gale when we finally got off Maui at night, and we were running before it under shortened sail, say a quarter mile offshore. We had this one other fellow, a sort of wise guy, who had been quite a swimmer in his youth—but he was an island boy and should have known. After nine or ten days in the boat, he thought he was still strong as ever; and he was determined to be the first man ashore, you know, to proclaim the glad tidings that we'd finally made it.

"He goes over the side and starts to swim, hand over hand, in a crawl, toward the shore. Of course, he didn't make it. There are sharks around at night. We tried frantically to come about, but with that weather we couldn't do it. We could hear him screaming when they had hold of him. Then there was silence. After a while, we got the sail up, just enough to keep us before the wind, and kept on going.

"Finally, we were off Spreckelsville, what the men called the Gold Coast because F. F. Baldwin, president of Alexander & Baldwin, lived there. It was just sunup. I said, 'Get the sail up. Let's get some speed and we'll go right through the breakers and land there.'

"One man said to me, 'Are you crazy? You want to kill us all?'

"I said, 'For crying out loud, you're so God-damned weak you can't even see me and now you holler because you're afraid to get your feet wet. Get that sail up! We're going in.'

"They raised the sail and I tightened the sheet. The wind made a *ssshh* sound. Waves were breaking against the hull and breakers underneath us; but full as she was, the boat kept on beautifully, didn't even take any water. It was surfing and dropped us right on the beach. We all tried to get ashore but . . . most of them had to crawl away from the boat. They couldn't walk until circulation started again in their legs. I had a heck of a time walking myself, and there was a terrible pain in my stomach. The second mate found a standpipe with a hose in it and yelled, 'Come over here. We've got some water. . . .'

"By that time there was a policeman on the beach, a night patrolman. He took one look and said, 'Are you crazy? Who are you people? Do you know where you are?'

"I said, 'We don't give a hoot where we are.' "

The starving men were taken into the Baldwin home, then to a hospital. At first they could not eat, only drink milk. Later, Matthiesen, like the others, was given a steak. "I think I fell asleep while I was eating," he said. "I woke up the next morning, a bright, beautiful day. That was marvelous. I thought, Isn't it nice to be alive?"

Matthiesen returned to San Francisco as a passenger on the *Maui,* now an army transport, and was assigned to the old *Manoa,* but promptly was beached by military intelligence. The reasons, when he finally learned them, turned out to be the fact that two of his brothers were German military officers and that he had written, but not mailed, a letter to one of them before American entry into the war. The letter, which was critical of the British, had been picked up by a shipmate and turned in to intelligence officers. The fact that Matthiesen was a U.S. Naval Reserve lieutenant apparently had less significance.

For a time, he washed bottles in a brewery to make a living, and could get no action on his case until he made a trip to the Navy Department in Washington, D.C. The ban against him then was lifted, and he was promoted to lieutenant commander. Assigned to active duty as executive officer of the U.S.S. *Deimos,* a navy freighter, he was torpedoed again off Guadalcanal and finished the war as captain of the U.S.S. *Ruticulus,* which promptly was dubbed "U.S.S. Ridiculous" by her crew.

"But we weren't so ridiculous," Matthiesen said. "We did a fine job of work through the Gilberts, Solomons, New Guinea, the western Pacific, Marianas, Philippines, Okinawa, and into Japan."

Mustered out in 1946, Matthiesen commanded Matson ships for another twenty-four years and retired as commodore of the fleet in 1970.*

---

*Captain Jonny Bruns also had problems with military intelligence, being beached mainly because he had written to inquire about relatives in Germany, which he had left before World War I. During a year before he could get permission to go back to sea, he worked as a motorman on San Francisco street-cars, then in a shipyard.

Jack Fischbeck, by then manager of the Royal Hawaiian Hotel, had no nationality problems but was out of a job the day the war started. On vacation, he was in El Paso, Texas, driving toward Florida, on December 7. He said, "I had a house, a job and a bank account in Hawaii, and I'm in the middle of Texas. We had Hawaiian license plates on the car and before the morning of the seventh was over, people were taking one glance and yelling

In the first twenty months of the war, twice as many Matson ships were lost as in the sixty years of the company's prior history. Before Matthiesen reached Maui, the old 3,000-ton *Manini,* under Captain George Sidon, went down in six minutes after being torpedoed in heavy seas off South Point on the island of Hawaii. For sixty-four hours from December 17, crewmen were at the oars of a lifeboat, spending an hour rowing and two hours resting, to keep it headed into the wind.

A mast finally was stepped and a shortened sail set on December 20. Two days later, an American bomber passed overhead at 800 feet. Sure that they had been seen and would be reported, the men celebrated with a feast of three cans of tomatoes. No rescuers appeared, however, until they attracted the attention of a patrol plane crew on December 24. One-fourth cup of water was served each man "to celebrate our good luck and Christmas Eve. We are all hopeful of being rescued tomorrow."

Again, no rescuers appeared. Messman Jules H. Simmons died on December 26 of thirst, hunger, and exposure and was buried at sea. Survivors joined in prayer on December 27 and in religious services on Sunday, December 28. Additional seaplanes appeared within the hour, and the crew was rescued by the destroyer *Patterson* later in the day. The men had been twelve days in the open boat.

Worse luck struck the *Malama,* a sister ship, three days later. Carrying new, secret, and sophisticated electronic devices—actually, very early radar—the ship had been delayed at Honolulu when war broke out, then ordered to take a roundabout southern course to Manila. Captain Malcolm Peters's request

for a pistol had been refused by the military government in Hawaii. On the last day of 1941, when the ship was 400 miles from the Tuamoto islands, a small seaplane was sighted.

Gordon Pollard, one of the mates and later both a captain and a shoreside Matson official, said:

"We couldn't identify the plane, really, and some thought it might be New Zealand or Australian, a pilot just out checking on us; but Captain Malcolm Peters decided he could not take a chance of having the ship captured. He ordered all but the essential nuts taken off a condenser so that it would be only a few minutes work to take off the rest and let a big stream of water come aboard."

On January 1, the seaplane came back, showing its Japanese markings and firing a machine gun across the *Malama*'s bow. Having no defense, Captain Peters ordered the ship stopped and the men into lifeboats. One of the last to leave removed the remaining nuts from the condenser, and water poured in as he scrambled out of the engine room. The little seaplane waited until the boats were away, then bombed the ship repeatedly. The *Malama* went down shortly before the Japanese auxiliary raider *Hokoku Maru* appeared. Formerly a passenger ship in the South American trade, she was well armed and commenced preying on South Pacific shipping as soon as the war began. She took aboard the seaplane and also picked up the *Malama* crew as prisoners. Nobody bothered to tell the pilot he had wasted his bombs.

Peters and his men were taken to a prison camp near Shanghai; later were moved farther north in China; down the Korean peninsula; and, just before the war ended, to the Hokkaido coal mines. Two men died and Pollard did not think "any of us could have made it through a winter [1945–1946] in that climate."

For the freighter *Mauna Loa,* nothing went right. Captain F. R. Trask was five days out of Honolulu, headed for Manila via Port Moresby, New Guinea, on December 7, 1941. Ordered to the nearest friendly port, he steered for Pago Pago but was slowed to nine and one-half knots when the ship

at each other, 'Come and see the refugees.' I finally got through by telephone to Syd Walton, one of the Matson executives, in San Francisco. He said, 'Wherever you're going, keep going. The hotel is taken over already by the navy, the navy has part of the ships, and the army has the rest. All we're going to do is to run an accounting department here to see who owes whom when this is all over.' " Fischbeck managed to get into naval aviation, "although I didn't know the front end of an airplane from the back," and was commandant of a naval station of 500 officers and 6,000 men at Clinton, Oklahoma, when the war ended. Chef Edgar Kina would not have been impressed by the menus.

dropped a propeller blade. He then was ordered to Suva and finally to Sydney for repairs. At the end of the month, he was headed for Brisbane with 3,800 barrels of fuel oil; but after that, things became more confused. "Between January 1 and January 6," Trask reported, "the U.S. Army loaded and discharged supplies for Darwin [on Australia's north coast] at least three times. . . . as one major told me, he knew more about the hardware business he had left in Salt Lake than his present duties."

By mid-January, *Mauna Loa* was at Darwin, where wharfies took nine days to unload the small cargo. During the next two weeks, the ship again was loaded and unloaded several times, receiving orders which often were canceled before they could be opened. On February 14, 500 Australian troops came aboard; and the next day a convoy of four troop-carrying merchant ships, escorted by the U.S. cruiser *Houston* (later sunk), headed for Timor, the Portuguese island at the eastern end of the Indonesian archipelago.

Waves of Japanese aircraft attacked, and Able Seaman Manuel M. DeSilva was mortally wounded. Several soldiers also were hit, and one later died. Trask found dozens of holes in the *Mauna Loa* above the waterline, and oil was leaking.

The convoy turned back to Darwin, where the troops went ashore but left their equipment on board. On the night of February 21 Trask's problems were increased by the excruciating pain of a kidney stone passing, but he put off a trip to a hospital until the next day.

On that day, there wasn't time. Japanese bombers hit the port and shipping in the harbor in midmorning, and a dive-bomber promptly located the *Mauna Loa*'s number 5 hold. The ship began sinking by the stern as aircraft, bombing and strafing, harassed the crew on the ship and in boats. Trask carried off the ship's papers, codebooks, and a sextant but forgot about money, watches, and his wallet in the ship's safe. All hands reached shore and were trucked to an army camp several miles out of Darwin for the night. Only then, Trask realized that his kidney still was hurting like mortal sin.

The men from the *Mauna Loa* begged truck rides seventy miles south to Adelaide River and, after three days there, boarded a cattle train on the narrow-gauge railroad for a 235-mile ride to rail end at Larrimah, mostly standing up because of the jam. The Australian army at that outback hamlet provided a meal, tea, and space on a truck convoy for Alice Springs, 650 miles farther south, "over a corrugated trail which was good for the backside."* A series of other trains of varying gauges took the crew another 1,000 miles to Adelaide, on Australia's south coast, then to Melbourne, where eventually they found sea transportation home.

The S.S. *Lihue,* 7,000 tons, was not in the best of condition when she left New York for Trinidad Bay on February 14, 1942. Captain W. G. Leithead reported, "zigzagging was started but it was found that due to all the defense work done and with no degaussing coil on the steering compass the vessel steered a better zigzag than could have been laid out."

She did have, however, a navy gun crew that was competent, lucky, or both. At midnight on February 22, the moon had just set. Seconds later a torpedo struck, well forward on the port side. The ship immediately developed a sharp list to starboard and was down by the head, but engineers managed to get it up to its maximum speed.

Leithead reported: "Shortly after [we were] hit, the sub started firing at us [with a deck gun]. His first shell fell short . . . and he sent up a flare to windward of himself. Our gun [a three-inch weapon in charge of Ensign Peter Wendt] blazed away at him as he fired another shell at our radio antenna. An impact was heard by quite a few of the crew and myself, and then there was no more of the submarine. We fired five shells at him and I was informed . . . that the gun pointer was point blank on . . . and that the sub was only four to five hundred yards off."

Ensign Wendt took photographs of the listing

---

*The U.S. Army later helped Australians to build a paved highway from Darwin to Alice Springs in the middle of the continent.

ship, the gunners, and the lifeboats into which the crew was ordered at noon the next day when the *Lihue* was stopped by water in the fuel tanks. She later sank. The crew was picked up by a British tanker. *Life* magazine published Wendt's photos under the heading, "U.S. Freighter's Gun Crew Sinks Sub by Light of U-Boat Skipper's Flare."

The old, tired *Kahuku,* with a 2,000-horsepower engine that, at full throttle, could push her at eight and one half knots, made a wartime trip to Suez via the Cape of Good Hope, then returned to Jersey City to have a deck gun installed and to load military cargo for the Persian Gulf. Harlan Soeten (later curator of the San Francisco Maritime Museum) went aboard as second mate, mainly to steady his nerves after several months on coastal oil tankers, which were preferred targets for German submarines.

"A five-inch gun had been mounted on the poop," he reported, "and quarters for the accompanying Armed Guard had been built in a hot and crowded storage space over the engine room. Some kind of mastic 'armour plate' had been poured around and on top of the pilothouse. The extra weight had started to cave in the roof, and four 4-inch timber supports had been hastily placed beneath. Many a dark night we mates cursed those four-by-fours as we banged into them while trying to get to the chartroom or from one bridge wing to the other in the dark and in a hurry. . . .

"The *Kahuku* was owned by Matson . . . but was husbanded by the Isthmian Steamship Company. The Isthmian mates condescendingly referred to the Matson ships as 'pineapple clippers.' She *[Kahuku]* was a 6,000-ton vessel. . . . She had a flush deck amidships, which put the pilothouse and bridge deck lower than on most ships. . . . the only way to get a good view ahead was to climb on top of the pilothouse. This made watch-standing . . . an extremely active operation, with frequent fast trips up and down a vertical ladder. . . . Captain Eric A. Johanson was a long-time Matson mate who had been given his first command, the *Kahuku,* when in his late fifties or early sixties. . . . the chief mate

was an Isthmian man who said half jokingly that he had been assigned to the *Kahuku* as punishment for turning down a job as mate of an Isthmian ship loading for Murmansk. . . .

"We left Chesapeake Bay 29 May, 1942 at 6 a.m. in convoy bound for Key West. As I recall, there were six rows of ships and five or six ships in each row, about half of them tankers. The *Kahuku* was next to last in one of the middle rows. . . . the convoy's speed was set at seven knots so she could keep up. . . . Our escorts were a converted British trawler and an American four-stack destroyer of World War I vintage. . . .

"On 8 June, nine days from the Chesapeake, I came on watch at midnight to find us off Rebecca Shoals Light to the west of Key West. The convoy had reduced speed and stopped zigzagging. . . . Some of the ships were almost stopped. . . . Captain Johanson was on the bridge and the third mate was on top of the wheelhouse, trying to figure out what was happening. It was an eerie night, with a half-moon shining through a thin overcast, not a breath of wind, and quiet as death. We could hear the water lapping against the hull as we drifted along on a slow bell. The debris in the water—part of a ship's settee, a door, hatch covers and the ever-present oil slick—added to the tenseness of the night. . . . while we were talking, the commodore's ship gave the signal, 'All ships proceed independently.'

"That really started a scramble. Here were about thirty-five ships . . . half of them bound for the Gulf on a west-to-northwest course, and the rest bound for Yucatan Channel in a southwesterly direction. As luck would have it, most of the vessels going north were on the south side of the convoy, and vice versa. It was a few hours before everyone was unscrambled. . . . We had been on our new course about an hour when we saw two flashes on our northern horizon, followed by the sounds of explosions. At least one tanker, possibly two, had gone as far as they were going to go. . . .

"On 11 June we reached Serrana Bank, a shoal of several miles, and once again our convoy commodore sent up the signal to proceed independently. . . . The commodore's ship and four others continued in the direction of the Panama Canal, [and] the rest of us turned hard left on the base course . . . zigzagging towards Port-of-Spain, Trinidad. The next day the *Kahuku* had the ocean to herself, the other ships having left us behind. That evening, our radio operator heard an 'SOS, we are torpedoed and abandoning ship' from one of the Panama-bound ships.''

On June 13 Soeten wrote, ''Sparks came to the bridge with another SOS, from a ship about 140 miles northwest of Port-of-Spain; and early in the morning of the 14th, we received an SOS from one of our former convoy mates at about the same position. From then on, Sparks was making frequent trips. . . . with reports of submarines sighted or distress calls from torpedoed ships . . . it seemed evident that the subs were onto a good thing—they simply waited astride the 'safety lane' and sank the ships as they came by. To the best of my knowledge, of the sixteen ships of the unescorted convoy that stood down the Yucatan Channel, only one reached port. None of the Panama bound vessels made it, and a United States Lines freighter that skirted the Venezuelan coast was the only vessel to reach Trinidad.

''About noon on the 15th, some 150 miles northwest of Trinidad, we were again running through heavy debris . . . when we sighted three lifeboats filled with men . . . and at about the same time we saw two vessels approaching from the south. They were the converted yacht *Opal* and the *YP-63*. The men in the lifeboats, to our not very great surprise, declined to be rescued by us. As we hove to, they waved us on, shouting, 'We're better off where we are. We've been sunk once and don't want to get it again.' . . . but the *Opal* signaled us to stop and ordered the men out of the boats and aboard the *Kahuku*. By 3 o'clock all were aboard, their lifeboats tied astern on long painters, and we were underway again, the *Opal* and the *YP-63* running alongside. The sixty-three men we had picked up

were survivors of two freighters . . . that had been sunk the night before.

''By 6 o'clock, steering a seventy-four percent zigzag pattern, we were feeling relatively relaxed with our escorts nearby, when gradually they widened their course and disappeared in the darkness to the south. At 8 o'clock, there was an explosion a mile or so to the north of us and a few minutes later we could see the waterlights of rafts bobbing in the darkness. This vessel we later found to be the American-Hawaiian Line's *Arkansan,* returning from the Persian Gulf. I went up to the bridge where the captain, mate and gunnery officer were having a conference. It was decided that the sub which had torpedoed the *Arkansan* would need at least an hour to get into position for a shot at us. . . . Then we noticed someone signaling by blinker on our port bow and it being answered by someone to starboard. . . . Apparently, two subs were choosing which ships to sink.

''At 9:20, I was sitting on my bunk . . . when someone yelled, 'Here it comes!' Before I could react, the torpedo exploded directly under me, and when I came to a few seconds later I was lying in the waterway on the other side of the deck. Getting up, I went to the bridge just as the captain sounded the signal to abandon ship. My lifeboat, the starboard one, was blown up . . . so I went over to the port side to help get that one away. . . . fortunately the sea was calm and the overloaded boat safely cleared the ship. . . . both forward rafts were already floating and men were jumping over to swim to them. I then started aft . . . and looked into the radio shack where Sparks was trying to repair his equipment. I told him he was wasting his time and to come with me . . . but he went on with his repairs and I never saw him again. I reached the poop where the gunnery officer had just ordered his men to jump—the vessel now had taken a starboard list and was down by the stern. Seeing a waterlight some distance astern, which apparently wasn't going to get any nearer, and all my options having run out, I jumped off the port quarter.

"As soon as I hit the water, I was sure I was in trouble. The *Kahuku* was still going slowly ahead. Two of the three lifeboats we were towing astern had swamped and were being towed along under the surface, with their gear trailing after them. Men . . . , knowing the boats were tied astern, had jumped or slid down the painters, only to find nothing at the end except a lot of tangled gear which, instead of supporting them, dragged them under.

"Fortunately, I got clear of this mess and after about an hour's swim reached the waterlight and found it attached to a raft with only three or four men aboard. . . . others kept arriving [until] there were twenty-two men on, or clinging to, the raft.

"The *Kahuku* was still afloat, and a submarine had surfaced and was firing tracers at the radio shack. After a few minutes of this, he started firing at the poop with a larger calibre gun. The third shot apparently hit the magazine, as there was an explosion, a flash of fire and the ship settled a little more by the stern. Sometime around midnight, a second torpedo was fired and the *Kahuku* finally went under, stern first.

"Several of the men on the raft had been picked up first by a German submarine, presumably the same one that sank us, and subsequently placed aboard a raft. The submarine's captain told them the *Opal* would be out the next day and pick us up. He also informed them he had been in Port-of-Spain a few days earlier and had gone to see a Gary Cooper movie. . . .

"About 2 p.m. [the next day] . . . the *Opal* and YP-63 hove to nearby, with rope ladders over the side. Clad only in my underwear and covered with fuel oil, I was helped over the rail. Six of the *Kahuku's* crew, including the captain, first mate and gunnery officer, were missing. Eleven were lost from the *Cold Harbor* and the *Scottsburg*.

"Down in *Opal's* chiefs' quarters, I asked the chief machinist's mate, 'Where were you last night? You must have seen the gunfire.' His answer, in summary, was, 'Yes, we saw you and the other

ships being sunk but there wasn't much we could do about it. We're no match for the subs, so we don't bother them; and they don't bother us when we come to pick up survivors.'

"It was a sort of gentlemen's agreement for which we were thankful.''

On July 5 in the Barents Sea, the sun dips toward the horizon at midnight but never goes below it. It makes for fine hunting weather but is not so pleasant for the quarry. On that date in 1942, hunters and quarry were hard to tell apart. The German battleship *Von Tirpitz* had slipped out of a Norwegian harbor, and all Allied combat ships anywhere near went looking for her—so she was one quarry. Some of those combat ships, however, had to leave Murmansk-bound convoys of freighters to fend for themselves. These quarries could only scatter for dubious safety. So an oiler on the Matson freighter *Honomu* acted understandably.

"He would only come down into the engine room long enough to make his rounds, check the water in the boilers and dash back up on deck,'' according to Alan L. Harvie, the ship's third engineer. "He was firmly convinced we were done for and that the engine room was the prime target. He'd stand by the forward starboard corner of the after house by the steward's room and wait until time to make another round.''

The frightened oiler was correct but unlucky. Without warning, a torpedo struck at 2:30 P.M. "There was a terrific shock,'' Harvie said, "and the lights went out. The engine started to labor heavily, deck plates bounced around and water started pouring down through the ventilators and skylight. The fireman dashed up the ladder and I ran over to the throttle and stopped the engine and the main circulator. The purpose was to stop the vessel so the lifeboats could be launched. Then I went out into the fireroom, secured the fires in the boilers and opened the safety valves to let the steam escape. . . .

"There was no word from the bridge. . . . the

mate had been pitched off onto Number Two hatch. . . . Unfortunately, the oiler's choice of location had been a poor one, since the first torpedo struck almost under him, and he was blown half the length of the house, breaking a shoulder blade and other bones. . . . about this time the ship received another torpedo in the port side. . . . the port lifeboat had been launched and was well out of the way. The four life rafts were launched and we managed to get away in them."

"Sarge" Kolence, ship's carpenter, added: "Nine of us, including the skipper, were on one raft. A swarm of German planes flew down and looked us over, then flew away. Three submarines came to the surface and one of them came close. The sub commander, in bum English, said he hoped we were all right and explained there was nothing personal in the sinking, that it was just part of war. . . .

"They took our skipper [Captain F. A. Strand] prisoner, gave us a dozen loaves of black bread marked 'Kiel,' a few cans of horsemeat and some bandages, and shoved off. . . . We put our feet inside each other's shirts to keep them from freezing. Water got low about the fifth day and we rationed it."

Harvie said:

"All rafts were tied together in tandem, with the lifeboat taking the lead. We set up watches of four hours on the oars and four hours rest . . . the weather was cold and at times a light drizzle set in, so we weren't dehydrated too much. . . . several times we could hear distant explosions . . . but couldn't see anything. . . .

"On the ninth day, a British Catalina plane spotted us and tried to land; but it was too rough, so she dropped some cigarettes and chocolate bars wrapped in a life jacket with a message that she would get us some help. However, a fog set in almost immediately and we couldn't see much nor could the searchers see us. On the tenth day, the lifeboat left us and headed for the coast. I understand that they eventually landed with several casualties.

"On the afternoon of the 13th day we heard

gunfire from a vessel's 20-mm anti-aircraft gun. It sounded quite close so we fired six rounds from my pistol. It sounded awfully puny but the gunfire ceased immediately. . . . Almost two hours later we saw a dim shape in the fog and up came a British minesweeper in company with another of the same type. They had heard us all right but were being very cautious since there were only four rafts and their information had been that there were five boats. . . . they assumed the four pips on the radar might be submarines. The HMS *Halcyon* was a most welcome sight, to put it mildly. They were on the last leg of their search grid when they found us. Their fuel was running short, and they would have had to return to port."

Honomu gun crews had been British. For his action in shutting down both engines and fireroom before leaving his post, Harvie was awarded the British Distinguished Service Cross and the U.S. Merchant Marine Meritorious Service Medal. Survivors of the sinking spent some time in a Russian submarine base hospital near Murmansk and later were taken to Archangel, enduring heavy bombing attacks in both places.

Kolence, in September, was a passenger on a log-carrying former Greek freighter headed back to the United States in convoy. This ship, too, was torpedoed, "sending logs flying like toothpicks in the air" and killing one man; but the rest of the passengers and crewmen were taken aboard a British rescue ship without getting their feet wet.

Matson's freighter *Olopana* also was far from the sugar and pineapple routes, in the same convoy with the *Honomu*. Six of the thirty-five ships were sunk by German aircraft before it could scatter. Captain M. C. Stone headed the *Olopana* due north until he ran into an ice barrier, then turned southeast, hoping for refuge at the Russian island of Novaya Zemlya. The ship was attacked by a German aircraft on July 5 but survived.

Stone then changed course again, trying to hug the mainland coast to Archangel (Arkhangelsk). At 11:00 P.M. on July 6, however, a torpedo struck the engine room, killing engineers John Durham and

John Sochacki, oiler Sam Aiau, and gunner Edward Owen. Messman Albert Percell and fireman Charles Kaialoha were lost overboard. Surviving crewmen took to three rafts as the submarine surfaced and shelled the ship until she sank. After three days, the crew reached a beach on Novaya Zemlya, from which they were lifted by a Russian Catalina seaplane.

En route from Nova Scotia to England on August 8, 1942, Captain Theodore H. Cunningham sounded a general alarm on the freighter *Kaimoku* when he saw two other ships in his convoy blown up off his port bow. Two torpedoes from a submarine wolf pack then struck the ship, which went down in four minutes. Engineer Joseph Gonzalez and fireman Peter McDermott were killed, but remaining crewmen were rescued by a Canadian corvette.

Weather was the enemy for the small freighter *Mapele* carrying supplies to a secret navy refueling station at Sand Point in Alaska's Shumagin islands on January 14, 1943. Attempting to negotiate Korovin Strait in a blinding snowstorm and with ice covering decks and superstructure, Captain John M. Fitzsimmons used the time-honored Alaska system of blowing the ship's whistle and listening for echoes in order to approximate his position. He did pick up a dead-ahead echo from a rock pinnacle off Cape Devine but could not stop the ship in time. The *Mapele* was impaled. All hands abandoned ship but two—Able Seaman John H. Taylor and navy gunner Francis H. Wallace—were lost from the boats landing on a surf-pounded beach.

The Liberty ship *Henry Knox* was bound from Australia to Bandar Shahpur, Iran, in the Persian Gulf when she was hit by two torpedoes on July 19, 1943. The heavy load of military supplies included explosives, which caught fire and showered the deck. Thirteen of the forty-one men aboard were killed in the fire or lost in the boats. The Japanese submarine surfaced after the torpedoing. It came alongside one boat and took away all the food, water, sails, and charts, then cut it loose. Captain Eugen M. Olsen, the last man off the ship, directed a search until he was sure all survivors had been located, then divided the remaining supplies between the three boats and set a northeasterly course. After eleven days the burned and wounded men sighted a small, uninhabited atoll, eventually getting ashore even though one boat upset on the reef in a sudden squall.

The next day the castaways attracted the attention of a passing native lugger, which took them to an inhabited island. The survivors finally reached Mali, the seat of the government of the Maldive islands, and later Colombo, Ceylon.

CHAPTER TWELVE

LINERS AT WAR
(1941–1946)

Speed, double bottoms, and fuel capacity were the most pertinent factors in the wartime history of Matson's four modern passenger liners: a history covering 1,460,000 miles of cruising through five oceans, Antarctic drift ice to Glasgow, Oran to Suez the long way around.

Their twenty-two-knot speed meant principally that they could outrun on the surface any submarines then operating and that a submerged submarine could be effective against one of them only if it were lying directly in the path of the ship.[*] The Armed Forces chose to accept this risk and sent the big troopships without escorts much of the time when they were in areas more or less safe from aerial attack. The ships also were better armed than the freighters, with batteries of 22 mm and Bren antiaircraft guns on their tennis decks.

The fuel tankage allowed very long voyages, and all four ships undertook them. After a few trips back and forth to Hawaii under convoy at the war's outbreak, the *Lurline* began running to Pago Pago and other South Pacific ports, escorted by combat ships only until the first nightfall out of Honolulu. The *Matsonia, Mariposa,* and *Monterey,* all serving

the South Pacific during the first months, also proceeded alone from the same point.

The *Lurline* continued this service, generally to Brisbane as a southern terminal but touching at most other U.S. bases in the South Pacific and once going all the way to Bombay, until the summer of 1945. Carrying up to 4,200 troops at a time westbound, she often had cargoes of wool, hides, pig lead, and tallow, as well as battle casualties, refugees, diplomats, and government officials (including Australian Prime Minister John Curtin on a trip to meet President Roosevelt), war brides, entertainers, and assorted civilians on her return trips. During the entire war, Commodore C. A. Berndtson and his crew saw only one torpedo wake, apparently a last hope shot from a submarine that couldn't catch up. The *Lurline* left the Pacific–Indian Ocean areas in 1945 to redeploy troops from the European to the Pacific war theater. During the trans-Atlantic trip to France after V-E Day, the ship was lighted at sea for the first time in nearly four years. She made thirty-one wartime voyages, steamed 388,847 miles, carried 199,860 passengers, and served 9,322,706 meals.

The other three liners had more varied experiences, although only the *Mariposa* traveled farther. This ship stayed in Pacific service until May 1942, then picked up 3,813 soldiers at Charleston, South Carolina, and sailed for Karachi by way of Cape-

---

[*]This was an outside possibility but could happen. The U.S. heavy cruiser *Indianapolis,* which carried the first atomic bomb to Tinian and had a top speed well above thirty knots, was torpedoed and sunk in open waters off the Philippines in just such a situation shortly before the war ended.

town, guarded mostly by British warships, including the battleships *Rodney* and *Nelson*. She left the troops at Karachi, loading scarce tungsten and mica, as well as seventy-seven American Volunteer Group pilots from the China–Burma–India war theater, eighty-eight missionaries, and fifty-four Chinese aviation cadets. Escorted to Capetown, she then proceeded alone to New York at 20.09 knots. On October 20 she sailed for Liverpool with 4,068 troops, unloaded them, picked up another 3,987 at Glasgow, and took them to Oran, Algeria, in a convoy harassed by submarine alerts and once bombed briefly. Returning to New York in November, she sailed again, from Newport News, on December 21 on a 110-day, 41,000-mile voyage with calls at Rio de Janeiro, Aden (reached by a route so southerly there was danger from Antarctic drift ice), Massawa, Suez, Djibouti, Somaliland, the Sudan, Bombay, Capetown, Glasgow, and New York.

On the leg from Djibouti to Suez, the *Mariposa* carried a contingent of black, French-speaking Senegalese troops, fresh off long desert marches, along with their dogs and chickens.

"[They] were quite surprised that they didn't have to cook their own food aboard ship," wrote Fred Stindt, then the *Mariposa*'s chief purser, "and couldn't figure out what made the ship go. They finally concluded she must have legs and walk along the bottom. . . . Staff members became accustomed to seeing chickens scratching on the rubber-tiled decks in the staterooms in search of food, troops balancing enormous packs on their heads and repeatedly walking into door mirrors, which were beyond their comprehension.

"The men camped on deck wherever they could find room to spread a blanket, and since they had been camping out so long, the desert dust from their belongings soon pervaded the ship. . . . each soldier carried his own small kerosene lamp, and the first night the ship was ablaze with individual beacons. With the aid of their officers . . . the lamps were all collected before anything caught fire, and within a few days the troops were behaving quite conventionally. . . .

"At Suez, a gang of eighty Arabs was employed to give the ship a thorough cleaning, after which 2,763 passengers were embarked for the homeward voyage."

In August 1943 the *Mariposa* lifted 5,507 troops from Boston and added another 90 at Reykjavik for her largest single passenger load to date. Later in the year she made two round trips to Bombay, stopping in San Francisco at the conclusion of the first—eighteen months and eleven days after leaving her home port. In 1945 she crossed the Atlantic ten times, bringing her total war service to twenty-nine voyages, covering 414,589 miles and carrying 202,689 passengers.

The *Matsonia* spent the entire war ferrying troops to Pacific combat areas, operating close to the battle lines in New Guinea and the Marianas, like the *Lurline,* and returning to the U.S. mainland with cargoes of wool,* as well as thousands of bags of mail. Passengers included refugees, battle casualties, and even a few Japanese prisoners. In all, she carried 163,732 passengers on thirty-three voyages, without serious incident, and continued in military service for some months after the Japanese surrender.

The *Monterey* carried the largest loads of passengers (6,855 on one voyage, making do with 3,841 bunks) and saw the most combat.

On her second trip to the Mediterranean, carrying 5,000 Canadian troops from Liverpool for Naples in a twenty-two-ship convoy, she had been designated a rescue vessel, although Captain Elis R. Johanson (a gentleman with a full-rigged ship tattooed on his chest) hadn't been told. R. J. McKenzie, later port captain for Matson at Honolulu, was aboard as chief officer. He said, "When the meeting of convoy officers was called before we left Liverpool, the captain was ashore and I wasn't available, so the navigator attended. Captain Johanson always had

*The most common cargo from Australia was baled wool. Captain Raymond Racouillet remembered being third officer on the freighter *Manukai* when it lifted a huge load. "We stored it every place, even in the iceboxes," he said. "If we had taken a torpedo, we all felt we would stay afloat with that cargo."

tried to avoid being named as a pickup ship because the *Monterey* was so high-sided that it was difficult to take on people at sea. But the navigator only had three stripes, and everyone else at the meeting was either a captain or an admiral. So there wasn't much he could do about it when the convoy commander picked the *Monterey* for the job. When he got back to the ship, he either forgot to tell the captain or was just plain scared to tell him. So the first the captain knew about it was when this flight of Junkers—about twenty-five planes—came over and hit two merchant ships and a destroyer. When the convoy commander signaled for a rescue ship to turn out of the convoy to aid the Grace liner *Santa Elena*, the navigator had to tell the captain, 'That means us.'

"Nobody was very happy about it. It was night and there was some confusion. I don't know how it happened, but I was shocked when all of a sudden all the deck lights were turned on. It was a few minutes before I could get to the switches and turn them off. It was a scary thing; but after the whole thing was over, one of the Canadians we rescued told me: 'That was the greatest thing. Here we were, hit and sinking in the dark, and morale just about as low as it could get. Then all of a sudden, there's that big ship, coming our way and with the lights turned on. I tell you, it made a hell of a difference. We thought: Somebody cares. Help's coming.' "

The *Monterey* lowered starboard lifeboats, which picked up survivors directly from the *Santa Elena,* from the water and from a destroyer which had taken people aboard temporarily. *Santa Elena* also got away some lifeboats. Survivors able to do so came aboard the *Monterey* on scrambling nets, lines, and ladders; the injured on litters were loaded through side ports. In all, 1,644 Canadians from the *Santa Elena* and 31 survivors from a small Dutch ship came aboard. The *Monterey* was just picking up her last lifeboat when an escort vessel advised that a torpedo had just crossed his bow and ordered her to get under way at full speed, which she did.

McKenzie adds, "After we had taken aboard the 5,000 Canadians at Liverpool, one of their officers told us they had an outbreak of trench mouth among the troops. We tried to get some dentists transferred from some of the other ships but had no luck. In the people from the *Santa Elena,* there was a whole contingent of dentists—but of course they didn't have a bottle of medicine or even a dental mirror among them.''

Captain Johanson received a commendation from the commandant of Squadron 16 and later the Merchant Marine Distinguished Service Medal for the operation. The records don't say what happened to the navigator.

The *Monterey* was credited with shooting down one Junker bomber during her European service. She also proved the value of her double bottom late in the war when she ran aground at Oro Bay, New Guinea, while groping through a fog composed of pumice ash from an erupting volcano some thirty miles away. The ship heeled 10 degrees to port. Her 3,900 passengers were transferred to two Liberty ships nearby; and a tanker and some landing craft attempted to pull her free, without success. Two large tugs arriving the next day had no more luck until 2,500 barrels of oil and 466 tons of water were pumped overboard. She then floated free, with only two slight dents in her keel and no leaks either in bilges or double bottoms.

The *Monterey* made two more trips to France and one to the western Pacific, returning from this one with 437 emaciated American prisoners of war who had survived the Japanese prison camps in the Philippines. She was headed for Manila when the Japanese surrendered.

Statistics are unavoidable. The four Matson liners made 119 wartime voyages, steamed 1,460,227 miles, carried 736,521 passengers, and served 35,084,317 meals. Meanwhile, all vessels operated by Matson completed 1,337 voyages. The company's maintenance and repair division worked on 1,850 American, British, Dutch, and Russian vessels during the four war years. In 1944 alone gross volume of such business was $30 million. Matson Terminals, Inc., had stevedoring and other facilities at Seattle,

Portland, San Francisco, and Los Angeles and handled 10,061,337 tons of military and essential civilian cargo during the war. More than 4,000 ship berthings were arranged all over the Pacific, and 7,000 accounts were rendered.

Financing was complicated. The government required immediate services from virtually all of the Matson organization but did not get around to a reasonable financing method for eight months. During that time, Matson advanced $20 million of its own funds to finance operations for which it could collect nothing directly. A revolving fund finally was set up by the War Shipping Administration in August 1942.

As a government agency, 1942–1946, Matson spent $128 million for ship operations and collected $144,280,000 in revenue from Lend-Lease and other cargo such as essential merchandise for Hawaii's civilian population. Although much of this was carried in the company's own ships, the money went to the government.

Government service for the company's personnel and ships did not end with V-J Day. All four passenger ships and most of the surviving freighters continued under government orders for about a year, and the air transport division worked on navy contracts until the beginning of 1946. The first of the passenger ships was returned to Matson on April 11, 1946; the last, on September 26. None was in any condition to resume passenger service immedi-ately. Of the thirty-eight freighters turned over to the government, eleven had been sunk and ten "requisitioned for title" (meaning that Matson would not get them back). Others needed work before they could go back into commercial service.

A partial about-face by the government also put Matson into the aviation business, although earlier it had been told emphatically to keep its nose out. That this reversal was arranged by the navy rather than the Civil Aeronautics Board did nothing to help the company's case later. At the navy's request, Matson set up an Air Transport Division in August 1943, with an aircraft modification center at the Oakland Municipal Airport. A navy contract covered servicing, modification, test flying, and ferrying of SO3C planes (Curtis scout and observation types). Matson modified 127 and salvaged and serviced another 199. Later, it overhauled and converted 38 four-engined R5D transports, naval versions of the DC-4 model, readied four more as "flag" planes for admirals and the like, and worked on several others.

Once more encouraged about its future in air travel, in September 1943 the company filed an application with the CAB to provide air service paralleling its shipping routes: Los Angeles, San Francisco, Portland, and Seattle to Honolulu. Matson never had a prayer but did not find out for nearly three years.

CHAPTER THIRTEEN

AN AIRLINE LOST,
HOTELS RESTORED,
SUGAR IN BULK
(1945-1947)

Matson's efforts in the Pacific over-ocean airline business were extensive, expensive, long drawn out, acrimonious, and frustrating. Because of the war, the 1941 rebuff from the new Civil Aeronautics Board had little immediate effect except to end Matson's financial interests in Pan American Airways. The air transport division, established in 1943, grew quickly to 700 employees in ground services and acquired enough reputation so that civilian business was available when navy contracts ended. In early 1946 it converted military transport airplanes to civilian use for the government of the Netherlands; Northwest, California Eastern, Chicago & Southern, and Alaska airlines; Transcontinental Air Express; Willis Air Service; Trans-Ocean and Trans-Pacific Airways, and the Atlas Supply Company. Matson also serviced planes for several of these clients, as well as providing line maintenance for United Air Lines on a subcontract from Trans-Ocean.

At least as much of the airline struggle took place in CAB and court hearings as in air operations. Matson's approach was an extension of the theory of complete transportation packages. Company attorneys stressed that Matson alone among the route applicants already had maintenance facilities in Oakland, plus hotels and amenities for passengers in Hawaii. It also could offer travel alternatives including a fly-one-way, cruise-the-other proposal to give vacationers four more days in the islands during a holiday of specified length while retaining for them the luxury and fun-and-games experience of a voyage on one of the great white ships.

The company also said it was prepared to spend $9 million for its air establishment, including aircraft and terminal facilities, that it would cover any financial losses on the air service from company funds, and that it would operate from Los Angeles and San Francisco to the islands without subsidy.

In contrast, Pan American, operating under the grandfather permits obtained in the mid-1930s, had a postwar annual subsidy of $6 million, including $1.20 per plane mile, or $2,880 for each one-way trip, when it resumed commercial flying from San Francisco to Honolulu. In its petition for the same route, United Airlines asked $0.50 per plane mile, or $1,200 per one-way trip.

In a curious cake topping for its application, Matson noted that its planes could get useful weather reports from Matson ships plowing the seas below them. The company didn't say the ships wouldn't give the time of day to United or Pan American planes, and it didn't say they would.

Matson also pointed out that it was spending $50,000 a year to promote Hawaii tourism, complained bitterly about the basic theory of the CAB (that ship lines should not, under any circumstances, own airlines), and predicted sourly that awarding certificates only to Pan American or United could mean the Hawaiian islands "may become mere dependencies of Wall Street and La Salle Street." It also estimated that in time tourism might bring 100,000 visitors a year to Hawaii by air.

None of this rhetoric impressed the CAB, which, after ignoring Matson's 1943 application for regular air service for nearly three years, rejected it on June 29, 1946. United was awarded authority for San Francisco–Honolulu but not for the other proposed routes.

Matson had taken one step prior to the decision by purchasing and converting one DC-4B transport. With this, it proceeded to set up a nonscheduled triangle service (not requiring specific route approval) to carry passengers and freight between Los Angeles, San Francisco, and Honolulu.

The decision to start nonscheduled service was a calculated risk. Maritime strikes under way at the time created an immediate demand for all the air service Matson or other operators could provide. More important, company officials believed that if it could demonstrate its ability to run a good airline, public pressure might build against the adamant CAB. So the first flights were made as spectacularly as possible. Flight number one had Captain E. L. Sloniger, an almost legendary pilot and instructor, at the controls, with two additional pilots, a radio operator, and a flight engineer in the cockpit. Four passengers and a heavy cargo of fresh strawberries occupied the cabin.

The *Honolulu Advertiser* of July 7, 1946, reported the arrival:

"A big four-motored plane, symbolizing new freight service for Hawaii and a new chapter in Matson Navigation Company history, rode in on the sunrise Saturday and sat down at Honolulu Naval Air Station just ten hours and twenty-one minutes after it took off from San Francisco.*

"As the plane's door opened, the fragrance of

*Military transport flights from Oakland or San Francisco to Honolulu were common during the latter part of the war, but most of them were made in partially converted PBMs or other flying boats and required eighteen or more hours, all uncomfortable. Land-based civilian aircraft used military airfields on Oahu in the postwar period until Honolulu's International Airport was completed.

garden-fresh strawberries, part of the cargo, followed the crew members and four passengers down the steps. An Hawaiian men's trio played as two hula girls draped leis over the shoulders of the airborne arrivals. The airplane itself was decorated with a forty foot paper lei representing Ilima, the 'Oahu flower.' "

The strawberries sold for $1.75 to $2.00 a box in Honolulu.

That was only the beginning. Matson was rapidly converting other DC-4s for its own use. A week after the first flight, an eastbound Matson plane descended from 9,000 to 500 feet above a Matson liner, also eastbound, and circled three times while passengers on each waved to the other.

On July 30 Captain Sloniger made the first direct civilian flight from Portland to Honolulu, bringing ten passengers and two tons of Oregon roses, potatoes, plums, tomatoes, watermelons, and berries on the *Sky Matsonia*. Portland newspapers also considered it important that copies of the same day's editions were on board. Honolulu's morning newspaper, the *Advertiser,* did not.

This flight was made shortly after the CAB had denied petitions both by Matson and Northwest Airlines to establish regular service on the route, with Seattle–Tacoma as a mainland coterminal. The CAB declared that a need for such service "does not exist" despite the fact that the direct flight could be made in approximately twelve hours, as compared with a minimum of more than twenty-four hours for Northwest–Hawaii service via San Francisco. Loud Northwest protests were ignored.

A passenger on the first flight was J. J. Holzman, president of a Hawaii produce firm, who owned some of the perishables in the cargo and expressed enthusiasm about such shipments by air. There is no record of his opinion after another flight, a few weeks later, which was carrying Holzman berries and vegetables when it ran into a weather front and had to return to the Pacific Coast. The entire shipment was spoiled.

Included in Matson's Air Division personnel were T. A. Schmidt, with long experience on several airlines, as operations manager; Leigh Murphy, former test pilot and airline pioneer, for general operations; Chalmar Hans, maintenance manager; and Ernest Gann as a command pilot. Gann, a widely published author, remembers the Matson operation as "the best airline in the world."

Recently he said, "There's nothing like it in service and refinements even today. The food was unbelievable, comparable only to that on the finest liners. They thought they were running a shipline, not an airline. All of the food was prepared under the direction of the same chef who supervised the food for the passenger ships. We had none of this brown-bag stuff or eating on your lap.

"You never saw such food . . . squabs with wild rice, a whole pig with an apple in his mouth, baked Alaska . . . just superb. The flights were about twelve hours but time went fast on those planes; the passengers were happy.

"We frequently rendezvoused with Matson ships in mid-ocean, coming down almost to deck level to circle them. We were close enough to see the steam coming out of the stack when they blew the whistle for us, although we couldn't hear it in the plane. The passengers loved it and so did the people on the ships, waving handkerchiefs, the whole bit. A band always met us in Honolulu."

As modified, the Matson DC-4s were finely finished with mahogany trim and equipped to serve meals at tables with linen cloths. Two stewardesses were uniformed by Mainbocher, and on some flights a steward helped with the serving.

The company's proposals for regular service had specified it would have eight aircraft, each with twenty-four berths for overnight flights, and twenty-five operating crews. It finally did have six aircraft, which made thirty-four flights from San Francisco, eleven from Los Angeles, and eighteen from the Northwest between August 1946 and the following February. Service continued through 1947 but obviously was doomed. As a nonscheduled airline, Matson could not advertise exact departure times but usually had a waiting list for seats. However, United started operating daily flights from San Francisco late in 1947; and Pan American had two a day on the same route, plus one from Los Angeles. Both airlines promptly dropped the one-way fare from $195 to $135, making competition ruinous for unsubsidized Matson. Even a $15 increase shortly afterward was not enough. (For comparison, Pan American's prewar one-way fare on the flying boats had been $278.)

Reluctantly, Matson withdrew from the Hawaiian air routes, chartered its planes for such odd uses as flying fashion models to Paris, and later for the miserable business of carrying Puerto Ricans, always crowded up to or beyond sensible limits, to New York. The planes later were sold and the Oakland air terminal was closed. The company looked once more at the airline business, briefly considering buying troubled Trans-Ocean Airways in 1956. Fortunately, it did not do so: Trans-Ocean eventually went bankrupt.

A Matson brief filed with the CAB during the height of the legal battles predicted that the company might not be able to continue its passenger liner service unless it also had a share in the Hawaiian airline business. The earlier prediction about 100,000 visitors a year going to the islands by air did not show exceptional foresight. This one did.

During the war, the two Matson hotels in Honolulu had provided a study in contrasts. The navy's requisition of the Royal Hawaiian as a rest-and-recreation center mainly for submariners hardly could have been better. For more than three years, crews of the underseas boats—nerves tightened and complexions faded during the long, dangerous, and claustrophobic voyages to Kurile Strait, the Japanese coast, or Southeast Asia—remembered and looked forward to its fine rooms, restaurants, expansive gardens, and the excellent girl watching on Kalakaua Avenue. (A late-war rest center on tropical Guam offered good food, quarters, and beer; but it just wasn't the same.)

For hotel watchers, the experience also was entertaining. Navy skivvies dangled from the Royal Hawaiian lanais; an occasional monel window

Wilhelmina, one of the first Matson passenger steamers, carried passengers before and between the two world wars.

The first liner *Maui,* here shown in 1930, was the last ship delivered to William Matson, in March 1917.

Mariposa and *Monterey* crossed courses at Pago Pago in the 1930s.

At the christening ceremonies for the luxury liner *Malolo*, launched June 26, 1926: Wilhelmina Tenney (left), Secretary of Commerce Herbert Hoover, Lurline Matson Roth and her twin daughters Lurline and Berenice.

Malolo arrives in Honolulu on her maiden voyage. November 1927.

Straw Hat Day. Launching of *Mariposa*, July 1931, at Bethlehem shipyard, Quincy, Mass.

Mrs. William P. Roth and Captain Frank Johnson receive ship's wheel memento, marking completion of *Lurline*'s postwar reconversion, from Lisle Small, president of United Engineering shipyard. April 1948.

Three Matson liners in port at San Francisco, 1959. Left to right: *Lurline* (no. 3), *Mariposa, Matsonia.*

Matson's Royal Hawaiian (right) and Moana hotels in between-war Waikiki. The Seaside Cottages show in lower left-hand corner. 1927.

The ''pink palace'' and the Moana still dominated the Waikiki area in 1947.

Top Left: Once the hotel opened, gala dinners were routine at the Royal Hawaiian.

Bottom Left: The Princess Kaiulani, which opened in 1955, was the modest off-beach Matson hotel—but hardly austere.

Below: Aloha Tower crowds shed tears and paper streamers as *Lurline* departs.

Top Right: Passengers on after-deck of *Lurline* in late 1940s.

Bottom Right: Evening entertainment in a Matson liner ballroom. Post-World War II.

Below: Hilo Hattie does the Hilo Hop on the *Matsonia* deck. May 1946.

Top Left: Matson's first civilian airliner is christened at Honolulu, July 1946, by Mrs. Carl Eastman of San Francisco.

Bottom Left: Flights took 12 hours, but passengers were happy.

Below: Stewardesses were uniformed by Mainbocher.

Left: Wailea resort hotel and condominium development on former Matson land on Maui's southwest coast. 1979.

Below: Luxurious living at Wailea.

screen, floating like a prototype Frisbee, sailed from an upper window through the palm trees. If contests to see who could throw a belt knife most accurately were hard on the room doors and more than a few cigarettes burned out on the carpets while somebody was trying to go all the way with a busted flush, well, the hotel watchers just didn't know so couldn't weep about it.

Just up the street, the Moana continued to be operated by the company throughout the war and presented a much different picture. That pleasant old hostelry was continuously jammed with military men on leave; droves of newspaper, magazine, and radio correspondents; plus assorted casuals who either couldn't get or did not want any military housing. As the only Waikiki hotel where a traveler ever could expect to get a room without being a chum of the manager or his cousin, it seethed with people. Long queues waited at the door of its dining room, and in late evening a submanager often was stationed beside the elevator to make quite sure ladies headed for the upper floors really lived there.

Typical of its problems were the woes of a maitre d' who begged an American correspondent, "Can't you do something about the English newspaper fellow? He never leaves a tip, so the waiters won't serve him, and I can't fire the waiters."

There also was a woman of strong opinions behind the registration desk. An observer watched one evening as she doled out keys to a very few vacant rooms and turned away dozens of other applicants. Eventually, his curiosity overcame his judgment and he said, "I've been watching. You've given rooms to sergeants and generals and civilians, but you've turned away every single major. Why is that?"

"There are never," she said without hesitation, "any rooms for majors. They're just big enough to be nuisances and not big enough to amount to anything."

The first postwar hotel job was to put the Royal Hawaiian back together again. At times, 600 men were on the job, and the gallonage of paint, miles of wire, and tonnage of materials at least ap-

proached the figures that had been so impressive when the hotel was built. Renovation cost exceeded $2 million, but one possible cost was avoided. Frank Palmer, a construction boss during the rehabilitation and later chief engineer for the hotel, remembers going into the basement with a security man, who drew chalk lines on a big concrete wall and said, "We want a hole right here—three feet wide and six feet high."

The jackhammer work took days, but Palmer was stunned when his crew broke through. "Here was this big room," he said, "about 40 by 100 feet. . . . It was the old wine cellar. There were all kinds of liquor, stacked cases of champagne, wooden on the outside and straw inside. The dampness had caused the wood and straw to rot; and so here were the bottles, standing upright and stacked four feet high. When the war started, some smart hotelman had stored all the exotic beverages . . . then had sealed up the only door so it looked just like part of the foundation. If the navy had known that stuff was down there, they'd have torn down the building. . . . they were drinking Five Islands gin." So restocking the bar cost a little less than it might.

Matson had signed its first contract with the hotel and restaurant workers' union in December 1940, agreeing to several improvements in wages and hours, vacations, and overtime pay; but navy occupation of the Royal and martial law regulations during the war decimated the union's membership. In July 1945 the union (officially named Local 5, Hotel and Restaurant Employees and Bartenders International Union) won an election among employees of the Moana and the Seaside Bungalows, also Matson owned.

The union called a one-day strike early in 1946, and at the Moana Matson signed a new contract including checkoff of union dues, paid sick leaves, and grievance procedures. This preceded the Royal reopening, however, and most of the employees of that hotel when it did reopen on February 1, 1947, were the same who had served it in the prewar years. Somewhat overage, they were described by an hotel official as "a very tired, patronage-type of employee. They lived on the grounds, where they once had gardens and raised chickens, even a fish-pond where they raised mullet. This was a hangover from the old days. They had housing and board. We had a Japanese camp, a Filipino camp, and a sort of motley camp behind the old Seaside Bungalows."

Labor problems were brewing all over the islands, but for the moment they appeared remote from the Royal and its acres of waving palms.

Wartime customers waiting in line for dinner were not the only hungry creatures interested in the Moana's dining room. For years, termites had been busy eating the whole dining room wing, from the bottom up. As soon as the Royal Hawaiian was reopened, the Moana was closed for renovation of the entire building.

The most spectacular event, however, occurred when a crew of Samoan workers severed all connections between the three-story dining room wing and the rest of the building—wiring, pipes, roofbeams, and timbers. They then put a cable around the wing and pulled with two bulldozers. The whole wing collapsed on its termite tunnels.

According to Palmer, managing this Samoan construction crew as he had workers giving the Royal its face-lift, Honolulu ordinances prohibited even trucking termite-ridden rubbish through city streets. Remarkably, however, an equally unauthorized fire broke out in what was left of the dining room after it had been hauled just across the street to a vacant lot. What wouldn't burn was covered in a trench, and an impressive building now sits atop the evidence.

The Moana's rehabilitation, which quickly restored the traditional popularity of the hotel, also prepared the way for further expansion, which was to come in the early 1950s.

After eighteen years as Matson's president, William P. Roth happily moved to the less frantic office of chairman of the board of directors on March 18, 1945. Frazer A. Bailey, elected president,

came to that job with thirty-five years' experience and a firm belief that Matson people could do anything. He stepped into two years of solid frustration.

Born at Spotsylvania, Virginia, Bailey had been hired away from the Newport News shipyard as personal secretary to Captain Matson and rose steadily to become company purchasing agent, secretary, and director. Fulton W. Wright, later a Matson vice-president, said of the 1930s: "Bailey was the sparkplug, who did it all. He was making $5,000 a year and running the company single-handed. I think he started doing that when Captain Matson died and Ed Tenney, mostly in Honolulu, was president. He had a lot of higher-ranking people around who didn't do the work, so Bailey did it. . . . when I went there, he wasn't married, lived at home with his mother. He worked all the time, far into the night, and more or less expected everybody else to do the same."

Bailey made many plans in 1945, but actual reconversion to peacetime activities could begin only in the next year. In addition to refurbishing of the hotels and the abortive efforts to get into the airline business, Bailey's problems included complete renovation of the liners and reestablishment of passenger service to the islands; modernization of the freighter fleet; and, after many years, inauguration of an entirely new method of carrying the company's principal eastbound cargo.

The temptation to call this last problem—moving raw sugar in bulk—a sticky business is irresistible. Traditionally, sugar had been bagged at the mills, loaded into ships via conveyor-gantry systems, lightered out, and handled with slings at some shallow ports and those without proper docks, or moved down an overhead wire at Kukuihaele. As cargo, the bagged sugar presented no special problems so long as it was kept dry; but the bagging and loading were slow and expensive. Just before the war, some experimenting with bulk loading of the *Makiki* had been done at Kahului.

By 1946 pressure for bulk shipment was overwhelming, even though it called for heavy capital expenditures by shippers and the carrier. Producers needed very large, specialized hopper trucks, some to carry twenty-six tons, for the trip from mill to pier. Bulk-sugar storage plants were complicated. The original Hilo dock plant cost $2 million and consisted of four eighty-foot-wide cylindrical bins, each seventy-four feet high, with elaborate conveyors to take sugar from the truck dump, weigh it, feed it into the bins from the top, and take it out and to the ships from the bottom. Conveyors also recycled the heavy, sticky stuff from bin to bin, to keep it from packing down into an almost immovable mass. (During one waterfront strike of several weeks, some Matson ships were idled with full loads of sugar in their holds. When the strike ended, stevedores had to use jackhammers to break up the solidified sugar before they could get it out.)

Some of the first bulk plants had storage bins with sides sloping inward at the bottom, funnel fashion; but sugar, unlike wheat or other grains, isn't slippery. A man who falls into a bin can walk out across the sugar with no problem, but the stuff simply would not slide down the funnel portions of the bins unless someone stood outside, beating on the metal with mallets. At longshore hourly wages, that got expensive.

Bulk sugar also requires careful distribution in the holds to trim a ship. At first, this was accomplished by a power trimmer lowered into the hold and guided there by a longshoreman who earned the title "Huli Huli" (around-and-around) man and finished his shift covered with spilled sugar. Later, the job was done by remote control.

Unloading the ships also was difficult. A conveyor could be set up to take the sugar from the hatches, but at first longshoremen had to shovel it from the corners of the holds to the hatch area. Later, scrapers somewhat like the horse-drawn Fresno scrapers used by prebulldozer highway crews were substituted, using power off the gantries. Small bulldozers followed them; and worm-geared, mobile conveyors then were built especially for the job. Nothing helped much, however, in the final clean-up when sugar had to be cleaned off decks, the

sides of holds, and even the overhead beams before the spaces could be used for other cargo.

"Otherwise," says a veteran of the operation, "the stuff would liquefy as soon as the ship got into hot weather, drip down on the cargo headed for the islands, and make a terrible mess. That liquid sugar can take the paint right off an automobile."

Restoration of attractive passenger service to the islands was important to travelers and appeared essential to Matson's hotels, but the big liners were in no condition to provide it. After abortive negotiations with several shipyards, Bailey finally decided to do the bulk of the huge ship rejuvenation job in Matson's own Alameda, California, yard, developed during the war at the government's request.

"They put three big passenger ships into a small yard to reconvert them," said Wright. "Bailey was talked into it by the man who was running the shipyard. He came up to headquarters and told Bailey, 'Sure, Boss, we can do anything.' It couldn't possibly work. Even the big yards wouldn't take all three of them . . . and didn't even bid on the jobs. The government gave a $2 million allowance for refurbishing each ship but that was just a drop in the bucket.

"This was a serious mistake, all right, and . . . it just got away from them, literally. I used to make up these cash projections for Bailey. We'd go around and find out from everybody what cash they would need for a fiscal period. We'd put down $2.5 million for each of the ships as Matson's portion of the expected cost. Every time . . . I'd say [to Bailey], 'Now this isn't going to work. This isn't enough cash. The boys in the shipyard tell me this isn't half enough.'

"Bailey would look at me, disgusted, and say, 'Put it in anyway.' So I'd put it in. Finally, this just caught up with him. Bailey took the beating and was more or less forced out."

Bailey went to Washington as chairman of the National Federation of Shipowners. Ray Hasenauer, a former company treasurer, felt Bailey was blamed unduly for several things and added: "The shipbuilding losses weren't really all that bad, and the company had at least $30 million in cash at the time.''

Bailey's resignation came on March 31, 1947. Reconversion of the *Monterey* and *Mariposa,* still far from finished, was suspended on July 12. The *Lurline,* which had cost about $8 million to build, was returned to civilian service in 1948, after approximately $19 million had been spent on reconversion. In a final settlement, the government paid $6,250,000 of the cost.

CHAPTER FOURTEEN

NEW SHIPS, NEW UNIONS
(1947–1952)

John E. Cushing came to Matson as president on May 8, 1947. The only real attraction was a three-year contract that would provide him with a pension he wanted. He had no intention of staying longer. No stranger to waterfront problems, Cushing had headed the American-Hawaiian Steamship Company during its difficult years as an intercoastal line. The problems at Matson, however, reached beyond ships and piers: the company was being sued for mismanagement by Walter Buck, a large stockholder and son of Captain Matson's onetime partner; the Royal Hawaiian Hotel was ready for visitors, but the liner *Lurline,* refurbished to carry them over, was not; the abortive airline required liquidating; the shipyard was costing a fortune to operate; directors as usual were squabbling; the company's main agency in Hawaii was disgruntled and disgruntling; a West Coast dock strike was almost inevitable; and serious labor troubles loomed in Hawaii for the first time. That Cushing did not depart immediately for the Tasmanian highlands (devils lurking there would be mere pussycats compared with those in his outer office) speaks well for true grit, if not a sense of self-preservation.

"He was a very able steamship man who had operated in the intercoastal trade in a period when they were lucky to earn the depreciation on their ships," Fulton Wright said. "He was a sharp-pencil man. His expense accounts were figured down to the postage stamps. We never had had a budget in Matson, but the first thing he said to me was, 'We're going to have a budget and you're going to fix it.'

"So I would go and sweat out a budget. We had a very tight period. . . . Cushing . . . just inherited it. The first thing he had to do was to shut down everything on the incomplete passenger ships. We used to refer to it as nothing but a slaughterhouse. The losses were tremendous. . . . those big ships were nothing but a cash drain.

"Walter Buck had something like 52,000 shares of Matson stock. . . . He decided that his interest had been jeopardized by this passenger ship deal. He sued the company and this went on for a long time. Buck sent his lawyers, really tough guys, down, and we were supposed to give them all the background. We did that very reluctantly, to some extent producing only what they insisted on having. . . .

"Buck changed courses a couple of times. He would go in and spend hours with Cushing, apparently be satisfied, and go away saying he was going to call off the whole thing. Then he'd get back to his own office and have a change of heart.

"Cushing would say, 'I'll never understand the workings of Walter Buck's mind.' He was just sweating blood, of course, taking the beating for something he had inherited. When Cushing first offered Buck a seat on the board of directors, Buck wouldn't take it, as I recall. Later he accepted . . . he was very mercurial and unpredictable.''

The Buck suit finally was dropped after he accepted a director's seat and Matson paid his legal expenses of $20,750. He remained a director for a number of years.

For nearly half a century, American shiplines had been partially dependent on government ships used in one war or another and sold as surplus afterward. In the late 1940s this again was the source for most lines, and the supply of vessels was greater than ever before. In 1946 Matson sold eight ships, too small or too venerable for the Hawaii trade, to Asian and South American buyers. Then it began assembling a fleet of war-built freighters: fifteen C-3 types, four smaller C-2s, and three slow Liberty ships.

Shifts between Oceanic's South Pacific freight service and Matson's Hawaii runs were frequent and confusing. The fine old Oceanic vessel names —*Sierra, Sonoma, Ventura,* and *Alameda*—were revived for the C-2s, later used on larger C-3s. The eight ships sold in 1946 were followed into oblivion by three more old freighters in 1948 and one in 1949. The names *Maunawili, Makaweli, Makiki, Makua, Mauna Kea, Waimea, Waipio, Maunalei, Mokihana, Mahimahi,* and *Manulani* sank without a trace or a tear shed. New names on company fleet lists included *Merchant, Planter, Banker, Craftsman, Educator, Retailer, Fisherman, Packer, Rancher, Farmer, Refiner, Pilot, Wholesaler, Citizen, Forester, Lumberman,* and *Logger,* each with ''Hawaiian'' as a prefix.

Not so charming, perhaps, but easier to spell. (The company opted for easy spelling during some thirty years but returned to Hawaiian ship names in the late 1970s.)

Hard for sentimentalists to accept was sale of the old liner *Matsonia,* sometime *Malolo,* which had made 350 voyages under the Matson flag, 310 of them peacetime trips to Hawaii including dozens during 1946–1948 when, partly and hurriedly

renovated, she had provided interim service. She made her last departure from Honolulu on April 15, 1948, was sold to the European Home Lines, and was renamed the *Atlantic,* then *Vasilissa Freideriki* (Queen Frederika). She operated under the Greek flag for years, and when she was scrapped in 1977, there is every reason to believe the ghosts of departed 1929 millionaires still dabbled their toes in the Pompeian-Etruscan swimming pool.

On April 16, 1948, the renovated *Lurline* sailed from San Francisco for the first time, to an accompaniment of steamship whistles, trailing serpentine, and adjectives. The 722 passengers explored public rooms with Polynesian decor, Raymond Loewy-designed staterooms, smoking rooms, bars, a veranda dance pavilion, a swimming pool, and an on-board shopping center. A crew of 444 served passengers who paid from $120 minimum fare to $850 for a lanai suite.

Hawaiian longshoremen long have enjoyed a reputation as some of the world's most efficient. Explanations differ: that they have an affinity for operating machinery; that they work best in groups rather than as competing individuals; that the *uku-pau* (hurry up, then rest) idea has a special attraction for Polynesians; that they enjoy jobs in which rhythm is important. Whatever the explanation, the reputation often is confirmed even by ship captains not given to praise of stevedores in general.

In the 1930s they also worked for less than any others in America. While West Coast docks seethed with unrest and erupted in head-knocking strikes, island ports were quiet, some 1,400 men were employed, and the most skilled apparently enjoyed demanding assignments such as working the wire port at Kukuihaele.

It was the same contented Kukuihaele experts, however, who first rocked the island waterfronts, listening to one Harry Kamoku, a Hawaiian member of the Sailors Union of the Pacific, who said they should have better pay and working conditions. The Kukuihaele gangs in 1935 formed an independent union to seek them, and island waterfronts never were quite the same again. This independent union later formed the nucleus for a small local of the ILWU and eventually became part of the all-island Local 142.

While Kamoku was organizing the island of Hawaii union, Jack Hall, a big and tough labor activist, was following a different organizing route. Having arrived in the islands in 1935, Hall managed to sign up 3,000 sugar plantation workers for a CIO farm workers union in 1937. He said, "I asked Harry [Bridges] and Lou [Goldblatt] for CIO support but they didn't think Hawaii was important. Not long after, though, they recognized that if the union [ILWU] was going to get at Matson effectively, they'd have to get at the Big Five."

It's not clear whether he did get any immediate support; but when a group of Kauai longshoremen went on strike, Hall hurried to help them and succeeded in getting a contract of sorts.

Hall's objective, odious to island employers, was also simple: one big union. Sugar and pineapple workers, many living in company housing divided by races, were the largest labor groups in Hawaii, were paid poorly, but never had mounted any effective unionization campaign. Strikes by them would have small chance of success unless they could obtain support from unions able to cut off plantation supplies and block movement of their produce.

In Hawaii's situation, this meant longshoremen above all others. By themselves, longshoremen were too few to keep strikebreakers away from the docks or to finance long disputes of their own; but they were in a strategic position to help the agriculturists. From the union point of view, the ideal combination should also have included teamsters. Hall never was able to arrange this, but his proposed two-component organization was fearful enough.

The Kauai dockers' contract, weak as it was, provided an opening wedge; and a Hilo dock fight in which fifty persons were injured became a cause célèbre. Castle & Cooke Terminals, Ltd., signed a contract with Honolulu longshoremen in 1940.

War soon stopped everything, but the days of serenity for island employers never would come back. Hall took a government job in the early days of the war but left it in 1943 to sign up majorities of workers at five plantations. The union demanded negotiations, but management held out for National Labor Relations Board elections. That strategy backfired when the board concluded that 50 to 60 percent of all plantation employees actually were industrial workers, entitled to vote; and in 1945 the territorial legislature dealt employers another blow by passing a labor law extending to all plantation workers the same right to organize that federal law gave to industrial workers.

From there, it was all downhill for the organizers, who signed an additional 30,000 pineapple and sugar workers in the next eighteen months. The big union, with a stranglehold on the ports and enough nonport members to make sure that hold could not be broken easily, was a fact.

The late C. C. Cadagan, former president of Alexander & Baldwin and a Matson director, remembered that at one point in the organizing drive Hall came on company property and Cadagan ordered him thrown off. The *Honolulu Star-Bulletin* editorially criticized the action; and Cadagan, never one to leave public relations to others, personally went to the newspaper office to complain about the editorial to editor Riley Allen.

"Allen listened," Cadagan recalled, "and then asked me, 'You think you were right to throw him out because he was on private property?'

"I said, 'Yes.'

"He said, 'Well, this is private property, too.' And he threw me out."

Jack Hall was named to the Honolulu Police Commission in 1945. The plantation workers branch of the ILWU struck for eleven weeks in 1946, gaining the first agreement covering the entire industry, as well as some wage increases. The elimination of free housing and some other paternalistic relics likely was of more value to the employers than to the workers, but a second strike shortly afterward solidified some union gains.

In San Francisco, a 1947 work stoppage by the ILWU was followed by negotiations in which employers again challenged union operation of hiring halls, and talks stalled on this issue. In September 1948 the ILWU joined a widespread maritime strike under an interunion pact. Employers were disorganized to the point that a Matson vice-president was quoted as saying, "After three days of those meetings I couldn't stomach any more. I just couldn't take the flag-waving speeches."

The strike tied up shipping from the U.S. West Coast for ninety-five days, although Hawaii received some cargo from the East Coast and British Columbia. President Harry Truman's unexpected election victory further demoralized the employers, who eventually split. Ship-operating firms met labor leaders without the participation of stevedoring contractors. A new agreement was reached in December, providing some pay raises but changing nothing else materially. Matson ships again could operate normally—but for just four months.

Then the once docile Hawaiian stevedores turned over the fruit basket again. A May 1, 1949, strike called for wage increases, arbitration, and improved working conditions.

Alex Budge explained: "The workers are paid $1.42 now and are demanding parity with the Pacific Coast, where the pay is $1.82 [per hour].

"We originally offered 8 cents, later raised it to 12. . . . We're against arbitration because it will play into the hands of the union. The union represents much more than the dock workers. It represents workers throughout the whole island economy."

More than any previous troubles, this strike did tie up the island economy. Shortly, 30,000 persons out of 100,000 in the work forces were unemployed, business was at a standstill, and householders were short of essentials. Matson hotels stayed open but had no room shortages.

Longshoremen had agreed to work navy, army, and relief ships; but as tensions rose, the governor of Hawaii, acting under some hasty legislation, seized facilities and equipment of Castle & Cooke Terminals in Honolulu and six other companies. Employees received paychecks from the territory as

strikebreaking groups were formed. A spate of confrontations, small riots, and arrests of pickets followed as some ships from Atlantic, Gulf, or Canadian ports arrived, having been loaded by AFL longshoremen. A few barges and small craft also operated, but the island economy wound down rapidly as West Coast ILWU longshoremen continued to refuse to load ships for the struck ports. The strike ended after six months. Stevedores received 21 cents more per hour in increments but did not reach parity with their mainland counterparts for another decade.

Cushing's sharp pencil and Wright's sweaty budgets brought some order into Matson's financial house, but neither could solve the whole problem. Laid-up, unfinished passenger ships continued to eat dollars, while the freighter fleet lay idle nearly 300 days in two years. The company lost 1,435 vessel days to strikes in 1948, 2,502 in 1949.

Matson hotels showed their first profits ever in 1947: a not-so-impressive $76,720 for the first six months of 1948, and $56,017 for all of 1949—this on a prewar investment of $6,597,000 plus $2 million reconversion costs.* In 1949 the company as a whole lost $4.5 million. In 1950, however, both hotels and ships did better, the hotels earning $335,517 for the first half and the freighters bringing in $1,129,000 for the entire year, as opposed to the 1949 deficit of $1,561,000.

It was a strange period. Freight rate increases of 20 percent in 1947 and 10 percent in 1948, while failing to put the service in the black, left island importers restive about their costs and sugar shippers making noises about finding somebody to carry their cargo more cheaply. They were especially unhappy about rates to Gulf and East Coast ports, being served by Matson and the Isthmian line as a joint venture.

Randolph Sevier was elected president of Matson

---

*The hotel profits of those years invite comparison with Oregon's famous Timberline Lodge at Mount Hood, which in one year of operation by a civic syndicate had profits almost exactly equalling the total income from its pay toilets.

on June 30, 1950, having been chosen by Cushing. Burly, optimistic, a joiner, and very much island oriented, he brought to the job a background of the docks. Born in Eureka, California, he had served in the navy in World War I, and first worked for Matson as a freight checker in 1923. By his own assessment, he would happily have been a strong unionist if there had been a union to join at the time. Donald McLean, a purser on the old liner *Maui* and later president of the California & Hawaiian Sugar Refining Corporation, Ltd., hired Sevier as a seagoing freight clerk a few months later, gave him the lasting nickname "Joe," and thus launched him on three years of sailing on Matson ships. Sevier, who took an assistant purser's job and then taught himself the typing it required, left Matson in 1927 to reorganize a Hilo tourist limousine service, moved to Honolulu in 1930 to head Castle & Cooke's steamship department and, later, the subsidiary Honolulu Stevedores. He remained with the parent Castle & Cooke as vice-president until hired by Matson as executive vice-president in 1948.

He had need of optimism when he took over the presidency just after outbreak of the Korean War. The *Lurline* was doing well in the Hawaii tourist business and helping the hotels, but very little else was smooth sailing. Cushing had applied a tourniquet to the company's bleeding artery by halting the passenger ship reconstruction, but it was an emergency measure, not a cure. The *Monterey* and *Mariposa,* intended to provide regular passenger service to Australia and New Zealand, still lay at Alameda, seagoing Percherons eating their heads off in upkeep. Although the 1949 Hawaii strike turned out to be the last really big dock stoppage until 1971, longshoremen and seagoing unions managed to keep up a drumfire of unauthorized walkouts, generally only a few days at a time, for all sorts of reasons: protesting government attempts to deport Harry Bridges; in sympathy with various other unions; sometimes over picayunish local work rule disputes. Two strikes in 1952 cost 952 vessel days, and various slowdowns and short strikes in 1954 cost 343 more.

Sevier, widely respected as an operations man, cut the company's shoreside losses by selling off the unprofitable subsidiary, United Engineering Corporation, and its San Francisco property. The Alameda shipyard was leased and later sold. In complicated maneuvering, the U.S. Maritime Administration was induced to take over the laid-up *Monterey;* and the *Mariposa* was sold (in 1953) to the Home Lines, which operated her as the *Homeric* in European service for twenty years. Damaged by a galley fire in 1973, she was then sold to a Taiwan shipbreaker.

On the other hand, Sevier led the company into further hotel investments. In 1950, a one-half acre property adjacent to the Royal Hawaiian Hotel on Kalia Road was purchased for $180,000. This was madness to the eyes of longtime islanders, an incredible bargain in hindsight. By 1970 what little Waikiki freehold real estate there was for sale had a price tag of $5 million an acre.

In 1952, the Surfrider, a 152-room hotel without a dining room but adjacent to, and connected with, the Moana on the ground-floor level, was built for $1,421,000, including furnishings. This was designed for less affluent guests, save for the top floor, which consisted of two elaborate penthouse suites.*

In the same year, the hotels produced one of the more strange labor incidents, described in "A History of Local 5," written by hotel union members and published by the Industrial Relations Center of the University of Hawaii. The history says:

" 'Led by an alien rabble-rouser, some 800 workers walked out of three Matson resorts here Thursday, leaving 1,500 guests of Hawaii in a state of confusion, frustration and disgust. . . .'

"These were the opening words of a front-page, bold-face *Advertiser* editorial soon after the beginning of our fifteen day strike against the Matson Navigation Company on February 14, 1952.

"The editor then went on to pay his compliments

---

*More than twenty-two years later, a former Matson director still was sputtering at the memory of discovering that one of the suites promptly was occupied by Matson's vice-president for hotels.

to our members by saying that they were 'in many instances earning far more than their intelligence, education or training entitled them to.'

"Why were Local 5 members on strike?

'It's the same old story—many of those 800 are perfectly satisfied BUT—a short-sighted few have secured control and, by threats or intimidation, are in a position to force the majority to do their will.'

"How should the strikers be punished? If necessary, all 800 should be 'dropped and forgotten' and their jobs given to scabs.

"These quotations show what sort of treatment unions used to get in the local press. . . .

"Generally our relations with Matson had not been bad but in 1951–52 management developed a hard-nosed streak, encouraged by the Hawaii Employers Council. So we came to a showdown. When the cooks walked out, the hotels closed the dining rooms and nearly the entire force hit the bricks.

"The guests reacted in various ways. Some called our strikers 'damned fools' and squawked when Matson refunded $8.00 a day and sent them to look for their own food in outside restaurants. Others walked alongside the pickets and assured them of their sympathy and support.

"This strike is in a class by itself for the type of strikebreakers recruited. Beside the ordinary kind serving for wages and the clerical workers forced to serve sandwiches, the cream of Honolulu volunteered its services—free. 'Expensive jewelry glinted from the hand of more than one 'temporary maid,' reported the *Star-Bulletin*. 'In charge of volunteers at the Moana was the president of We, The Women [*sic*], and in charge at the Royal was an equally prominent wife of a bank president.'

"At least these jewel-laden volunteers learned that a room maid's life is no picnic. 'Most of us who went down to volunteer our help wore street clothes,' said one of the women, 'and though it isn't really dirty work, we were drippy wet when we got through.'

"After two weeks, the strike was settled. More important than actual gains was the respect that Local 5 won for its strength and militancy. What we got included:

Five cents an hour for food handlers, plus free meals; Eight cents for other classifications;

Our first medical plan: Matson paid half the cost of HMSA for workers and their dependents;

Language on hiring which practically amounted to a hiring hall;

Three weeks vacation after fifteen years' service."

Arthur Rutledge, president of Local 5, interviewed in 1974, still thought the strike had little effect on the hotels or their subsequent troubles.

"The Matson hotels," he said, "just weren't run on a businesslike basis. They were run like a ship. One guy did nothing but wash glasses and wouldn't touch a dish even though the man next to him had them stacked all around him. Matson wasn't too tough; it was too easy. Nobody looked at the bottom line.

"You know, if a waiter brought a customer a fish when he'd ordered steak, the waiter would say, 'Oh, go on and eat the fish and then I'll bring you your steak.' There are a thousand stories like the man who ordered Kool cigarettes and presently the waiter brought him a package of cigarettes nicely packed in ice. Nobody was checking those things."

CHAPTER FIFTEEN

HOTELS, NEW LINERS, AND BACK-HAUL
(1952–1959)

The hotels had other problems, not the least being the Royal Hawaiian's Chinese fire drill on days when the *Lurline* arrived. As soon as the ship appeared off Diamond Head in the morning, Royal representatives rode a launch out and went aboard to meet special guests and to make room assignments before the 10:00 A.M. docking at the downtown Aloha tower to band music and welcomes from hula dancers.

Then the fun began. The trick was to get passengers and their luggage off the ship as rapidly as possible so that the tremendous cleaning task could begin, but not to get them to the hotel too soon or to permit boredom to set in. Bored people like to go to their hotel rooms, but the rooms weren't ready. So while one group of bonifaces was alternately rushing and delaying the newcomers, others a few miles away at the hotel were trying to speed departing guests out of the rooms six hours or so before they were to board ship for the mainland.

Neither job was easy; but with judicious applications of Mai Tais, soft music, and soft soap, they did get done. On a good Boat Day, the Royal doorman might pocket $1,000 in tips.

At the ship, 65 to 70 carpets were exchanged, more than 850 bags of laundry removed, and clean linens brought aboard. The ship carried 6,600 pillowcases, 11,000 club towels, and matching supplies of other linens. Plant experts freshened the $5,000 display of greenery in the public rooms. Galleys were stocked; 2,100 pounds of fresh papaya, 1,800 pounds of fresh pineapple, and 350 pounds of island fish were typical items.

In addition, as many as eleven longshore gangs handled cargo and mail before the ship sailed at 4:00 P.M. in showers of confetti, more music, and the required buckets of nostalgic tears.

The late Edwin K. Hastings, named Matson vice-president for hotels in 1955, said: "I had a mandate to make them profitable—but don't make any changes. Now, how the hell can you do that?*

"They were giving away the finest rooms in the Royal to owners and their friends, things like that. In those days, we had five months' business: February and March, July and August, then a week or so in October and the traditional last half of December.

"One of the first things I had to do was to take the Royal off the American plan. People didn't really want to stay at the Royal because they had to eat all their meals there, or at least pay for them. There were a couple of good restaurants down the street.

---

*Such mixed directives in the islands were not peculiar to Matson. Cadagan remembered suggesting to Alexander & Baldwin directors that an unprofitable cattle-feeding operation be closed down. Directors agreed; but as the meeting adjourned, "a board member came up to me and said, 'That's all fine, but don't fire Joe. His wife taught me to dance.'"

"So I took it off. Before that, the deal was to give the kids nine plates of ice cream and the man five steaks—I mean, whatever they wanted. One great problem was to get those old-line waiters, Filipinos and Japanese, to take an order, write it down, and then have it charged properly. That was much more difficult than just going into the kitchen and saying, 'Give me another soup, give me another steak.'

"To change a condition like that with the local people was very, very difficult. They'd say, 'Yes, yes,' but nothing would happen. The old story is that the third time you'd tell them to do something, they'd say, 'Oh, you wanted it painted red?' "

Matson built its fourth hotel, the 252-room Princess Kaiulani, a block back of Waikiki Beach, at a cost of $3,250,000. It opened in 1955, with Perle Mesta as its first guest (nonpaying, naturally) and Duke Kahanamoku, Hawaii's famous Olympic swimmer, taking the first official plunge into its pool. He then was sixty-five years old. The eleven-story building was the tallest in Waikiki and was planned for guests who didn't fancy the lush cuisine and prices of the other houses. After a slow first year, it operated at a profit.

This gave Matson 1,000 of the 3,580 hotel rooms at Waikiki, required a staff of 1,200, and brought to $10 million the company's postwar investment in remodeling and new hotels. Matson hotels registered 54,594 of the 109,600 island visitors in 1955; but the *Lurline,* making twenty-nine cruises, carried only 20,000 passengers, an average of 690 per trip. The rest came by air or on a few through vessels.

The Sevier-directed expansion also included purchase of 1,492 acres of land with 8,500 feet of waterfront between Kihei and Makena on Maui for $500,000. Formerly owned by the Baldwin family, this was held for future development.

On the mainland, the Matson Assurance Company was established primarily as an intermediary agency to write and then reinsure the Matson Navigation Company's various policies. For its capital, title to the Matson Building on San Francisco's Market Street was transferred and $2 million in cash supplied. Later, 93 percent of the stock of the Pacific National Life Assurance Company, of Utah, was bought; and that company was merged into the Matson firm under the Pacific National name.

Other transactions created confusion. Treasurer Ray Hasenauer first was asked to investigate whether the trucking industry offered a logical inland expansion of the total transportation system Matson always had sought, and he was directed to look especially at the Pacific Intermountain Express Company. This he did, reporting that the industry was chaotic and that the PIE company's prospects were poor. Whereupon, without further consultation, Matson bought a 10 percent interest in the trucking firm.

On Oahu, Matson long had coveted the Halekulani, a graceful old cottage-type hotel with its buildings, none over two stories, scattered through a grove of palms and exotic imported trees adjacent to a corner of the Royal property. The Kimball family reluctantly decided to sell because of a tax situation and received a bid for $4 million. Matson could have had the property for almost anything over that but delayed a decision. Eventually, prodded by Hastings, the company decided to buy, just as the Kimballs were receiving another offer of $4,250,000. Again, the Matson negotiators stalled; and the property, later worth several times that price, went to a syndicate headed by Norton Clapp, a director of the Weyerhaeuser Company.

"We also missed in Tahiti," Hastings said. "Gardner Dailey and I went down there around the first of December 1955 and selected twelve or fourteen acres on One Tree Hill [Tahara]. We could have had it in fee simple for $30,000 and did put down $3,000 on it. Matson had an open door in Tahiti. They were going to restore the passenger ship service there and it would have made sense. . . . Now, Tahiti's gone another way, but Matson could have had everything their own way for ten years. Instead, we lost our down payment. Eventually, the same property sold for $250,000."

Running alone to Hawaii, the *Lurline* sold 95 percent of its passenger space in 1950 and like percentages in the next several years but had trouble showing a profit because of the expense of shoreside services. Laundries, furniture repair shops, ticket offices, and other service units could be neither eliminated nor kept really busy by her twelve-day round-trip schedule. Necessary overhauls and even small breakdowns could disrupt the entire operation. Competitors nipping at the freight services since 1946 repeatedly threatened to do likewise in the passenger field; and the requirement for regular passenger services to Australia and New Zealand, mostly without them since the war, was increasing. If Matson did not restore this service, a U.S. subsidy would be lost.

Infallibility is a welcome visitor in any company's board room but doesn't often appear. Nothing is easier to criticize than a thirty-year-old decision that went wrong; but the vote of shipping men to spend more money on passenger ships in the early 1950s is easy to understand. Propeller-driven aircraft did serve the Pacific islands but were severely handicapped on the longer routes, trying the patience of crews and passengers alike on the 2,200-mile trip to Hawaii and depending on island specks—Canton, Samoa, Kwajalein, Wake, Guam, the Semichis—as way points on other long overwater flights. A vacationer indeed could reach Hawaii in one fourth of the time a passenger ship required but needed a couple of days' rest to get over the experience.

Civilian jet aircraft, in hindsight so obviously the answer, appeared so then only to a few experts. British engineers launched Comet jets, only to lose two of them, with their passengers, to design failure. Internationally known aeronautics pioneers freely predicted additional jet disasters all the way from metal fatigue to fatal ingestion of gravel and birds by the engines. In the United States, only the Boeing Company had even a flying prototype of a civilian jet liner, and it received its first firm orders in October 1955.

By then, Matson management had made its decision. In Newport News, the old *Monterey*,

reclaimed from the government, got a $20 million face-lift to match or outdo her sister ship, the *Lurline*. In Portland, Oregon, two "Mariner" freighters, mostly idle since their construction several years earlier, were purchased and converted to passenger vessels, increasing their gross from 9,217 to 14,812 tons without extending the hull dimensions. The first cost $23,486,640, the second $24,029,563. Government construction subsidies totalled $20,498,057.

Predictably, Matson then played name games again: the old *Monterey* became the *Matsonia* (no. 3 in that succession), while the sometime freighter *Free State Mariner* became the new *Monterey* (no. 3 with *that* name), and the *Pine Tree Mariner* was rechristened as the newest *Mariposa* (also no. 3) late in 1956. The next year, the *Matsonia* went in service opposite the *Lurline* on the Hawaii shuttle, thereby putting all those expensive laundries and ticket sellers on a six- rather than a twelve-day schedule. The other ships began making forty-two-day round-trip voyages to the Antipodes, via Hawaii and other islands. They could carry 365 first-class passengers each, plus 209,340 cubic feet of dry cargo and 30,254 cubic feet of refrigerated freight, at a twenty-one-knot cruise speed. These were the first U.S. ships equipped with Sperry gyrofins to reduce roll, hydraulically operated hatch covers, and twenty-nine waitresses in place of the usual dining saloon waiters. Air conditioning, swimming pools, theaters, and 500 loudspeakers for the high-fidelity sound system contributed to passenger luxury—at least, for those who like loudspeakers.

Matson's freight business grew steadily after the strikes of the late 1940s. Gross freight revenue went from $33,525,000 in 1951 to $59,414,000 in 1960, although earnings fluctuated wildly from a high of 7.83 percent on the rate base in 1951 down to 1.17 percent in 1959, to 3.46 percent in 1960, then climbed again to new highs. Passenger ships contributed to a net loss on shipping in 1956, although the company had $300,000 net profit. The imbalance was shown more clearly in 1958, when the company listed its assets as $40,179,000 depreciated value of Matson vessels and related equipment; $25,065,000 for ships operated by Oceanic; $8,276,000 for hotels and shipyard properties, also a depreciated valuation; the strange figure of $429,000 for 500,000 shares of Honolulu Oil Company stock; $1,820,000 book value for 163,291 shares in Pacific Intermountain Express Company; $10,191,000 book value for 674,821 shares of Pacific National Life Assurance Company; and $4,420,000 in government securities.

Income for 1958, however, was $73,000 from the hotels, $1,156,000 from dividends (mostly Honolulu Oil), and $176,000 from other sources. Matson shipping operations lost $196,000; those of Oceanic, $866,000. Thus, the consolidated net profit was only $343,000 on $90,380,000 assets at book value. These figures were shown in the company's annual reports. If the Honolulu Oil shares had been carried at their approximate marketable value of $43,000,000, the profit-on-investment picture would have been even more bleak.

Dissension on the board of directors was inevitable. Directors representing Castle & Cooke were not too worried about Matson's profit picture so long as their own company received handsome returns for stevedoring and agency operations. Sugar representatives were still aggrieved by the freight rates as well as the lack of profits, and hence were torn two ways. Directors without other island interests were just unhappy.

The late Frederick Simpich, Jr., then representing Castle & Cooke on the Matson directorate, said:

"Joe Sevier tried to serve too many masters. Put him in an operating situation, whether it was labor relations, development of containerization, or management of his skippers, and he was great. His deficiency arose because he tried to carry water on both shoulders where his stockholders were concerned. This of course is the root of the whole Matson problem. . . . Sevier just got caught in a veritable maelstrom, and he thought that his personality, which had gotten him out of a lot of things, might lead to a solution of this. But there wasn't any solution."

The passenger ship/hotel business was the worst dilemma. Whereas prewar accommodations, afloat and ashore, stressed luxury regardless of price, now there were entirely new factors. Nobody was likely to ride a ship for four and a half days unless that trip was much more pleasant than any airplane ride merely hours long. This meant good service and food, music, fun and games, hula lessons, attentive deck stewards, captain's dinners, floating beauty shops, and bars with prices much, much lower than those ashore. Profitable or not, much of the same service was expected by passengers in the cheapest cabins as by those in upper-deck suites.

One result was that high expectations also came ashore with the passengers at Honolulu. Hastings said, "You couldn't treat people like dukes on the way over and then put them into a drummer's delight of a hotel just like the one back in St. Louis. They had been spoiled for days and wanted it to go right on."*

Matching shipboard luxury with similar delights in the Honolulu hotels was fine for the few who really didn't care what anything cost, not so fine for the majority who quickly discovered a whole covey of new, non-Matson hotels in Waikiki, with attractive prices.

Thus the dilemmas: the ships had to be more attractive than airplanes but not *much* more expensive; the hotels had to be as luxurious as the ships but still compete with hostelries that did not have flocks of gardeners pulling coconuts off palm trees

*Shipboard passengers were not easy to please. During January–March 1958, the *Lurline* made an Orient cruise. Later the company solicited comments and got them: 50 percent of those answering thought the shore tours were good but too expensive; 25 percent complained about a crowded ship, the worst factor being that women couldn't get into the beauty shop promptly and considered the operators uppity when they did get in; many disliked the two-sittings dining arrangements (early diners missed the cocktail hour; late diners couldn't get into the movie); 22 percent thought bar prices too high; half a dozen complained, oddly enough, that the ship served too much free champagne and too many drinks on the house, thus running up prices for everybody; others mentioned dirty linens and the miserable personality of a ship's doctor. The real problem? Sixty percent of the passengers were female, 70 percent at least sixty years old.

before they fell on somebody's head, or such amenities as the Royal employees who did little except to take wet bathing suits from rooms, dry them quickly, and return them before the guests took a notion to go swimming again.

Perhaps the greatest problem in the freighting part of Matson affairs was back-haul. Basically, this consisted (and still consists) of sugar and canned or (recently) fresh pineapple, with some papaya, household goods, and odds and ends. The Hawaiian sugar crop has approximated 1 million tons annually for most of the postwar years unaffected by strikes. In 1953 Matson ships moved 750,000 tons to California and about a third as much to Gulf and Atlantic ports. This compared with total cargo tonnage of 2,860,028 for the year. Later years showed great increases in total tonnage but virtually none for either of the eastbound cargoes. Pineapple in 1967 provided 497,000 tons of cargo, 297,000 tons being carried by Matson.

The fact that a steamship line to Hawaii cannot operate profitably without back-haul has been demonstrated repeatedly: the Pacific Transport Line's thirteen sailings in 1950; the S.S. *Leilani* (ex-*Gen. W. P. Richardson* and *La Guardia*) making twenty-three trips with passengers and cargo in 1957 for the Hawaiian Steamship Company and the Hawaiian Textron Company; Pacific Hawaiian Line (a lumber carrier) and Hawaiian Marine Freightways with sailings in 1958 and 1959; plus efforts of several barge lines.

The important question for Matson, however, was how much of the ship costs should be assigned to this back-haul freight. The principle that rates need not be the same as charged for freight in the crowded direction has been well established in the Alaska one-way trade and elsewhere: the ships must come back anyhow, so carrying back-haul increases operation costs only slightly. This situation is diluted in the Hawaii trade by the necessity to detour to outer islands to pick up part of the cargo. That part of the service never has been envied by Matson competitors.

But the weakness in Matson's position on back-haul was exploited in endless rate hearings: on the back-haul it was serving its own people, the producers who either owned large blocks of Matson stock or otherwise were connected with the company. Island businessmen not involved with sugar or pineapple, aided by politicians interested primarily in island consumer prices, hammered again and again on the theme that if sugar and pineapple paid their fair share of costs, westbound freight rates to Hawaii could come down. Matson's mainland stockholders generally stood with them, but for differing reasons: if sugar and pineapple paid more, Matson might make some money.

Sugar and pineapple interests replied simply: if eastbound rates went too high, they could find somebody else to do the freighting or do it themselves. Later, they did both for parts of the crops.

For N. S. Laidlaw, Matson's former vice-president for freight traffic, one result of the dispute was simple: "I must have spent the equivalent of five years of my business life on the witness stand," he said. "I mean that literally."

Matson had one other enormous disadvantage in rate matters: all that income from Honolulu Oil stock and other nonshipping investments.

"You could argue until you were blue in the face before the Maritime Commission that Matson was losing its tail," said one veteran of the rate wars, "but they'd say, 'Why, look at those earnings!' It was the same thing with the people of Hawaii, who were convinced Matson was making a killing on the ships."

Sevier made desperate efforts to bring order out of chaos; and his first move was a true shocker: the four Matson hotels were sold to the Sheraton hotel chain for $17.65 million. The transfer was completed on June 4, 1959. Comment in the islands ranged from incredulity to condemnation, and opinions of the company's directors were nearly as diverse.

Hotel union leader Arthur Rutledge was succinct: "It was Joe Sevier's biggest mistake."

Director Simpich partly agreed: "I felt it was a terrible mistake. They plowed thirty-five years of effort into the development of Waikiki. Fifty years was the term of their lease. Then they got a case of buck fever and abandoned properties that had incredible value.''

Alex Budge basically disagreed: ''The hotels didn't make any money and were difficult for Matson to operate. There were constant problems in management and operations, and it was hard to keep on top of it.''

The late J. Walter Cameron, then president of Alexander & Baldwin, said: ''I wasn't really for the hotel sale, but the Royal was losing money. So when the sale came up, we suggested that Alexander & Baldwin didn't need cash but would take Sheraton stock. That was fine with Sheraton . . . but one of the chain's big creditors, an insurance company, objected violently; so we never did get an interest in that firm. We had to take the cash.''

Matson's original sale plan included the Baldwin property on Maui, but in the end that was withheld. Hotels manager Edwin K. Hastings claimed credit: ''I had a lot to do with keeping that Maui property . . . out of the sale to Sheraton. The other Matson people said, 'We can't go into the hotel business down here as long as we've sold to Sheraton.' I said, 'Yes, we can. We can't go into the hotel business on Oahu [according to the terms of the contract].'

''Sure, I was unhappy about the hotel sale. I'd put in five years changing those hotels around. . . . We'd turned the corner. I don't know why they were sold, but there are always people who like to make *deals*. It was the wrong time, painful. Figures on tourism were going up, and Hilton and Sheraton both were trying to buy. . . . the pity was all that

fee simple land. I can laugh about it now, but there were some glorious opportunities and some magnificent blunders.''

Allen C. Wilcox, later president of Matson and of Alexander & Baldwin, said simply: ''It was a stupid mistake.''

Sevier told a newspaper reporter: ''When you try to do too many things at the same time, you can't do a good job on one thing.'' He also said the company had not decided what to do with the Maui beach property but had several offers for it, including a bid of $1,250,000.

Twenty-one years later, it is difficult to understand how management so close to the total Hawaiian picture could have failed to see that the Waikiki boom was just beginning; but a conservative would have to recognize both that the sale did represent a modest profit for Matson on the depreciated properties and that the only operating profits had been considerably less than bank interest.

In the view from the board room, the predictable pain of renewing the Royal land lease in 1975 may have loomed large—the Bishop Estate not being widely known for charitable treatment of land tenants at renewal time—and directors simply had no way of guessing that the properties could be resold in the meantime for approximately $60 million. This sale was a two-part maneuver, Sheraton selling the Moana, Surfrider, Princess Kaiulani, and some other properties to the Osano group of Japanese investors for $30 million in 1960; the Royal and a newly built Sheraton-Waikiki on the same property, for $105 million in 1974. Breaking out of that the precise valuation placed on the Royal and its ground lease might interest accountants, but few others.

CHAPTER SIXTEEN

FLEET PROBLEMS,
STOCK PURCHASES,
SHORE SERVICES
(1959–1961)

Sale of the hotels represented only one step—the most publicized but not the most important—in a continuing effort to do something about an outsized organization badly in need of help. The problem could be stated in either of two ways: nobody knew what to do about Matson, or at least a dozen top people knew, and no one agreed with anyone else. A management consulting firm discovered in 1957 that twenty-three separate activities were managed directly by the company president and that major departments operated without any requirement to show contributions to company profits. These obvious faults were corrected, but little else changed in the next two years.

Some sea operations went smoothly, but others contributed to the furore. Matson and the Isthmian Line were carrying sugar to Gulf and Atlantic ports in an uneasy joint venture, moving about a fourth of the crop but satisfying nobody. The ships in the East Coast service, in contrast to those in the Hawaii–Pacific Coast trade, had enough eastbound cargo but seldom could fill their holds going west. So although these ships lost money, sugar producers complained constantly about rates for their product.

Meanwhile, Sevier was seeking acquisition or mergers involving United States Lines, Isthmian Steamship Company, States Line, Luckenbach

Steamship Company, and others. In the end, nothing came of any of these negotiations. Pacific Far East Line lost a bid to compete in the Hawaii trade, and the other lines remained independent.

During 1955 rate hearings, Matson executives testified that a Matson freighter carried 19,874 tons of cargo on an average California–Hawaii round trip but that the margin of profit was so small that loss of 2,000 tons to a competitor would wipe it out. In Northwest–Hawaii voyages, they said the margin between profit and loss was only 200 revenue tons.

At about the same time, the Committee on Merchant Marine and Fisheries of the U.S. House of Representatives issued a statement at the conclusion of some (1955) hearings. This said:

"With respect to the non-subsidized segment of our American flag fleet, the outlook is tragic. This applies to the coastal, inter-coastal, ocean and tramp trades. The operating costs for vessels in these services has risen to a point that there is no prospect whatever for future replacements. Services that are merely breaking even or making a small profit today with ships that were purchased from the government at knocked-down prices . . . could not possibly survive . . . if they had to cover the capital investment required for new vessel construction.

"Hence, the gravity of the picture for the subsidized lines is far out-shadowed by the grim outlook for the unsubsidized segment of the fleet. The simple truth . . . is that ten years from now the American dry-cargo fleet of 674 vessels well may be reduced to 276 or less, unless drastic steps are taken now.''

No very drastic steps were taken; but Sevier told Matson stockholders at their annual meeting held aboard the *Monterey* in San Francisco on April 10, 1959, that Hawaiian statehood would benefit the entire maritime industry, and added: ''The future for shipping in the Pacific and Far East has considerable promise. Matson plans to be a productive partner in that future . . . and has every expectation of a profit from its shipping operations.''*

Not the least of Sevier's problems was his board of directors. The 1959 annual report listed eighteen directors and could have listed, but did not, almost as many points of view. The aging W. P. Roth, as chairman; forty-three-year-old William Matson Roth, who had managed to stay away from the company until he was thirty-five but now was vice-president for finance and planning; and J. F. Coonan, his brother-in-law, represented the Matson family, controlling about 275,000 shares of stock. They wanted the line to produce profits of its own, and they also lived in fear of corporate raiders who very well could be slavering over the Matson assets and cash. Almost any good internal Matson battle could produce the opportunity for a raid.

Also on the board were J. Walter Cameron, longtime head of the Maui Pineapple Company and now president of Alexander & Baldwin, and that company's Vice-Presidents C. C. Cadagan and J. G. McIntosh. For some time Cameron had been buying

up for A&B any Matson stock available, so that firm's investment now was 293,706 of Matson's 1.5 million outstanding shares. A&B's paramount interest was favorable rates for moving sugar and pineapple from the outer Hawaiian islands to the mainland.

C. Brewer & Company, likewise interested in sugar rates from the outer islands (Hawaii, in its case), as well as in westbound rates for merchandise, was represented by its president, Boyd MacNaughton, and Vice-President Starr Bruce. Holding 125,000 shares, Brewer also earned auxiliary profits from Matson stevedoring and agency services at the outports. Castle & Cooke, owning 204,720 Matson shares, had among the directors its own chairman, Alexander Budge, highly critical of Sevier's management; Vice-President Frederick Simpich, Jr.; and George G. Montgomery, a Castle & Cooke director and chairman of the Kern County Land Company.

Minority interests were represented by C. Hutton Smith, president of American Factors, which held only 22,620 shares and mostly wanted low rates for its island merchandising divisions; Walter E. Buck, no longer the active dissident he had been; W. W. Crocker, chairman of the Crocker-Anglo National Bank of San Francisco; E. G. Solomon, vice-president of Provident Securities, a Crocker company; R. J. Chandler, representing the old Los Angeles Steamship Company people; and Herman Phleger, a San Francisco attorney.

Seldom has so much talent been so hopelessly deadlocked. Basically, all the island owners except Amfac were mostly interested in low eastbound freight rates. Enjoying high stevedoring and agency profits, Castle & Cooke people would as happily have seen Matson liquidated (tax considerations aside), since it was confident it could attract all the shipping Oahu needed and at favorable rates, no matter who provided the vessels. Brewer and Alexander & Baldwin were sadly convinced they never could get reasonable outer-island service from any shipline they did not own; William P. Roth was a tired man in failing health; William Matson Roth, more and more speaking for the family, never had

---

*Sevier's flair for public relations was indicated by these shipboard stockholders' meetings, which annually drew several hundred participants, compared with a handful attending previous meetings ashore. He also made fast friends for the company when the sailing of one of the liners was prevented by a quickie seamen's strike after several hundred passengers were aboard. Instead of sending passengers ashore with refunds and ruined vacations, Sevier invited them all to stay aboard as the company's weekend guests, while the ship, although still at dock, served meals and provided entertainment as if at sea.

For half a century, bagged sugar was lowered by overhead cable to ships at Kukuihaele on Hawaii Island.

Twin slings speeded the job, always threatened by stormy seas.

Left: From isolated shallow ports such as Hana (Maui) and Mahukona (Hawaii), bagged sugar was lightered to anchored ships.

Below: Modern bulk sugar loading is automatic, limited to ports with elaborate equipment, as here at Kahului, Maui.

Break-bulk loading of cargo before the advent of containerization.

Trans-Pacific racing yacht *Westward* gets a ride home from Hawaii.

Thirty-one ton desalting unit for Standard Oil Company leaves *Hawaiian Logger*.

Containerization comes to Hawaii in 1958 as *Hawaiian Merchant* takes deck cargo of containers out of San Francisco Bay.

Hawaiian Monarch made her first Seattle call, taking on a load of containerized general cargo for Hawaii. November 1969. (Courtesy of Port of Seattle)

The ro-ro freighter *Lurline* (no. 5) draws a wake pattern in San Francisco Bay.

Manukai (formerly *Hawaiian Enterprise*) was the first of Matson's new containership fleet.

Matson's overhead container handling system at Port of Richmond, California. 1979.

Matson developed its own gantry cranes, such as these at Honolulu.

Honolulu's Diamond Head terminal has been a center for container operations.

Sand Island at Honolulu is being expanded to combine Matson's cargo handling operations at one facility.

When small ships aren't available, big ones go into tiny ports. *Lurline* loads molasses at Kawaihae, Hawaii Island.

Not quite all the cargoes roll on or off a ro-ro freighter. Some walk.

Left: R. J. Pfeiffer, Matson president 1973–1979, beside containership *Maui* (no. 2) on maiden voyage. Kahului, Maui, 1978.

Below: Kauai, sister ship to *Maui* (no. 2), is christened November 1979 at Sun Ship Inc., Chester, Pennsylvania.

wanted in the shipping business and now wanted out.* Buck, Chandler, and others were looking for options.

Corporate thrashing of this sort did not go unnoticed. Investors betting on some sort of liquidation or other distribution of assets ran up Matson stock from a 1957 low of $20.00 to $26.25 on October 8, 1959, but mysteriously quit buying at that point.

The next day, Matson made a public offer to buy 677,780 shares of its 1.5 million outstanding shares of common stock. Alexander & Baldwin, Castle & Cooke, Brewer, American Factors, Provident Securities, the Western Renaline Corporation (a Roth family company), and the Lurline B. Roth Charity Foundation waived their redemption rights.

Other stockholders were offered $33.69 in cash, one-third share of Honolulu Oil stock, one-fourth share of Pacific Intermountain Express stock, and one share of Pacific National Life Assurance stock for each Matson share surrendered. The Matson annual report for 1959 valued these components at $70.78. People who had bought the stock at $12.00 in 1948 or 1949 shed very few tears. The distribution cost Matson $20,954,439 cash, 207,326 Honolulu Oil shares, 155,494 shares of Pacific Intermountain, and 621,978 shares of Pacific National Life Assurance.

Matson executives avoided direct quotations concerning these maneuvers; but Sevier did tell one interviewer, "In disposing of its non-shipping assets in this manner, Matson will be in a much stronger position to [concentrate] on shipping operations in the Pacific." In his annual report to stockholders six months later, he added: "Matson begins the new decade of the sixties as a steamship company, carrying on a tradition born more than seventy-five years ago when Captain Matson launched the service."

*William Matson Roth and his mother had in mind very special urban renewal projects; it was he who conceived and financed the Ghirardelli Square development in San Francisco. After resigning his Matson office, Roth went into government service as U.S. deputy representative for trade negotiations, with the rank of ambassador. In 1974 he ran for governor of California but was defeated in the Democratic primary.

Sidney P. Allen, financial editor of the *San Francisco Chronicle,* mentioned that Sevier had refused to talk to the press there but added: "Now the die is cast. Matson has set its course to go full speed ahead as a shipping concern without supercargo [*sic*] and without all the multiple distractions of a major investment company."

The impression was widespread that: (1) the hotels had been sold to get cash to pay off the stockholders under the October offer; (2) the company was now just a shipline without shoreside entanglements; and (3) the island owners, with 646,046 out of 878,022 shares of stock still outstanding, would have unquestioned control, thus ending the board room strife.

All very neat and tidy but not quite true. When the distribution was completed, Matson still owned 292,674 shares of Honolulu Oil, carried on the books at their cost of $353,725 but with a market value of more than $13.4 million. This, plus retained shares in the life insurance and trucking companies, plus healthy investments in state and federal bills and bonds, added up to at least $24,652,000 in cash and marketable securities; so Matson didn't really need the hotel sale money. The company also retained the undivided Wailea waterfront property on Maui, so it was not precisely devoid of shoreside interests.

Nor was peace and quiet guaranteed to the board of directors. Roth interests still held 115,000 shares of the stock; Provident Securities had another 61,000; and various owners who rejected the October offer clung to another 55,000. Control still depended on shaky alliances and a first-class cat fight was possible at any time. Only one danger, real or imagined, had been definitely eliminated: an agreement between major stockholders provided that none would sell its holdings without giving the others a chance to buy, thus effectively ending the probability of any corporate raid. No such shield protected against continued internal wrangling or governmental criticisms.

The long dispute over long-haul eastbound rates

came to a head in 1961 when the California & Hawaiian Sugar Company, a cooperative that refines and markets the island crop, canceled its contracts with the Matson-Isthmian combination for raw sugar deliveries to Gulf and Atlantic ports, handing that business to the Reynolds Aluminum Company, which had ships hauling ore from the Caribbean to Portland, Oregon. These oreships sailed in ballast from Oregon to Honolulu and there picked up sugar for the eastbound back-haul.

Matson's principal mainland nonshipping investments were liquidated during 1960. Shares of Pacific National Life Assurance were sold at their approximate cost of $1,094,374, and those of Pacific Intermountain for $114,336. The 292,674 shares of Honolulu Oil were distributed to remaining Matson stockholders on the same basis as in the stock redemption: one-third share of oil stock for each Matson share owned. The Matson annual report showed the cost of this as only $352,727; but Honolulu Oil sold out, literally lock, stock, and barrel, one year later to Standard Oil of Indiana and (the California properties) to Tidewater Oil Company for $358 million. In the decade during which the Honolulu Oil Company shell was dissolved, Matson would have received—had it retained its 7.7 percent interest—approximately $27,566,000.

Matson officials long had supported the cause of Hawaiian statehood and applauded when it was achieved in 1959. The new state government, however, turned out to be largely Democratic (Big Five support of Republican causes was traditional), labor oriented, and impatient to flex its new muscles against establishment privilege, corporate injustices if any, and all cabals except its own. Matson, the island companies owning most of the shipline, and a few other groups such as Dillingham and Theo. H. Davies were obvious targets for all this energy. Legislative investigations of them were under way almost as soon as the legislators could find their way to committee rooms.

One result was a state antitrust law considerably stronger than the federal statutes; but the main thrust of the state effort turned out to be against interlocking directorates affecting the large banks, trust companies and the Big Five, rather than Matson. For the most part, the new government was content to intervene in rate cases (seldom on Matson's side) and to wait and see what might happen next to the steamship line.

Several things did. Sevier had been a longtime Castle & Cooke man, but as Matson president he became more and more restive over the Honolulu firm's handling of Matson business. Budge said, "He gradually drifted toward Dillingham. We used to have some real battles." One such battle resulted in cancellation of the Castle & Cooke agency contract—the one drawn up at the insistence of attorneys circa 1917 after more than a decade when the two companies had cooperated with only a handshake between Captain Matson and E. D. Tenney in lieu of formal agreement.

On May 11, 1962, William P. Roth retired as chairman of the Matson board of directors; Sevier moved into his place; and Stanley Powell, Jr., became the company president.

In one of his last statements as president, Sevier said:

"In hazarding an opinion of the future of Matson as a steamship company, I cannot help but be realistic. In doing so, I'm inclined toward optimism despite current problems. We have eighty years of experience as a bulwark. In terms of operations we are one of the largest [steamship] companies under the American flag. We serve an essential foreign trade route. We are the largest of the unsubsidized operators in domestic trade, with no dependence on Federal financial aid. We supply the supporting transportation network for the economic well-being of the state of Hawaii, a position we have earned by the calibre and consistency of our service and our high degree of dedication. Certainly there are critical problems ahead—that is the nature of the free enterprise system."

Randolph Sevier was not an easy man to discourage.

From the earliest days, concentration of Matson's shipping business in a very few ports made feasible the husbanding of its own ships. Shore facilities for ships' business grew steadily; and existence of these facilities led the company into development of longshoring methods and tools, cargo distribution, and representation of other shiplines at Pacific Coast and island ports.

The organization built up during World War I to serve U.S. Shipping Board vessels at San Francisco was kept together in the 1920s and 1930s. Jess Rose, who was Matson's general stevedoring superintendent when he retired, went to work on the company's docks in 1924, when most cargo was hoisted by rope slings, the only powered mobile equipment being a couple of electric jitneys. Lift trucks were manually operated, and steel beams forty to fifty feet in length were pushed by longshoremen to outer corners of ships' holds on greased rails.

Rose remembered that Matson dockers, both supervisors and gang members, "were always looking for something mechanical to do the job. Longshoremen with cargo hooks hanging out of their hip pockets suggested many of the improvements and solved some complicated equipment problems."

The pre-1942 improvements included special pallets for canned pineapple, worked out by longshoremen on Maui, open boxes for brick and tile, and "Jensen boxes," forerunners of the containerization that eventually would change the whole pattern of waterfront operations as well as the shape and sizes of ships. Simple enough in retrospect, these boxes were plywood containers, six by six by four feet, fitted with hinged doors and locking devices including numbered aluminum seals similar to those used on railroad boxcars. Named for J. Harding Jensen, then head of Matson Terminals, Inc., the shoreside company subsidiary, these boxes were stuffed with liquor, candy, and any other cargo especially subject to damage or pilferage. They cut losses sharply and also speeded loading.

Expanded by government request a second time during World War II, Matson's stevedoring contin-

ued to function at Los Angeles, San Francisco, Portland, and Seattle in the postwar period. By 1959, Matson Terminals, Inc., held eleven contracts for terminal service to other shipping companies and nine for stevedoring. The Matson annual report did not break out financial results for the subsidiary, but dock operations contributed considerably to the $101,474,610 shipping revenues.

In 1961, when the parent company was losing $1,067,000, the terminals had twelve stevedoring and twenty terminal contracts, reporting gross business of $4,830,000 and a profit of $185,000. In the following year, their outside contracts totalled $5,970,000, and again there was modest profit. In 1963, however, financial details of the terminal operations disappeared into a consolidated financial statement for the entire company. The Matson annual report to stockholders for 1964 showed only that Matson Terminals had taken over all of the parent company's container and specialized automobile operations in Honolulu and that a $20 million, two-year contract for Matson Terminals to do all the cargo handling for the joint Army–Navy Ocean Terminal in the San Francisco area had been signed.

In the late 1950s and early 1960s, the company also docked and serviced round-the-world passenger ships and freighters of the P&O Lines, Cunard, Holland-American, Grace, and other lines, as well as its own passenger liners—some seventy to eighty vessels a year at the San Francisco passenger ship docks. Writing to Hawaii State Senator Randolph A. Crossley in 1961, Sevier said: "In 1960, the Matson fleet—this does not include our Oceanic subsidiary—made 307 round trip voyages, carrying nearly four million tons of cargo and sixty thousand passengers. By contrast, the three major trans-Pacific companies headquartered in San Francisco— American President Lines, Pacific Far East Lines and States Steamship Company—had a combined total of only 252 voyages; and only U.S. Lines, the biggest of the American flag carriers, had a voyage total in excess of ours. . . . such are the requirements of the Hawaiian economy. To operate such large, fast turn-around freight and passenger service [bills of lading totalled 248,000 in 1960] obviously requires a shoreside organization of some size and efficiency.''

Another Sevier statement, made to a congressional committee, noted that cargo handling was 48 percent of the total cost of handling Hawaii's seaborne commerce. Labor, he said, accounted for 56 percent of the total cargo-handling and vessel costs.

Total cargo-handling costs increased 167 percent from 1946 to 1961, and vessel operating costs per day went up 115 percent in the same period.

The crying need to lower those costs was obvious and was to lead to perhaps the most dramatic changes of shipping in modern times, as well as to some of the most difficult labor negotiations.

Containerships were coming, scores of revolutions in cargo handling with them.

CHAPTER SEVENTEEN

CONTAINERSHIPS AND NEW OWNERS (1957–1965)

Matson established the steamship industry's first integrated research department in early 1956, with Foster L. Weldon as director. The group, including L. D. Yates, F. B. Graham, P. D. Bradley, and D. W. Papez, first made an intensive study of Hawaii's special freight problems, reporting its conclusions in mid-1957.

The recommendations included a two-phase program to develop seagoing container service to the islands. Phase 1 would involve conversion of six Matson freighters to carry 24-foot containers on deck, with conventional break-bulk cargo in the holds. Phase 2, contingent on the success of Phase 1, called for introduction of all-container vessels, conversions or new ships, plus special-purpose carriers for bulk sugar, automobiles, and outsized cargo.

The freighter *Hawaiian Merchant,* sailing from San Francisco on August 31, 1958, with a deckload of twenty containers filled with everything from beer to baby food, inaugurated the service. Sea-Land Service, Inc., had pioneered the use of containers on the East Coast two years earlier; now Matson brought the shipping revolution to the Pacific. Differences in systems included sizes of containers and Matson's use of shore-based gantry cranes, as opposed to ship's gear.

Matson had a selling job to do, and Sevier recognized it. He told reporters: "To put such a

system into operation would call for the utmost cooperation. . . . directly concerned would be Hawaii's consignees and shippers. . . . Certainly it could not be successful unless labor cooperated, too. If it is put in effect, the changeover . . . will be gradual. We have to feel our way. However, the new system appears to be the only hope on the horizon of achieving some stability in the costs of moving cargo to and from Hawaii.''

In the first year, six C-3 freighters were altered to carry seventy containers each on deck. Conversion of the C-3 *Hawaiian Citizen* into the first full containership on the Pacific was completed in 1960 at a cost of $3,787,000. Lease obligations on containers and chassis brought the outlay to $17.8 million by March 1962 and to $30 million by 1964. Management then decided to spend another $14 million for more vessels and containers.

Matson's development and use of the A-frame gantry cranes was soon copied by other containership operators, but there were other problems. San Francisco's famous old finger piers, supported only by pilings, could not support the weight of cargoes and cranes; and nothing like the needed space for container storage and yarding back of the piers was available. Hence, the company first moved containers through the Todd shipyard at Alameda, then transferred operations to the Encinal Terminal, also at Alameda. At Los Angeles, Matson advanced the port $1 million, interest free, to get new facilities constructed. Repayment was made from wharfage tolls. At Honolulu, the Dillingham-owned Oahu Railway & Land Company terminal was used both for traditional cargo and containers, which were moved by narrow-gauge railway flatcars to inland storage areas, thence to road chassis. Use of the railway, not so incidentally, provided the Dillingham organization some justification for holding its rights-of-way in Honolulu. Most of the rail line around the island was being abandoned, but the Honolulu rights still were important to Dillingham operations.

The industrial marriage, however, was anything but smooth. Matson complained about lack of storage space, rising rates for the awkward rail link, and various other details. Unable to reach an understanding, the shipline executives then approached the Hawaii State Board of Harbor Commissioners and obtained an agreement for improvement of the downtown Diamond Head terminal to accommodate container traffic. Operations were transferred there as soon as the facilities were ready.

The *Hawaiian Citizen* could carry 400 containers, including 72 with refrigeration. Two C-4 bulk carriers, the *Californian* and the *Hawaiian,* were converted to carry 286 containers each westbound as well as 16,000 tons of sugar and 3,000 short tons of molasses on eastbound trips. These were added to the fleet in 1961. The C-3 *Hawaiian Fisherman* was converted to become the nation's first specialized seagoing automobile transport in the same year and was renamed the *Hawaiian Motorist.* An automobile could be driven into a special cage on the dock, lifted to any one of five holds, and driven off onto garage decks, including special platforms between the integral decks. At first, the vessel could carry 464 autos, all below decks. Capacity later was increased to 517, with deck space for 226 containers. Chiefly because of special ventilation, the U.S. Coast Guard permitted the vessel to carry autos without draining their fuel tanks or disconnecting batteries.

The floating garage operated between San Francisco and Los Angeles on the West Coast and Hawaii on a fourteen-day turnaround. Although it sailed for a decade, it did create storage problems at all three ports and was unresponsive to the needs of a Honolulu dealer whose customer decided on Tuesday that she wanted her new Cadillac to be pink instead of the blue ordered but still expected it to be delivered the next Monday.

The vessel was sold in 1973. The buyer converted her to a bulk carrier and realized a tidy sum by selling as scrap the steel that had been used in the extra parking decks.*

One essential to the development of containerization and other port mechanization was an accord between waterfront employers and the longshore union. For years, the union fought almost all new methods of cargo handling for fear of losing jobs, while employers battled just as stubbornly for each and every laborsaving device, regardless of its side effects.

This impasse really was broken for the first time in 1959 when the Pacific Maritime Association (employers) and the ILWU initialed a pilot agreement under which employers contributed $1.5 million to a Mechanization and Modernization Fund, which became known as the "M&M fund"; and the union agreed to lift certain work rules and to accept new laborsaving methods. Put into final form in 1961, the agreement provided that for five and one half years, employers would put $5 million annually into the fund, basically to allow early retirement and pay for mandatory retirement. The significant paragraph regarding the union's new position reads: "It is the intent of this document that the contract and working and dispatching rules shall not be con-

---

*Ventilation equalling that of the *Motorist* now permits carrying of "live" automobiles on Matson's newer containerships and its roll-on, roll-off freighters. On the ro-ro ships, most of the cars and small trucks are driven aboard after highway trailers, buses, and odd-sized cargo are in place on the various decks. The autos then fill connecting ramps, which have room for 207 of ordinary size.

Over 20 percent of all automobiles sold in Hawaii are small Japanese cars, well adapted to short island trips and Honolulu's horrendous traffic. These arrive in Japanese bottoms, to Matson's continuing regret.

strued as to require the hiring of unnecessary men.''
In the longshore wars, this was something new.

Stanley Powell, Jr., was unique among Matson
presidents in that his entire business career had
been spent with the company. Graduating from the
University of California in December 1940, he obtained his first Matson job as a seagoing apprentice
clerk. Later, when he was a cashier on the passenger
liners, his duties included the care and repair of the
ship's slot machines, one of the more popular enter-
tainments.

Commissioned as a navy ensign, Powell spent
three war years in uniform, was discharged as a
lieutenant in 1945, and returned immediately to
Matson as a passenger ticket salesman. His rise in
company ranks was classic: salesman to finance
clerk, to investment analyst, to assistant treasurer, to
treasurer in 1957. In these last two positions he was
in close touch with Weldon's planning group, the
hotel sales, and the stock redemptions. He was at
least one of the architects of the last-mentioned
plan. His appointment as vice-president for the
freight division in 1959 and as executive vice-
president in early 1961 were logical preparations for
the presidency he assumed in 1962. Other company
presidents had been men of wide experience, but
none knew the company as well from the inside.
None had ever fixed its slot machines.

Powell also had a dream for Matson, and it was
like nothing Matson ever had been before. He had
about six months to contemplate it before little
nightmares and bigger ones began to intrude. At
the end of 1962, he was able to tell stockholders the
company had earned $2.24 million for the year,
compared with a loss of more than $1 million in
1961. He also predicted the company would earn $4
million in 1963. It did earn $4.95 million.

Other news, however, was less rosy. On February
3, 1963, failure of her main turbines left the *Lurline*
dead in the water at the entrance to Los Angeles
Harbor. The damaged ship, which had cost $8.3
million in the early 1930s and had been renovated
in the late 1940s for another $19 million, lay idle

for months while the company sought government
approval to sell her abroad. This was necessary
because of the subsidy involved in the postwar
renovation.

Passenger business to Hawaii in the previous year
had been unsatisfactory, and the liner *Matsonia* had
been laid up. Now she was put back in service and
renamed once more: *Lurline.**

The year was unkind to Matson vessels. The 295-
foot barge *Lumberjack,* designed to get into any of
the Pacific Northwest ports, large or small, and
equipped with its own lifting gear, was launched
with considerable interest in the trade. Operating
C-3 freighters, Matson had been carrying some 20
million board feet of lumber and plywood annually
to Hawaii. Another 90 million board feet moved
mostly on barges of the Pacific Hawaiian and Oliver
J. Olson fleets. With the *Lumberjack,* Matson
hoped to siphon off another 30 million board feet
because of its size, convenience, and economical
operation.

The concept was excellent, the performance a
disaster. On one of the first trips the *Lumberjack*
was being towed out of Humboldt Bay, California,
into high seas. The tug lengthened its towline too
soon, and winds drove the *Lumberjack* onto the
south breakwater, where she was destroyed in eight
hours. More than 4 million board feet of lumber
littered eight miles of beach.

The *Lumberjack* disaster hampered Matson's
relationships with American Factors' lumber department for years. An overeager freight salesman had
assumed that because Matson's container tariffs all
included cargo insurance, the same would be true
for lumber tariffs on the *Lumberjack.* An Amfac
buyer was impressed and made a heavy cargo com-

---

*Just to get all the naming headaches in one place, *Lurline* no.
3 was sold in 1963 to the Chandris Line, which made repairs and
put the ship into Europe–Australia service as the *Ellinis.* *Lurline*
no. 4, launched as the *Monterey* and renamed *Matsonia* in 1957,
also was sold to Chandris in 1970. Renamed *Britanis,* this vessel,
too, went on the Europe–Australia run. Both vessels were still
operating in the late 1970s, and if a Greek crewman couldn't say
for sure whether he was on the third or fourth *Lurline,* it didn't
really matter.

mitment, pointing out to his superiors the savings so obtained. Unfortunately, the barge rate did not include insurance. The frosting on the buyer's bitter cake was that Amfac at that time operated a large insurance agency fully capable of obtaining coverage and collecting a commission.

Many observers believed that if Matson had not lost the *Lumberjack* it would now be carrying most of the lumber from the Northwest in barges, as competitors are doing. The trauma of the loss, however, hurt chances of building a second such barge, and Powell's need for funds for the Far East container fleet doomed them.

Frustration rather than disaster dogged the 300-foot *Islander,* a barge with a ship's hull, a giant on-board crane, and capacity for 155 containers. As conceived, the *Islander* could be towed from outport to outport as it distributed cargo picked up at Honolulu from the transoceanic vessels, or it could operate on its own power with only a six-man crew.

Seagoing unions, however, flatly refused to man the powered barge with such a small crew, so propulsion equipment never was installed. As a barge with crane, the *Islander* gave good but somewhat awkward interisland service, and later was used between Kobe, Japan, and Inchon, Korea, at which port it could fit into locks leading to a closed tidal basin, whereas larger competing vessels had to stand far offshore and lighter their cargo. More recently, the *Islander* has served military bases at Kwajalein, Majuro, and other outpost islands, and has earned its way in this business.

Originally, Stanley Powell had the support of Randolph Sevier, William M. Roth, and C. C. Cadagan, enough to ensure control of the board of directors. He had come up fast, however, and also needed support of operating people, many of whom he had passed on the way. One of them said:

"Powell was a great boss. He was the one who initiated all those incentive plans, stock options and bonuses, all the things big companies use to motivate their top people and other employees. When we were taken over by A&B, our personnel plans were so far ahead of A&B that they had to be reduced. . . . Powell was a great motivator and had

them all fired up. I hope history will record that in his favor."

On the eve of Thanksgiving, 1963, long-distance telephone operators finally located the president of Castle & Cooke, Malcolm MacNaughton, at a vacation spot on Maui. The caller? Stanley Powell, Jr., in San Francisco, choosing that time to warn that he would recommend to Matson directors on December 12 the cancellation of Castle & Cooke's Honolulu terminal and stevedoring contracts, despite the fact that Castle & Cooke owned 23 percent of Matson's stock.

MacNaughton thought this, as well as several other Powell moves, was a great mistake and said so repeatedly. Directors nevertheless approved the cancellation at the December meeting.

Cadagan thought directors should find good management for a company and then give it freedom to operate, adding, "I have every confidence in Matson's management. It has established an earnings record and I think any director in his right mind would think twice before overruling such a management."

Powell said only that he was convinced Matson's own people could do a better job for less money.

For this moment, he appeared to have the situation under control. Even Matson's passenger department, consistent loser and currently weighted down by lay-up costs on the damaged *Lurline,* showed signs of better health. Vice-President Walter Sternberg, a former airline executive, had mounted an advertising and sales campaign on the theme that the ships themselves were unique vacation destinations. This did improve business, and Sternberg could estimate the 1963 loss at only $500,000, compared with $2.2 million the year before. He thought the passenger department could make a modest profit if it could rid itself of the idle vessel.

Matson was drawing attention from many quarters —unions, travel agents, financial analysts, other steamship companies, and management consultants. *Business Week* magazine on July 6, 1963, quoted an anonymous consultant as saying, "They've got more guts than any steamship company in the country. Faced with a fleet replacement program, they didn't just get more ships; they . . . are taking a close look at the service they're providing and they are using all the best techniques to improve it. They are establishing the criteria other lines must inevitably follow.''

Of course there were varying opinions, including the negative. "Those people," said one customer, "worked on the theory that if it won't go in a box we don't want it. I actually heard one Matson executive stand up in front of the room full of sugar plantation managers (who would not set policy but had bosses who would) and say, effectively, 'If you don't like the way we handle your sugar, put it in a rowboat.' ''

There also was considerable attention from a dogged cadre of federal government attorneys who had spent some months in Honolulu. On January 20, 1964, the U.S. Department of Justice filed a civil antitrust action, charging that control of Matson by Alexander & Baldwin, Castle & Cooke, C. Brewer & Company, and American Factors constituted illegal restraint of trade.

Shortly afterward, C. C. Cadagan, president of Alexander & Baldwin, went to Washington, D.C., to discuss the litigation. He said, "The very first question a government attorney asked me was, 'Who blew the whistle on you?' ''

William Matson Roth had severed his last personal connection with Matson in 1963, resigning as director. This left James Coonan to represent the Matson family's remaining 13 percent interest. Hung Wo Ching, president of the interisland Aloha Airlines and a director of the Bank of Hawaii, and Dr. Thomas K. Hitch, a vice-president and director of economic research for the First National Bank of Hawaii, as well as chairman of the governor's advisory committee on finance, were elected to the expanded Matson board of directors, along with John H. Scott, a Castle & Cooke vice-president, and Wade E. Sheehan, executive vice-president of Alexander & Baldwin. Ching was the first Asian-American to be a director of Matson; and he and Dr. Hitch were the first islanders without direct connections to the Big Five companies to serve on the board.

By 1964 the board had set up an executive committee including Powell, Cadagan, Budge, Coonan, Boyd MacNaughton of C. Brewer & Company, and Donald C. Lahey representing the Crocker interests. This committee would decide what to do in the face of the antitrust action.

Although various board members assured news reporters they were unworried about outcome of the court action, within weeks they were publicly discussing alternatives to meet that threat. Newspapermen saw these as three: outright sale of the company, liquidation of it, or distribution of Matson shares to the stockholders of the four island companies named. There is no indication the third alternative was seriously considered.

Outright sale might have been dandy if Matson owners could have found a buyer willing and able to pay a fair price and to make certain very special guarantees: service to the "neighbor" islands; reasonable freight rates both ways; maintenance of capacity to handle sugar, canned pineapple, and especially molasses eastbound, as well as the varied westbound cargoes.

Malcolm MacNaughton, a Matson director and president of Castle & Cooke, said, "We would negotiate to sell to a proper buyer at a lower price than we would realize on liquidation" and defined the most proper buyer as "several hundred or a few thousand island residents." No hundreds or thousands stepped forward. One offer, $20.00 a share for stock with a book value of $63.15, was not long considered.

Liquidation had some steady adherents. Both MacNaughtons advised their stockholders of the possibility, but Amfac officials were quoted as expressing doubt that any other steamship company would equal Matson's service. Cadagan, informed of the liquidation sentiment among board members, had a simple response: "They can't liquidate Matson. They don't have enough shares."

In the end, none of the publicly discussed alternatives was adopted.

In July 1964 Alexander & Baldwin purchased the shares of the other three defendants in the antitrust suit. These constituted just over 40 percent of the outstanding stock and gave A&B 74.22 percent. The price was $21.6 million, or approximately $60.93 a share.

At the end of the month, U.S. Attorney General Robert F. Kennedy announced agreement on a consent decree entered in the U.S. District Court in Honolulu. This approved the A&B purchase, enjoined the other companies from reacquiring their shares and Theo. H. Davies & Company, Ltd., from buying any, although that company was not a party to the suit.

The government reserved the right to move at any time after ten years to force A&B to divest itself of all its Matson interests and specified that the court should order such divestiture "unless A&B shall show . . . that competitive conditions exist in the transportation of freight from Hawaii to the West Coast of the United States, or, if substantial competitive conditions do not exist, that this situation does not exist as a result of A&B's stock and other proprietary interest in Matson."[*]

The purchases naturally changed the Matson hierarchy. Cadagan replaced Sevier as board chairman, but Sevier remained a director. Budge, Coonan, both MacNaughtons, George C. Montgomery, John H. Scott, and C. Hutton Smith left the board; and Edward B. Holroyde, an A&B vice-

[*]The government never has moved against Alexander & Baldwin under the court order, so the company never had to prove its right to a good conduct medal. By the end of 1964, A&B also had purchased the shares of the three large mainland stockholders, increasing its holding to 93 percent. In the next five years it purchased the outstanding 7 percent from some 600 small stockholders, thus making Matson a wholly owned subsidiary in 1969.

president, was elected to it. Although public interest in Matson during 1964 was focused on the legal and financial maneuvering, the operating company was in the best of health. The long arguments with Castle & Cooke over pineapple rates to the Gulf and Atlantic coasts ended in divorce. Matson pulled out of the service, leaving Isthmian to carry on alone.

Powell was untroubled. He told a reporter the rates "were non-compensatory and it didn't make sense for us to continue to carry the cargo. Isthmian thought differently and I don't know why, but that's the way the ball bounces." Matson also transferred its stevedoring and terminal services in Honolulu from Castle & Cooke Terminals to its own subsidiary, Matson Terminals, Inc., which obtained most of its work forces from the firm of McCabe, Hamilton & Renny Company, Ltd.

Powell told his stockholders in the annual report that the consolidated net profit for 1964 was $6.49 million and added: "Matson has now emerged from its long period of transition from a diversified company to one principally in the transportation business. The time has come to explore possible areas of expansion in the field of transportation so that operational risks, now confined to one area of the Pacific, can be more diffused. In the development of the ocean freight container system, now serving Hawaii so well, Matson has also forged a high degree of technical and managerial know-how in its staff of able and experienced people. This is an additional reason to undertake a program of expansion."

There, in a paragraph, was his dream.

CHAPTER EIGHTEEN

JUST YESTERDAY
(1965–1980)

At the beginning of Matson's eighty-third year, 1965, the liner *Monterey* managed to hang up on a coral head in Bora Bora's tricky reef. Several million land crabs on the beaches may have been amused, but company officials were less so. The ship required dry-docking at San Francisco, and cancellation of one South Pacific cruise was avoided only by shortening each of three others by five days. The *Lurline* did cause cancellation of one Hawaii voyage by developing turbine trouble.

The passenger service, however, offered new features. The *Lurline* began calling both at San Francisco and Los Angeles on several trips, using an overnight mini-voyage between the cities as a teaser to interest new passengers in sailing to Hawaii. On three trips to the islands, the ship also made fourteen-day, four-island cruises, visiting Kauai, Oahu, Maui, and Hawaii, with the ship serving as a hotel at each port. All three trips were sold out.

The *Monterey* and *Mariposa* offered their long-distance passengers "special-interest" trips featuring shipboard instruction in art, photography, golf (thousands of old golf balls were driven into the ocean), bridge, navigation, and flower arranging.

In freighting, there was some new trouble. The secretary of commerce in July 1965 authorized the States Line, a privately owned, subsidized American flag carrier serving the Far East from the Pacific Northwest and California, to increase its annual calls at Hawaii from twenty-six to fifty-two. Matson sued in federal court to have the secretary's ruling overturned; and the case dragged on until 1970, when the defendant, which had sent in only a few ships, dropped its request for the additional service. This line went bankrupt in 1979.

Matson's income from both passenger and freight services declined slightly in 1965, but that from Matson Terminals again increased.

Two former military transports, C-4s, were converted into combination containerships and automobile, molasses, and bulk-sugar carriers by inserting 110-foot midsections to make each 630 feet long, with 29,300 tons displacement. Each ship could carry 690 containers and 192 automobiles westbound and on the return could lift either 12,000 tons of sugar and 134 containers or 3,800 tons of molasses and 470 containers. The *Hawaiian Monarch* joined the fleet in September 1965, the *Hawaiian Queen* in December. The two-vessel project cost $17 million.

Developments came fast in 1966. Powell reported 1965 profits of $7,230,000, book value of a share of stock as $72.70, up from $68.06 a year earlier, and stockholders' equity as $64,300,000, up $4 million for the year.

Ground was broken for a new eleven-story Matson office building at 100 Mission Street in San Francisco; and a new interisland feeder vessel to carry

212 containers, as well as 1,600 tons of molasses, was ordered.

The most dramatic development, however, was the Maritime Administration's approval in February of a Matson proposal to operate a nonsubsidized freight service between the Pacific Coast, Hawaii, and the Far East. This was the beginning of the diffusion and expansion Powell believed essential.

Rationale for the Orient service depended on the premise that Matson had a three-year head start on competitors in container technique and equipment. Since Japan, Korea, Taiwan, the Philippines, and Hong Kong all originated cargo well suited to containers—television sets, watches, clothing, electronics, canned goods, and the like—it should be possible for Matson to become a preferred carrier before competitors, especially the Japanese shiplines, could catch up.

This expectation, which did not work out well, fitted into Powell's dream for the company: a master system using ships, barges, trains, trucks, and perhaps even the larger air freight carriers, all made possible by the ease of transferring containers from one carrier to another. Management foresaw fast loading of merchandise in the Orient, speedy ships across the Pacific, integrated container trains crossing the United States, and other fast ships crossing the Atlantic. This awkwardly named "intermodal system" could cut days from delivery time for Japanese merchandise carried all the way to Europe by water. Use of the unit trains to move automobiles and mixed cargo for Hawaii and the Orient across the United States to ships on the Pacific appeared feasible; and, at least for a time, military cargoes would help to fill the westbound ships.

In April 1966 Cadagan became chairman of the Alexander & Baldwin board of directors and Powell was elected president, retaining the same title in the steamship company. Matson directors approved $46 million for the Far East service, and two C-3 freighters were converted to containerships in Japan. Two new, high-speed containerships were ordered in Germany for 1969 delivery. Matson leased a container yard and dock facilities at Oakland, to be occupied in 1968 or early the following year. Matson and Nippon Yusen Kaisha (NYK), in a joint venture, set up container facilities in Japan.

The Far East service began in September 1967, with the *Pacific Banker* and *Pacific Trader* on the Japan route. The first Japanese containership was launched only seven months, rather than the predicted three years, after its owners had decided on containerships; but the launching at a Honshu shipyard passed without much fanfare. More important was a 1968 recovery from a slump that had affected all Matson routes the previous year. Some recovery was due to generally improved business conditions, a part to the Isthmian Lines' conclusion that carrying pineapple to Gulf and Atlantic ports really hadn't been such a brilliant stroke of business. The company abruptly canceled its service, and Dole pineapple came back to Matson ships, at least for a while. That situation could not be expected to last, however, since Seatrain Lines, Inc., an East Coast tanker and freighter operation, had announced its plan to enter the San Francisco–Hawaii–Guam trade with containerships in 1969. These would be operated by a subsidiary, Seatrain Lines, California. To predict that this company would do everything possible to get the Dole pineapple business, and well might succeed, required no crystal ball.

One more attempt to expand Matson into a multiocean giant was made early in 1968 when the company joined with United States Freight Company and Waterman Industries Corporation in offering to buy control of United States Lines, Inc., largest American flag operator, with routes both in the Atlantic and to the Far East. Negotiations ended when owners of United States Lines found another buyer.

Matson's passenger services remained a borderline financial operation despite varying schemes to make them pay. The four-island cruises were expanded; the *Lurline* took a side trip to Mexico; the *Mariposa* and *Monterey* added Melbourne, Australia, and Nukualofa, on Tonga, to their ports of call and initiated Alaskan and South American cruises. Business generally was good but not good enough to meet spiraling labor and other costs. Passenger services broke even some years but lost money in 1968, when Alexander & Baldwin reported consolidated net income of $15 million.

One A&B decision in that year was prophetic, although it appeared then to have no special connection with Matson operations. Over the years, A&B had acquired 54.1 percent of the stock of the Maui Pineapple Company, Ltd.; and J. Walter Cameron, president of that company, also had served as president and chairman of the board of A&B. The connection had been somewhat uneasy, however, and became more so. The pineapple company management (the Cameron family) was very much aware of the fantastic tourist boom on Maui. The company had large landholdings virtually next door to the Lahaina and Kaanapali properties developed by American Factors as luxury resorts. Some of the Amfac land, bought for $150 an acre, was priced at $8 million an acre by the 1970s.

Understandably, the Camerons favored A&B investment to develop that West Maui property, whereas other A&B managers were reluctant to put development money into property in which they had only a half interest. A&B therefore offered to buy out the minority stockholders in Maui Pineapple. When this was refused A&B proceeded with plans to develop the old Baldwin property between Kihei and Makena, which Matson owned.* Powell said the 1,452-acre development, to be called Wailea, would cost $850 million and would include hotels, apartment buildings, golf courses, homes, and stores, as well as beach improvements. There could be little doubt about the use to which A&B intended to put any spare money in the near future. The company's total assets were $244.6 million.

Powell told a *Forbes* magazine writer in January 1969: "My frustration here [in A&B] is in trying to get a group of family stockholders to go along with

---

*Alexander & Baldwin a year later traded its Maui Pineapple stock to the Camerons. That family continued its profitable custom canning of the fruit but changed the company name to the Maui Land & Pineapple Company and in the 1970s began developing the West Maui properties on its own.

converting an insular, sheltered old company into a real mover. . . . I've still got a lot of persuading to do. I keep pointing out that we're way over-capitalized, that if we are going to fight it out in the jungle we've got to use our capital better."

The late Fred Simpich, Jr., a writer also long involved with the island companies, said in an interview shortly before his death: "There has been a great reluctance on the part of these old companies to use debt. I really don't know enough about it; but Powell, who was a sophisticated manager, probably was of the school where it was not considered hazardous to use debt as a source of a third to 45 percent of your capital. Knowing the A&B directorate pretty well, I can see that there are a lot of people there who never a lender nor a borrower want to be."

At first, the Far East containership service did well in spite of some problems with the ships. Both vessels were carrying capacity loads in each direction by the end of the first year of operations, and in early 1969 Matson moved toward extensions of container service to Manila, Taiwan, Hong Kong, and Korea. Company advance agents went out to establish shore facilities and representation and to identify the special problems to be expected in each place.

These were many and varied. In Korea, for example, Matson had an advantage in that the *Islander* barge could use the port of Inchon, near Seoul, whereas lines with larger vessels effectively were restricted to Pusan, at the south end of the Korean peninsula. Although Pusan involved shorter sea runs from Japan, cargo moving between that unlovely city and industrial centers in the Seoul area had to go via a rickety railroad or mountainous highways, subject to the attentions of superior thieves every foot of the way.

All was not peaches and cream, however, for Matson's advance man in Korea. George E. ("Pete") Goss spent nearly two years inching through red tape such as a Korean government requirement that a road tractor be imported with each cargo trailer. When the *Islander* brought in its first load of containers, they were sent off in truck convoys with a guard riding shotgun on each vehicle. Six months later, the entire operation was suspended. Eventually, Goss could laugh at the frustration.*

The ILWU struck the Pacific Coast container docks on March 17, 1969, demanding that all containers except shipper loads be stuffed and unloaded by longshoremen rather than warehousemen of the teamsters' union. A federal court ordered the longshoremen back to work under their existing contract.

This strike, another threatened by offshore unions, and a later walkout by marine firemen all affected the Far East container service, in which the threat of a strike could cause cargo diversions even though the strike never materialized. A breakdown of the *Pacific Trader* also helped to put the service in the red for the entire year. Other vessel casualties caused cancellation of six regular voyages in the Hawaii freight service, subtracting some $2 million from its expected revenues.

At midyear, Powell announced the purchase by Alexander & Baldwin of Acme Fast Freight, Inc., and some subsidiaries for $5 million. This would add measurably to Matson's ''land bridge'' capabilities, he said, since Acme had terminals in 116 cities throughout the contiguous states and held authority for services in Alaska and Hawaii. Acme moved more than 70 percent of its tonnage in trailers or containers on rail flatcars. Subsidiaries included Acme Fast Freight of Canada, Ltd., with terminals in five cities; Carloader Corporation; and organizations in Mexico, Colombia, and Venezuela.

Acme obliged its new owners by losing $303,000 in the remaining six months of the year. Seatrain Lines, California began services to Honolulu from San Francisco in October 1969 and quickly garnered enough westbound freight to affect Matson profits on its most lucrative route. A&B earnings for 1969

were $7.9 million, down nearly 50 percent from the previous year.

The *Hawaiian Enterprise* was delivered to Matson in December 1969. This was the first of four 34,000-ton ships on order, including two for The Oceanic Steamship Company's Antipodes routes, where conventional freighters had been losing money. These two vessels qualified for U.S. construction subsidies, which had been refused for proposed conversion of existing freighters; but the contracts raised A&B's capital commitment for new ships to $40 million.

M. H. Blaisdell, A&B vice-president for land management and development, resigned without public explanation on January 31, 1970. On March 18, directors accepted Powell's resignation as A&B president and named Allen C. Wilcox, Jr., to the post. In April, Wilcox replaced Powell as Matson's president as well. A month later Wilcox became Matson chairman, and Blaisdell became company president.

The bloodletting had begun.

Suggested reasons for the policy changes were as numerous as the persons offering them. One former executive said: ''I think the statement that A&B did not want to be in worldwide transportation is true, but I also think A&B wanted to retain its identification as an island company. Any effort to move headquarters or any important segment of their business to the mainland was resented by the old A&B group. But there were other factors—the fast freight, the endeavor to get into the Far East trades. [Powell] had a couple of stinkers.''

(Several vice-presidents had offices in San Francisco during this period, but A&B headquarters never were officially moved from Honolulu.)

Another Matson watcher saw the shipping company as ''a sort of hobby'' with A&B, not making enough money or having profit prospects to justify the capital required. He thought A&B was not big enough to capitalize Powell's planned land bridge system, although the ideas could have worked, and have for Sea-Land Services, Inc., backed by the

---

*Goss had a curious family connection with Matson history: his missionary maternal grandmother once told him she had been courted by Captain William Matson but could not consider him ''because he was a drinking man''.

tobacco capital of the R. J. Reynolds Industries. His point was that A&B, although firmly founded and profitable, would have had to jeopardize all its projects and capital to pay for the Powell schemes. By 1970 maritime strikes were imminent, expensive ships were on order, and the entire situation had become precarious.

Blaisdell listed important misconceptions: the idea that Matson could hold a three-year lead in containerization; the belief that Far East cargo would be available either for the trans-Pacific vessels or for land movements across the United States. "By 1970," he said, "Matson was getting only the bicycles" eastbound while high-revenue cargo moved in Japanese bottoms. He added that the unit train idea, when thoroughly studied, was less promising than at first believed: it could work for automobiles from Detroit but little else.

"The profit potentials were vastly overrated," he said, "and certain other factors were ignored. The passenger thing never did make sense after the war. The coming of air travel was obvious. Passenger ships are a sort of ego trip for the owners, something to show off to their friends."

Matson's friends were in for a series of shocks.

The first and greatest was sale of the liner *Lurline* to Chandris Lines. This was announced May 27, 1970, to take effect after a final early summer cruise to Hawaii. On board during that trip, Wilcox said, "It was a very emotional thing. I was afraid I might get lynched for my part in the sale, so I finally wrote a public letter expressing my personal regret but giving the reasons the sale had to be made." In the classic manner of travel buffs, islanders had used the ship infrequently but hated to lose it, the last seagoing American flag passenger vessel operating without a subsidy.

One favorable development in 1970 was the added value given to existing ships and those being built under firm contracts by escalation of shipbuilding costs. Although Matson announced at the time of the *Lurline* sale that "plans are being developed" to use Oceanic's *Monterey* and *Mariposa*

for Hawaii cruises, these two vessels, along with the freighters *Sonoma* and *Ventura*, were sold to Pacific Far East Lines, Inc., seventy days later. PFEL took over the subsidized South Pacific service and—quite happily—contracts for two 34,000-ton containerships being built at Sparrows Point, Maryland.

Matson's Far East service was suspended in midsummer 1970; and the two vessels in the trade, along with two more under construction in Germany, were sold. NYK (Nippon Yusen Kaisha) took over the Japanese container facilities without resentment toward its vanished partner. (In 1973, NYK chose newly formed Matson Agencies, Inc., as its general agents in all U.S. Pacific Coast ports, Hawaii, and Alaska.)

There was some truth in the charge that "if it isn't in a box, Matson doesn't want the cargo." In the late 1960s the company secured approval of increased tariffs for all conventional cargo except bulk or liquid materials such as sugar, molasses, bunker fuel, or fertilizer. Of ships in service in 1970, only the *Hawaiian Enterprise* and *Hawaiian Progress* (which joined the fleet in midyear) had one comparatively small hatch each for conventional cargo, as well as container facilities. Matson Terminals, Inc., divested itself of conventional cargo-handling contracts and equipment in August 1970, thus making the buyer, Crescent Wharf & Warehouse Company, an overnight power in West Coast stevedoring. At this time Matson had nine ships to carry containers, six of them with molasses tanks, six with fuel oil tanks, and four fitted to carry automobiles. The *Hawaiian Princess,* on the interisland feeder run, could handle containers, conventional cargo, molasses, or fuel oil. Matson's bulk carrier *Kopaa,* along with the similar *Sugar Islander* owned by the C & H Sugar cooperative, had most of the space for eastbound sugar; but four other Matson ships also could carry it. The company admitted insufficient capacity for lumber, structural steel, buses, trucks, and heavy machinery; and much of this business was being lost to barges and competing shiplines.

Also unfortunately, only four Matson ships really could be called modern. Each year, the company had to apply to the Cargo Re-insurance Association for a waiver to prevent penalty rates for cargo on all those ships more than twenty years old.

Alexander & Baldwin directors could breathe more easily by the end of 1970,* but Matson was shell-shocked. Shipline operating revenues slipped to $133 million in 1970 and $65 million in strike-hampered 1971. Blaisdell, with no steamship background, named as executive vice-president a seasoned operating man, Robert J. Pfeiffer. Pfeiffer had served with Inter-Island Steam Navigation Company, Ltd.; Overseas Terminals, Ltd., of Honolulu; Matcinal Corporation; Pacific Far East Line, Inc.; Matson Terminals, Inc.; and as head of Matson's Far East service.

Matson revenues improved to $70,360,000 in 1972; and the first significant profit since 1968 was earned in 1973, a rare strike-free year that produced $103 million revenues. A&B earnings per share of stock bounced from a low of $0.63 in 1971 to $1.72 in 1973 before the skyrocketing price of sugar ballooned them temporarily in 1974. In this last bonanza, however, Matson had no part: its pay for hauling expensive sugar did not increase with the commodity price.

In 1972 Lawrence S. Pricher had been named A&B president when Allen C. Wilcox, Jr., became chairman of the board. In April 1973 Pfeiffer was named president of Matson, and he and Blaisdell

---

* A favorable development for the parent company was an agreement between the subsidiary Wailea Land Corporation and the Northwestern Mutual Life Insurance Company for a joint venture in development of the Wailea resort project. This would ensure enough capital without heavy borrowing by Alexander & Baldwin.

Simpich once said, "So many landowners either try to treat land development as a conventional business venture where you go out and borrow money against an asset, keep the profit for yourself, and pay off out of earnings; or they try—if they're fat cats like A&B—to finance it all themselves. Both lead to disaster. The thing you want is a partner with a bottomless pocket, and give him half of it. He can take depressions, take unexpected drainage costs, strikes, and all the other things that upset the rugged individualist. The insurance company is the ideal partner. You couldn't do better. He does have a bottomless pocket."

both were elected senior vice-presidents of A&B. Wilcox resigned his chairmanship at the end of that year, leaving that post vacant but retaining a director's seat.

In the first seven months of 1973, Acme Fast Freight managed to lose another $1,230,000, keeping its record of no profits unsullied if not delightful. The company was sold to Alltrans, Inc., a California subsidiary of an Australian corporation.

In 1973 Matson freighters were offering one direct sailing a week from Los Angeles to Honolulu; U.S. Lines, using fast vessels, went from Los Angeles to Honolulu via San Francisco; and Seatrain moved Los Angeles cargo overland to San Francisco and into its slower vessels for the islands. Obviously, there was a tempting opportunity for any line prepared to offer four-day direct service from Los Angeles to the islands. There were many other indications that the fleet must be upgraded unless the company chose to face ultimate liquidation, but the Los Angeles situation cried loudest for solution.

Various methods were considered and eliminated: no suitable vessels were available for charter; useful mergers appeared dubious; to build new ships involved a long, risky lead time as well as hard-to-estimate expense. The conclusion was that acquiring two roll-on, roll-off freighters then under construction by the Sun Shipbuilding & Drydock Company was the only workable solution and that they should be put on the direct Los Angeles–Honolulu run.

In the end, the company did not buy the two vessels for $62 million but leased them for twenty-five years from trusts established by the First Chicago Leasing Company and the First Hawaiian Bank.

The new ships, delivered late in 1973, were the fastest in the fleet and could handle many shapes and sizes of noncontainer cargo (long steel and pipe, wallboard, trucks and tractors, tour buses, even elephants and giraffes), with space for forty-foot "high cube" road trailers as well as the standard Hawaiian twenty-four-foot containers—in fact, anything that could be hauled overland. Unequalled speed in loading and unloading was possible because cargo came on board over shore-based ramps on its own wheels, moved between decks on ship's ramps, was simply lashed down for the voyage, then departed on its own wheels at the end of the trip. In-port time for the big ships, when everything went well, was less than half that for comparable containerships.

The new ships, named *Lurline* (no. 5) and *Matsonia* (no. 4) also had molasses tanks. The intent was to carry molasses from the outer islands to Honolulu on the interisland *Hawaiian Princess,* store it in shore tanks, then pump the odoriferous goo into the ro-ro ships without delaying their departures. Sometimes the system worked.

Much of the westbound, odd-sized cargo was diverted from slow barge services, but the remainder loaded at Los Angeles undoubtedly was at the expense of Seatrain and United States Lines. For Seatrain, such cargo losses were close to the last straw. In spite of an aggressive sales campaign, this line never had been able to generate enough westbound cargo to compensate for the fact that it could not touch the eastbound sugar. The less frequent service to Guam had similar problems: mixed military and civilian cargo westbound, nothing available for back-haul. In April 1974 President Howard Pack of the Seatrain parent company announced withdrawal from the Hawaiian and Guam services and the pending sale to Matson of 3,400 twenty-seven-foot cargo containers and 1,500 chassis. Matson also took over charters on three elderly and trouble-prone ships, the *Transontario, Transoneida,* and *Transchamplain,* along with leases on a terminal at Honolulu's Sand Island. Confirming the announcement, Pfeiffer said the price exceeded $14.5 million and that Guam would be served by a sailing every ten days.

The purchase did little to dispel the murk of a gloomy Matson year. All three Seatrain vessels required almost immediate major repairs, and start-up costs put the Guam service in the loss column from the beginning.

Expectations for Matson's future suffered another blow late in the year when the Alexander & Baldwin board of directors voted down all proposals for new ships.

One observer noted: "They did it [refused authorization] for sound reasons so far as A&B was concerned. The amount of capital [and debt] involved was big enough to change A&B's emphasis from sugar and land to shipping. . . . Matson . . . is now inexorably headed to the day when the World War II hulls and hardware depart for the cemetery or, more accurately, cremation on a beach in Taiwan. The moment that happens, the vacuum created in terms of westbound lifting capacity is going to get filled. It simply must be filled for Hawaii to exist. When it does, the odds are that it will not be filled by some fly-by-night but a viable United States flag giant like Sea-Land or United States Lines. The only way to escape that confrontation is to buy new ships today."

The company shifted one of the old Seatrain ships to Panamanian registry to reduce its crew cost and put it on a feeder service, mainly to pick up pineapple in the Philippines for transshipment at Guam to the other two vessels, sailing to California. This strategy, plus some other successes in finding eastbound cargo in Southeast Asia, allowed the Guam service to break even in 1975. In 1976, however, all three vessels were out of service for two months with breakdowns, and Guam facilities were damaged by a typhoon. These events wiped out the progress of the previous year. In 1977 more losses were suffered in the Guam trade as the dreary succession of breakdowns continued.

There also was trouble with Matson's new ro-ro ships. These vessels lack the tonnage capacity of containerships, so depend on speed and reliability at sea and especially on quick turnarounds to make them profitable. The *Lurline* broke down once, requiring a tow; and the essential longshoring efficiency never was achieved at the port of Los Angeles, although Hawaiian longshoremen consistently met their schedules. After more than a year of frustration, the company moved its mainland ro-ro terminal to Oakland.

Meanwhile, experts continued bearish. One said:

"There will be no place [in the future] for small shiplines. The sensible thing would be to merge Matson with a larger shipping firm, so that A&B would have a small part of a big show instead of the whole of a little one. . . . The one great mistake Matson made was in handling the sugar producers. They worked so hard getting the rates up that it eventually drove C&H [the sugar cooperative] into building their own ship. This [the *Sugar Islander*] carries enough . . . so Matson's smaller ships can handle the rest, but the real cream is lost."

A second Matson watcher said, "I think Matson should be a public utility owned by the state. Puerto Rico acquired its shipline by condemnation; and Alaska, British Columbia, and Washington state all operate public ferry systems approaching the size and importance of transoceanic lines. Only very large combines or governments can afford the new ships and inherent risks of shipping business. If they could sell Matson to the state for what they paid for it, it would make sense from A&B's point of view. Matson's problems have rested not in its management or its market: it's in the carving up that is being done by the state of Hawaii."

Ownership of Matson by a company whose traditional business was sugar resulted in a curious seesaw. In 1974, when Matson's freight business was beginning a two-year decline, sugar prices soared and so did A&B's consolidated net income; but the 40-year-old Sugar Act, imposing quotas on sugar grown outside the mainland U.S. or Hawaii, expired when prices were skyrocketing. No politician dared propose a new quota system when candymakers and housewives were in shock at the grocery shelf prices.

Hence, sugar prices dropped abruptly as "offshore" sugar was rushed to the unregulated U.S. market. In 1975, A&B profits were held up by the sale of the Matson Building (second of that name) and contiguous property on San Francisco's lower Mission Street; but sugar profits continued to decline in 1976, and A&B agriculture and food-processing operations became unprofitable. In that year, however, Matson reported a 43-percent increase in operating income.

A&B sugar profits increased in the last half of

1977, with the help of one-time government subsidies. In 1978, however, no subsidies were received; and the U.S. Congress rejected legislation to stabilize prices and protect the domestic industry from the dumping of foreign sugar.

More important in the long run, however, was belated government recognition of some of the huge problems of financing new ships. The Maritime Administration and the Internal Revenue Service issued joint regulations for establishment and administration of a permanent capital construction fund. This meant that the Matson company now could defer income taxes on funds set aside for new ship construction. Matson promptly transferred to such a fund money it had been holding in a temporary building fund and $5.48 million from 1976 operations.

In the same year, a keel was laid for a 38,800-ton, 720-foot containership at Bath, Maine. This newest Matson ship, to carry 1,200 containers and 2,400 long tons of molasses at 22 knots, was launched in December 1977 as the *Maui* (second of that name). While it basically is an updated version of the design for the *Hawaiian Enterprise* and *Hawaiian Progress,* which each cost $23 million in 1970, the *Maui* had a price tag of $65 million, including related equipment and financing.

The Alexander & Baldwin annual report for 1976 said Matson would continue to deposit pretax income for new ship construction. In an address, company president Lawrence Pricher said some older ships would be retired as soon as the *Maui* entered service, leaving the company with five modern ships and three to five old freighters, all but one of which would be retired by 1981. A sister ship to the *Maui,* this one to cost nearly $76 million, was launched in November 1979 and entered service in September 1980. Her name: *Kauai.* *

Operation of the ro-ro ships was made more practical when the state of Hawaii in 1976 spent $190,000 remodeling Hilo piers for the shore-based

*The Hawaiian language may never vanish permanently from Matson terminology, although the spelling is confusing and precise meanings of words often are debatable. In 1978, four ships in the operating fleet were renamed. The *Hawaiian Enter-*

loading ramps, which Matson moved from Los Angeles. The port commissioners later provided similar facilities at Kahului, Maui.

Despite these developments, officials still were cautious. Matson President Robert J. Pfeiffer, discussing containerization, said: "The blunt fact is that further mechanization of intermodal transportation is inevitable. It is the task of leaders of management and labor to clear the way for the new methods. . . . The unions cannot reasonably halt the progress of maritime technology while the United States flag gradually disappears from the oceans . . . nor should employers expect or want to deny the workers any of the social and economic benefits of the new machines and of progress in the industry. . . .

"I believe that our industry, both management and the unions, will generate the managerial talent—unencumbered by ancient hostilities and prejudices—that will be capable of evolving practical and fair means to solve the problems of employing machines for the benefit of all Americans."

Pricher told a World Trade Association meeting at Honolulu in July 1977:

"I must be hopeful but I cannot be optimistic. With good fortune, improved traffic, union forbearance, government cooperation, technological ingenuity, the liberal risk of capital and the tolerance of the [Hawaii] community for necessary rate increases, I am hopeful that we can return to adequate levels of profitability so that we can re-equip ourselves to continue our service at present levels and accommodate hoped-for increases.

"In the last extremity, the state of Hawaii or the Federal government may someday have to enter the picture to keep the life-line intact. If subsidy is required, this is where it must come from—not from the pockets of private investors, but from the taxes of everyone. . . . This state needs ocean transportation. Indeed it cannot exist without it. Whether it be Matson or any other company, it is vital that this life-line be perpetuated and strengthened."

In an interview, he added: "The time may come when I would be remiss if I did not walk up the street to the state government, show them our predictions and say, 'Gentlemen, this is *your* problem.' "

On January 1, 1978, Pricher assumed the vacant position of chairman of the Alexander & Baldwin board of directors and chief executive officer. Robert Colson, who had moved from Matson to A&B management early in 1977, became president of the parent company. Both men later resigned. Gilbert E. Cox, formerly president of Amfac, became president and chief executive officer for A&B in June 1978. Pfeiffer, A&B executive vice-president as well as president of the Matson subsidiary, was named to the board of directors of the parent company.

With a prospective tenure of five years until retirement, Cox moved rapidly to sell the subsidiary Rogers Foods, Inc., and to phase out unprofitable operations: Princess Orchards, Inc., a papaya-growing and marketing organization; A&B Agri-business Corporation, a consulting and management firm; and the Guam operations of Matson Navigation Company. Problems with old leased ships, a typhoon that damaged Guam installations, and the continued lack of eastbound cargo had kept this service from ever making a consistent profit. It was discontinued in September 1979, and the leased ships were returned to their owners.

Service to Hawaii, on the other hand, continued to be improved. The most important feature was design and construction of computer-controlled overhead crane systems for loading and unloading containers at the ports of Los Angeles and Richmond, California, and consolidation of the company's terminal operations on Sand Island, Honolulu. The $28 million Terminal Island system at Los Angeles involves four 336-foot overhead cranes to move containers to and from a ship's side and a conveyor to transfer them to the ship-loading crane.

---

prise became the *Manukai* (sea bird); the *Hawaiian Progress* became the *Manulani* (heavenly bird); the *Hawaiian Monarch* became the *Maunawili* (winding mountain), and the *Hawaiian Queen* the *Maunalei* (wreath mountain).

Omens should be favorable. The same four names were used for 1920s-vintage freighters that served Matson long and well, surviving World War II without a casualty. Later, all four were sold, and the first three soon scrapped, but the *Maunawili* lasted until 1958 before meeting the same fate.

Straddle carriers will be eliminated. This system was designed to be in operation in 1980. The smaller version at Richmond began operations earlier. Completion of the Sand Island facilities, at an investment of $15 million each by the state of Hawaii and Matson, was scheduled for early 1981.

Gilbert E. Cox became Alexander & Baldwin's chairman in October 1979, and Robert J. Pfeiffer was named A&B president, also chairman of Matson. James P. Gray was chosen as Matson president. In mid-January 1980 Cox resigned; and Pfeiffer, as A&B president, took over the additional responsibilities of chief executive officer. In October 1980, Pfeiffer also became chairman of the board of A&B.

POSTSCRIPT

In less than a century, Matson, a shipping line with only one little freight schooner, grew up to build and operate heavyweight fleets. Barkentines, barks, and full-rigged ships were followed by great white liners with unprecedented numbers of bathrooms and huge appetites for used golf balls. Salty sailors got sugar on their boots and lovely, profitable oil on their hands and won citations in wars, while luxury hotels were raised where only swamps had been. Epic battles bloodied wharves, and blood of a different sort was shed in sweltering courts and paneled board rooms. Great dreams were dreamed, some to be realized, some to come tumbling down in misadventure.

The parade of Matson men grew and grew. There were William Matson, who manufactured his opportunities and never looked back at his tragedies; E. D. Tenney, in his way as magnificent as his stuffed gooney bird; William P. Roth, the quiet man; a whole clutch of windjammer skippers who faced perils of the sea and won, sometimes with the considerable aid of a square-faced bottle of gin. Among Matson men have been longshoremen with cargo hooks hanging out of their hip pockets; joyous Hawaiians riding up and down a cable over the pounding sea; runaway Germans turned Yankees; many a brawny Swede; a Czarist Russian still tasting mastodon meat; a wonderful Englishman who described the life of a sea captain as "innocuous desuetude." Each did something for the shipline with the seven-starred flag.

The big white liners are gone now; the airline is a memory; and someone else deals with the weird problems spawned by luxury hotels. No hula girls greet Matson ships. It has been a long time since Matson sailors, victims of war or storm or fire at sea, have had to make their way home over hundreds of miles of ocean in open boats, although only a fool would assume it could not happen again. Today's Matson is a mechanized organization whose containerships and specialized freighters operate with the regularity of ferries and little more excitement. Glamour now is hard to find. And yet—

On a bright October morning soon after the present *Lurline* joined the Matson fleet, her captain left the bridge of the westbound ship with a radio message in his hand and descended to the fifth deck of the amidships house. His smile toward a junior officer there was relieved. "I said some Hail Marys last night and they must have helped," he said. "We're going straight on to Honolulu, not to Kawaihae."

The junior's face was deadpan. "A pity," he said. "Great place, Kawaihae . . . nightclubs, girls, golf. . . ."

That was Tuesday. On Thursday morning, trade winds sliced off the tops of waves northwest of the island of Hawaii; but the 25,000-ton *Lurline,* her

decks solid with lashed-down highway trailers loaded in twelve hours at Honolulu, acknowledged the
weather only with a slight pitch. All appeared well,
but Captain Paul Heard's luck had run out. He was
off his eastbound course for Los Angeles, heading
once again for Kawaihae.

All he needed to do was to steer for half a mile
up a 500-foot-wide channel, to turn the 105-foot-
wide, 700-foot-long ship around in a basin with a
diameter of 1,100 feet, then to ease over against a
540-foot dock. Two tugs helped, and the *Lurline*'s
bow thruster made possible a ponderous sidewise
movement. The ship was made fast, spring lines
helping to keep the stern, that would not fit the
dock, away from a gaggle of anchored small craft.
Bow tanks were opened, and the ship began to take
through hoses the 1,863 short tons of molasses for
which she had come.

Kawaihae is only a niche in the forbidding Kona
coast of Hawaii, serving a hamlet and a few surviving sugar mills and plantations. On this day, however, it had too much molasses. No small ships with
proper tanks were available, so the big *Lurline* went
in. The day-long detour wrenched the tight schedule that makes profits from such a specialized ro-ro
ship possible; and a $31 million vessel was subjected
to hazards no underwriter could love, all for a cargo
probably worth less than the expense of picking
it up.

For nearly a century, Matson ships have been
going to Hawaii ports where others did not go,
sometimes for high profits, sometimes to help customers, occasionally for high principle.

The *Lurline* is no glamour ship; but for one
Thursday, she was in the grand tradition.

She didn't make a dime, but she got the molasses.

APPENDIX

MATSON SHIPS

(Listed chronologically by year acquired. Oceanic ships listed separately.)

1882–1934

EMMA CLAUDINA, 196 t, 3 m wood schooner, blt. San Francisco 1881 by Turner for C. A. Spreckels. Matson bought 1/4 1882. Sold Nov. 1886 to George Chandler. Wrecked off Moclips, Wash., Nov. 1906, crew of 8 rescued.

ELEU, 71 t wood tug, blt. San Francisco 1883 (ex-ALERT), sold by Matson to Shipowners & Merchants Assoc. 1908. Scrapped 1921.

LURLINE (#1), 389 t wood brigantine, blt. by Turner for Spreckels at Benicia, Calif., 1887. Matson owned 1/4. Sold 1896 to Hawaiian Commercial Co. Disabled 1915 off Mexican coast, crew rescued by steamer. Drifting vessel last seen Sept. 1915 at 109°W. Conflicting stories about final fate.

HARVESTER, 754 t wood bark, blt. Newburyport, Mass., 1871. Bought by Matson 1891, sold c. 1897 to Alaska Improvement Co. As 4 m sch., owned by Charles Nelson, departed Vavau, Tonga, 4 Nov. 1920. Missing at sea.

DAISY KIMBALL, 275 t wood sch., steam powered, blt. Alameda, Calif., 1892. Matson bought 1894, sailed to Hilo, sold immediately to Wilder SS Co. for local service. Renamed KILAHANI. Lost in heavy weather at Hakalau, Hawaii, on first coasting voyage 26 Jan. 1895.

SANTIAGO, 979 t steel bark, blt. Belfast, Ireland, 1885 as nitrate carrier for Chile trade. Matson bought 1894, sold to Associated Oil Co. 1906. Converted to oil barge and used by U.S. Navy in Alaskan waters during World War II.

SUMATRA, 1060 t wood bark, blt. Chelsea, Mass., 1856. Bought by Matson 1894, sold to Wilder SS Co. and broken up at Honolulu Nov. 1895.

ANNIE JOHNSON, 1409 t ship, blt. Harrington, England, 1872 as ADA IREDALE. Abandoned in South Pacific 15 Oct. 1876 when coal cargo caught fire. Reached Tahiti 9 June 1877. Repaired and re-rigged as bark, sold to Matson 1895. Rerigged as schooner 1912, auxiliary engines installed 1916. Sold to L. Ozanne, Papeete 1926. Crew rescued when sank off Washington coast 1929.

RODERICK DHU, 1534 t iron ship, blt. Sunderland, England, 1874. Matson bought 1896 and installed first electric plant in a sailing vessel in 1900. Sold in 1906 to Associated Oil as tanker. Wrecked off Monterey, Calif., 1909.

FALLS OF CLYDE, 1807 t, 4 m iron ship, later bark, blt. Port Glasgow, Scotland, 1878. Matson bought 1898 (via A. M. Brown), installed oil tanks. Sold to Associated Oil Dec. 1906. Cut down to oil barge at Ketchikan, Alaska, 1922. Restored as museum ship in 1960s, still on display at Honolulu.

ANTIOPE, 1496 t iron full-rigged ship (later bark), blt. Port Glasgow, Scotland, 1866. Matson acquired in 1899 in name of F. Whitney, Liverpool (this may have been only a charter). Sold to Capt. P. J. R. Mathieson. Captured by Japanese in Vladivostok blockade, Russo-Japanese War. Sold to Canadians. Was storeship at an African port in 1922.

INTREPID, 123 t tug, blt. Ballard, Wash., 1900 (ex-

CHARLES COUNSELMAN). Matson bought from Shipowners & Merchants Association in early 1900s, sold 1919. Last owned by Bellingham Tug & Barge Co., scrapped c. 1965.

MARION CHILCOTT, 1737 t iron ship, blt. Port Glasgow, Scotland, 1882 as KILBRANNAN. Aground at Point Wilson, Wash., 1896, repaired as MARION CHILCOTT. Bought by Matson 1900, converted to oil tanker, sold to Associated Oil 1910. Sailed as Trinidad molasses carrier c. 1923, used there as barge until 1940s.

ENTERPRISE, 2675 t iron and steel steamer, blt. Newcastle, England, 1882 as German EHRENFELS, later renamed ST. GEORGE. Matson bought 1901, sold 1 Mar. 1937 to General Steamship Co. Scrapped in Japan.

ROSECRANS, 2618 t steamer, blt. Port Glasgow, Scotland, 1883 as METHVEN CASTLE, then COLUMBIA. Used as military transport 1898. Matson bought in 1902, converted to tanker, sold to Associated Oil 1906. Wrecked off Peacock Spit, Washington (mouth of Columbia River), 7 Jan. 1913, with 33 men lost.

MONTEREY, 1854 t, 4 m iron ship, blt. Southampton, England, 1878 as CYPROMENE. Damaged in storm at Salina Cruz, Mexico, 1903. Matson bought 1904, sold to National Oil Transport as barge 1905. Refitted as 5 m barkentine 1919, scrapped at Los Angeles 1934.

HILONIAN, 2914 t iron steamer, blt. Middlesbrough, England, as TRIUMPH 1880, later became Spanish GAGITANO. Abandoned on U.S. East Coast. Matson bought and rebuilt in 1905, sold in 1916 to Swedish Rederiaktied Nord Atlanten. Sunk by submarine off Irish coast 16 May 1917.

AMY TURNER, 991 t wood bark, blt. East Boston, Mass., 1877. Matson bought 1906, sold to Woodside 1910. Reduced to barge, then refitted as bark, finally as barkentine after 1918 fire at Lyttleton, New Zealand. Foundered off Guam 27 March 1923.

FORT GEORGE, 1756 t, 4 m iron ship, blt. Belfast 1884. Matson bought from Planters Line 1907. Departed New York 28 July 1908. One possible sighting in South Atlantic but never seen again.

GERARD C. TOBEY, 1459 t wood bark, blt. Bath, Maine, 1878. Matson bought 1907, sold 1910 to J. M. Woodside. Reduced to barge, wrecked at Seymour Narrows, B.C., 5 July 1914.

HAWAIIAN ISLES, 2097 t, 4 m steel bark, blt. Port Glasgow 1882. Matson bought 1907, sold 1910 to Alaska Packers. Renamed STAR OF GREENLAND, next Swedish training ship ABRAHAM RYDBERG in 1929. In 1943 she was Portuguese FOZ DO DOURO. Scrapped 1957 in Italy.

ANDREW WELCH, 885 t iron bark, blt. Port Glasgow 1888 for C. Brewer & Co. Matson bought 1908, sold to G. W. McNear 1915. Ship took cargo of food for Belgium but was intercepted by British c. 1916. Drifted to Germany. Sold to Swedes and renamed OLGA, then to Norwegians and named SOPHUS MAGDALON, then CANIS, with Bergen as home port. Engines installed 1919. Sold to Skips 1948, renamed EINVIKA, home port Trondheim. In November 1950, when owned by Ingv. Christianslund of Frederickstad, Norway, she ran on rocks in gale off Raufarhofn, Iceland. Crew was saved by Icelandic Life Savings Association, but hull disintegrated and was barely visible in 1968.

GEORGE CURTIS, 1838 t wood ship, later rerigged as bark, blt. Waldoboro, Maine, 1884. Bought by Matson 1908, sold 1910 to North Alaska Salmon Co. Sailed until 1922, scrapped at Seattle 1929.

LURLINE (#2), 6571 t passenger steamer, blt. Newport News, Va., 1908 for Matson. Sold 1928 to Alaska Packers, renamed CHIRIKOF. Sold again to U.S. Maritime Commission, then to Yugoslavs in 1947, renamed RADNIK. Scrapped 1953.

R. P. RITHET, 1080 t steel bark, blt. Port Glasgow 1892 for C. Brewer & Co. Matson bought 1908, installed auxiliary diesel engines c. 1916. Burned and sank in North Pacific 24 July 1917.

ST. KATHERINE, 1264 t wood bark, blt. Bath, Maine, 1890. Matson bought from Planters Line 1908, sold 1910 to Red Salmon Canning Co. Sailed until 1924, scrapped at San Francisco 1927.

W. H. MARSTON, 1164 t, 5 m wood sch., blt. San Francisco 1901. Matson bought 1908. Suffered accident at sea, abandoned, then towed to port. Sold to Charles Nelson 1912, was owned in Portland, Ore., in 1913, and in Mobile, Ala., in 1920. Lost 2 Dec. 1927, in Gulf of Mexico.

IRMGARD, 671 t wood barkentine, blt. Port Blakely, Wash., 1889. Bought by Matson 1909, sold to Atkins Kroll Co. 1912. Refitted as 4 m sch. 1915. Wrecked at Fiji 1920.

MOHICAN, 852 t wood bark, blt. Chelsea, Mass., 1875. Matson obtained from Planters Line 1909, converted to barge to take two 57-ton guns to Pearl Harbor. Used as molasses barge 1913, sold to state of California 1919 to store vegetable oil, later was oil barge at San Pedro and San Diego. Burned out at National City, remains removed 1940.

S. G. WILDER, 604 t wood barkentine, blt. Port Blakely, Wash., 1887. Matson bought 1909, sold 1911 to J. P. Baetje. Dismasted and sinking off St. Johns River, Fla., 2 July 1922; Matson's leased liner HAWKEYE STATE towed her into river. Repaired as barge, foundered 1933 off Virginia coast while under tow.

WILHELMINA, 5974 t passenger steamer, blt. Newport News, Va., 1909 for Matson, sold 1940 to Lochinever, Ltd. (British Ministry of Shipping). Torpedoed 2 Dec. 1940, no lives lost.

HYADES, 3753 t steel steamer, blt. Sparrows Point, Md., 1900. Matson bought 1910, sold 1925 to Naknek Packing Co. Resold to Japanese 1935 as HYADES MARU. Scrapped at Osaka.

MANOA, 6806 t passenger steamer, blt. Newport News, Va., 1913 for Matson, sold 1942 to U.S. Maritime Commission. Delivered to Russians, renamed BALKASH. Lloyd's Register of Ships listed her through 1969.

MATSONIA (#1), 9402 t passenger steamer, blt. Newport News 1913 for Matson, sold 1937 to Alaska Packers, renamed ETOLIN. Became World War II troopship, scrapped 1957 at Baltimore.

MAUI (#1), 9801 t passenger steamer, blt. Union Iron Works, San Francisco, 1917 for Matson; sold 1941 to U.S. Maritime Commission, scrapped 1949.

MAHUKONA, 2512 t "laker" ftr., blt. Ecorse, Mich., 1919 as COVERUN. Matson bought same year, sold 1940 to Cie. Gen. Trans., France, but sale canceled Sept. 1940. Resold Dec. 1940 to Navebras S.A., Rio de Janeiro. Foundered 600 miles off Jacksonville, Fla. 17 Mar. 1941.

MANUKAI, 7409 t ftr., blt. Oakland, Calif., 1921 for Matson. Sold to Panama 1948, renamed SOROL. Later owned in Hong Kong as VINCENT. Broke down at sea 1952, scrapped in Japan.

MAKAWELI, 2552 t "laker" ftr., blt. Ashtabula, Ohio, 1919 as COWEE. Matson bought 1922, converted to oil and molasses tanker in 1930s, sold 1946 to Great Lakes Navigation Co. She was the only "laker" ever to return to Great Lakes after construction there. Scrapped Italy 1967.

MAKENA, 2642 t "laker" ftr., blt. Ashtabula 1919.

Matson bought 1922, sold 1940 to J. P. Goulandris. Renamed NADA under Panamanian registry 1947, became Finnish KALLE same year and Greek SARONIKOS in 1957. Scrapped in Greece 1960.

MANULANI, 9556 t ftr. with tanks, blt. by Moore, Oakland, Calif., 1922 for Matson, sold 1949 to Fratelli Rizzuto, Genova, Italy, renamed PROVIDENCIA under Panamanian flag. Became PREVIDANCE 1963. Scrapped at Split, Yugoslavia, 1967.

MAKIKI, 6096 t ftr., blt. Bath, Maine, 1917 as RHODE ISLAND. Later named WOONSOCKET. Matson bought 1923, sold 1946 to Panama owners. Renamed RIO CHAGRES 1952. Scrapped in Japan 1954.

MAUNA ALA, 6805 t ftr., blt. Bath, Maine, 1918 as CANIBAS. Matson bought 1923. Wrecked on Columbia River Bar 10 Dec. 1941, no lives lost.

HELENE, 927 t, 4 m wood sch., blt. Port Blakely, Wash., 1900 for Puget Sound–Hawaii lumber trade. Matson bought 1925, converted to pineapple barge, sold same year to Inter-Island Steam Navigation Co. Dismantled 1928.

MAUNALEI, 7159 t ftr., blt. Chester, Pa., 1921 as MOUNT CLINTON. Matson bought 1925, sold 1948 to Piaggio & Rovano, Italy. Renamed SANTA MARIA, then CAPO MANARA, of Genoa. Scrapped in Japan 1953.

MAUNAWILI (#1), 7409 t ftr., blt. Chester, Pa., 1921 as MOUNT CARROLL. Matson bought c. 1925, sold 1946. Became Uruguayan SOCRATES, British SOUTHERN ALBATROSS, still later PORTARIATISA. Scrapped in Japan 1958.

MALIKO, 6847 t ftr., blt. Sparrows Point, Md., 1918 as CAPE MAY. Matson bought 1926, sold 1947 to Wallem & Co., Hong Kong. Renamed SHAHIN with Panamanian registry, then BHARATEATNA of Bombay 1948. Scrapped in Japan 1953.

MANA, 3283 t ftr., blt. Newark 1920 as MORAVIA BRIDGE. Matson bought 1926, sold Dec. 1941 to U.S. Maritime Commission. Transferred to Honduran registry. Owned by Walter W. Johnson, San Francisco, 1948.

MALAMA, 3275 t ftr., blt. Newark 1920 as MILWAUKEE BRIDGE. Bought by Matson 1927, sunk by Japanese aircraft and deliberate scuttling 1 Jan. 1942 in South Pacific. Crew became prisoners of war.

MAPELE, 3545 t ftr., blt. Newark 1920 as PITTSBURGH BRIDGE. Matson bought 1927, first named MALA, renamed MAPELE 1936. Ran aground at Cape

Devine, Shumagin Islands, Alaska, 14 Jan. 1943. Two men lost in surf.

MATSONIA (#2), 17,232 t passenger liner, blt. Philadelphia 1927. Matson bought on ways, first named MALOLO. Sold Dec. 1948 to Home Lines. Renamed ATLANTIC 1949, VASILISSA FREIDERIKA (Queen Frederica) 1955. Scrapped 1977.

MAKAWAO, 3253 t ftr., blt. Newark 1921 as SUJER-SEYCO. Matson bought 1928, sold 1941 to U.S. Maritime Commission. Transferred to Honduran registry. Scrapped 1946.

MAKUA, 3543 t ftr., blt. Newark 1920 as SUHOLCO. Matson bought 1928, sold 1946 to Hung Ziang Shing, Shanghai. Renamed MEO HWA, then in 1947 TAI KONG.

MANINI, 3253 t ftr., blt. Newark 1920 as SUSHERICO. Matson bought 1928. Torpedoed south of island of Hawaii 17 Dec. 1941.

KALANI, 5506 t ftr., blt. Seattle 1918 as WEST LAINGA. Los Angeles Steamship Co. bought 1929 and operated as HELEN WHITTIER. Matson acquired 1931, sold 1940 to British, renamed EMPIRE CHEETAH.

DIAMOND HEAD, 5603 t ftr., blt. San Pedro, Calif., 1918 as WEST ERRAL. Bought by LASSCO, transferred to Matson 1931, sold to Wallem, Hong Kong, 1946. Became SHAHROKH, then Panamanian NORBERG 1949, EASTERN PRIDE 1950, HIGASHI MARU of Osaka 1951. Wrecked at Balingtang, Philippines, 19 June 1958.

KAINALU, 6021 t ftr., blt. Oakland 1920 as MURSA. LASSCO operated 1929 as M. S. SHERMAN. Matson took over 1931, sold 1940. Transferred to British flag as PACHESAM. Became Panamanian FENIX 1948, Japanese NISSHU MARU 1951. Scrapped in Japan 1961.

LILOA, 5523 t ftr., blt. Seattle 1918 as WEST HOSOKIE. Operated by LASSCO 1929 as CONSTANCE CHANDLER. Matson took over 1931, sold 1945 to U.S. Maritime Commission. Transferred to Russia, renamed BELORUSSIA and listed by Lloyd's Register until 1969.

LURLINE (#3), 18,564 t passenger liner, blt. Quincy, Mass., 1931 for Oceanic line. Matson took over immediately, sold to Chandris Lines 1963. Renamed ELLINIS. Still listed by Lloyd's Register 1980.

ONOMEA, 5510 t ftr., blt. Seattle 1917 as WEST HAVEN. LASSCO operated as MARIAN OTIS CHANDLER. Matson took over 1931, sold 1940 to British Maritime Ship & Trading Co. Torpedoed in North Atlantic 1 Nov. 1942.

YALE, 3818 t passenger liner, blt. Chester, Pa., 1906 for New York–Boston route. Chartered 1910 for Los Angeles–San Francisco service. Operated to Alaska 1916, taken by U.S. Navy for English Channel military ferry 1917. LASSCO bought 1920, transferred to Matson 1931. Sold 1941 for construction company floating barracks, returned to navy next year for Alaska troop carrier. Scrapped 1949.

CITY OF LOS ANGELES, 12,642 t passenger liner, blt. Danzig 1899 as GROSSER KURFURST. Seized by U.S. 1917, renamed AEOLUS. Bought by LASSCO 1921, operated by LASSCO and Matson 1931–32, transferred to Matson 1934. Sold 1937 to Japanese shipbreaker.

MAUNA KEA, 6064 t ftr., blt. Bay Point, Calif., 1919 as DIABLO. Oceanic & Oriental line acquired 1929, renamed GOLDEN RIVER. Transferred to Matson 1934, sold 1946 to Cia Centauro de Vapores S.A., Panama, renamed CENTAURO. Scrapped in Italy 1955.

MAUNA LOA, 5435 t ftr., blt. San Pedro 1919 as WEST CONOB. Oceanic & Oriental line acquired 1928, operated as GOLDEN EAGLE. Transferred to Matson 1934. Sunk by Japanese bomber at Darwin, Australia 19 Feb. 1942.

1935–1941

COMMODORE, 1526 t, 4 m wood sch., blt. Seattle 1920 as BLAATIND. Matson bought 1935 for use as barge. Refitted 1941, took lumber cargo to South Africa. Renamed COMMODORE II in 1943. Scrapped at Capetown 1947.

COQUINA, 2140 t "laker" ftr., blt. Manitowoc, Wis., 1918. Matson bought 1935, sold to Oliver J. Olson line 1940. Renamed CYNTHIA OLSON. Sunk by Japanese submarine off Washington coast 7 Dec. 1941.

CORRALES, 2146 t "laker" ftr., blt. Manitowoc 1918. Matson bought 1935, sold 1940 to Olson, renamed BARBARA OLSON. Sold to Peru 1957, renamed RIO PASTAZA. Sank off Pimental, Peru, Oct. 1964.

TIMBERMAN, 2059 t "laker" ftr., blt. Manitowoc 1918 as CORSICANA. Matson bought 1935, sold 1936 to

Schafer Bros. SS Lines. Renamed MARGARET SCHAFER, sold to Panama 1955, renamed GREAT OAKS, then PEGGY, then BORNEO. Scrapped at Hong Kong 1962.

KAILUA, 5342 t ftr., blt. Los Angeles 1919 as WEST CAJOOT. Oceanic & Oriental operated 1928 as GOLDEN BEAR. Matson bought 1936, sold 1942 to U.S. Maritime Commission. Became Russian VIBORG 1943. Listed by Lloyd's Register until 1969.

LAHAINA, 5645 t ftr., blt. San Francisco 1920 as WEST CARMONA. Oceanic & Oriental operated as GOLDEN STATE from 1928. Matson acquired 1936. Torpedoed in Pacific 11 Dec. 1941.

EWA, 7003 t ftr., blt. Seattle 1919 as ELDRIDGE. Later TACOMA of Tacoma-Oriental Line. Matson bought 1937, sold 1942 to U.S. Maritime Commission. Listed by Lloyd's Register until 1968 as Russian NOGIN.

HAMAKUA, 6403 t ftr., blt. Seattle 1919 as CITY OF SPOKANE. Later OLYMPIA of Tacoma-Oriental Line. Matson bought 1937, sold 1945 to U.S. Maritime Commission. Listed by Lloyd's Register until 1969 as Russian KUIBYSHEV.

HONOMU, 6403 t ftr., blt. Seattle 1919 as EDMORE. Later GRAYS HARBOR of Tacoma-Oriental Line. Matson bought 1937. Torpedoed en route Murmansk 15 July 1942. Captain made prisoner.

KAHUKU, 6062 t ftr., blt. Bay Point, Calif., 1919 as CUPRUM. Later SHELTON of Tacoma-Oriental Line. Matson bought 1937. Torpedoed in Caribbean 15 June 1942. Captain and several others lost.

KAIMOKU, 6367 t ftr., blt. Seattle 1919 as CRISFIELD. Oceanic & Oriental operated 1928 as GOLDEN HORN. Matson bought 1937. Sunk by German wolf pack submarine en route Nova Scotia to England 8 Aug. 1942.

LIHUE, 7001 t ftr., blt. Seattle 1919 as WHEATLAND MONTANA. Later named SEATTLE of Tacoma-Oriental Line. Matson bought 1937. Torpedoed in Caribbean 22 Feb. 1942.

MAHIMAHI, 7460 t ftr., blt. San Pedro, Calif., 1921 as WEST CHOPAKA. Oceanic & Oriental operated as GOLDEN DRAGON. Matson bought 1937, sold 1948 to Italian owners. Renamed MONGIBELLO, then POLIFEMO in 1949. Scrapped at Osaka 1959.

MOKIHANA, 7460 t ftr., blt. San Pedro 1921 as WEST PROSPECT. Oceanic & Oriental operated 1928 as GOLDEN SUN. Matson bought 1937, sold 1948.

Renamed Panamanian FRIXOS. Scrapped in Japan 1954.

OLOPANA, 6069 t ftr., blt. Vancouver, Wash., 1920 as BEARPORT. Oceanic & Oriental operated as GOLDEN MOUNTAIN. Matson bought 1937. Attacked by German planes and torpedoed in Barents Sea near Novaya Zemlya, en route to Murmansk 5 July 1942.

WAIMEA, 5670 t ftr., blt. San Pedro 1919 as WEST SEQUANA. Oceanic & Oriental operated 1928 as GOLDEN CLOUD. Matson bought 1937, converted to first bulk carrier in Pacific, sold 1946, when ship received Panamanian registry. Renamed MARMAR 1950, CARMAR 1952, TRIANA 1954, and Lebanese MADELEINE 1955. Scrapped at Split, Yugoslavia 1958.

WAIPIO, 5548 t ftr., blt. Seattle 1919 as WEST EL CAJON. Oceanic & Oriental operated 1928 as GOLDEN KAURI. Matson bought 1937, sold 1946. Renamed Panamanian PARALOS II. Scrapped in Japan 1954.

KOHALA, 5833 t ftr., blt. Seattle 1919 as WEST HENSHAW. Oceanic & Oriental operated 1928 as GOLDEN CROSS. Matson bought 1937, sold 1945 to U.S. Maritime Commission. Listed by Lloyd's Register as Russian PETER TCHAIKOVSKY until 1968.

HAWAIIAN MERCHANT, 7500 t ftr., blt. Kearney, N.J., 1941 for Matson. Sold to U.S. Maritime Commission 1943. Commissioned as navy's U.S.S. EURYALE (AS-22). Decommissioned as sub tender at San Francisco Oct. 1946.

HAWAIIAN PLANTER, 7200 t ftr., blt. Newport News 1941 for Matson. Sold same year to U.S. Maritime Commission. Became navy's U.S.S. BRIAREUS (AS-12) 1943. Decommissioned Norfolk, Va., 1955.

HAWAIIAN PACKER, 7200 t ftr., blt. Newport News 1941 for Matson. Sold same year to U.S. Maritime Commission. Commissioned as U.S.S. DELTA (AK-29), later redesignated as AR-9 (1942). Decommissioned Tacoma, Wash., 1 Dec. 1955.

HAWAIIAN SHIPPER, 7500 t ftr., blt. Kearney, N.J., 1941 for Matson. Sold same year to U.S. Maritime Commission. Sailed briefly as British EMPIRE BUILDER, then returned to U.S. Became Pacific Transport Line's AMERICAN TRANSPORT 1948, States Line's WASHINGTON 1958 and MICHIGAN 1959, then Waterman SS Co.'s MORNING LIGHT 1969. Scrapped in Japan 1973.

1945–

HAWAIIAN EDUCATOR, 7886 t C-3 ftr., blt. Pascagoula, Miss., 1945 as SEA HARE. Matson bought 1946, sold 1964. Renamed GREEN RIDGE.

HAWAIIAN FISHERMAN, 7886 t C-3 ftr., blt. Pascagoula 1945 as SEA FALCON. Matson bought 1946, redesigned as specialized auto carrier 1961, renamed HAWAIIAN MOTORIST. Sold 1973 to Valor SS Co., converted to bulk carrier.

HAWAIIAN LOGGER, 7176 t Liberty ftr., blt. New Orleans 1944 as ALES HRDLICKA. Matson bought 1946, sold 1960. Renamed CAPE COD, Greek ARTMISION 1961. Casualty and constructive total loss 1964.

HAWAIIAN LUMBERMAN, 7246 t Liberty ftr., blt. Houston 1944 as LAURA DRAKE GILL. Matson bought 1946, sold 1960. Renamed CAPE HENRY, then Greek TRIKERI 1961, Liberian DAHLIA 1965.

HAWAIIAN PLANTER, 7896 t C-3 ftr., blt. Pascagoula 1945 as SEA PEGASUS. Matson bought 1946, rebuilt to 14,246 t in 1967, renamed PACIFIC TRADER. Sold 1970.

HAWAIIAN BUILDER, 7898 t C-3 ftr., blt. San Francisco 1945 as SEA BLENNY. Matson bought 1947, sold 1970 to U.S. Department of Commerce.

HAWAIIAN CITIZEN, 7958 t C-3 ftr., blt. San Francisco 1945 as SEA WREN. Matson bought 1947, rebuilt to 12,589 t in 1970. Still active 1980.

HAWAIIAN CRAFTSMAN, 7885 t C-3 ftr., blt. Pascagoula 1945 as MARGUERITE LE HAND. Matson bought 1947, renamed PACIFIC BANKER, rebuilt to 14,161 t in 1970. Sold 1972 to Atlantic Far East Lines, Inc. (Liberian).

HAWAIIAN FARMER, 7914 t C-3 ftr., blt. San Francisco 1944 as SEA STURGEON. Matson bought 1947, sold 1971 to shipbreakers.

HAWAIIAN FORESTER, 7240 t Liberty ftr., blt. Jacksonville, Fla. 1944 as GEORGE F. WALDO. Matson bought 1947, sold 1955 to Weyerhaeuser Co., Tacoma, Wash. Renamed C. R. MUSSER, sailing under Panamanian flag 1969.

HAWAIIAN MERCHANT, 7887 t C-3 ftr., blt. Pascagoula 1945 as SEA SKIMMER. Matson bought 1947, rebuilt to 8300 t in 1951, sold 1971 to American Ship Dismantlers.

HAWAIIAN PACKER, 8348 t C-3, ftr., blt. Pascagoula 1944 as SEA SCAMP. Matson bought 1947, sold 1964 to U.S. Maritime Commission. Renamed PECOS 1966.

HAWAIIAN RANCHER, 8353 t C-3 ftr., blt. San Francisco 1944 as SEA RAY. Matson bought 1947, sold to shipbreakers 1971.

HAWAIIAN REFINER, 7958 t C-3 ftr., blt. San Francisco 1944 as SEA FIDDLER. Matson bought 1947, rebuilt to 8405 t 1950, sold to dismantlers 1971.

HAWAIIAN RETAILER, 7940 t C-3 ftr., blt. Pascagoula 1944 as DARE. Matson bought 1947, sold 1964 to U.S. Maritime Commission. Out of documentation by 1970.

HAWAIIAN TRADER, 7606 t ftr., blt. Portland, Ore., 1945 as BILLINGS VICTORY. Became Pacific-Atlantic SS Co.'s WASHINGTON 1950. Matson bought 1955, sold 1961 to Rachel V SS Corp., New York. Renamed RACHEL V, then KATHY, and again RACHEL V in 1964.

HAWAIIAN TOURIST, 7606 t ftr., blt. Portland, Ore., 1945 as MIDLAND VICTORY. Became BLACK EAGLE in 1948, SEACLIPPER 1951, ALASKAN 1952. Matson bought 1956, sold 1962. Renamed SMITH TOURIST, then U.S. TOURIST. Scrapped in China 1970.

HAWAIIAN TRAVELER, 7606 t ftr., blt. Portland, Ore., 1945 as ADRIAN VICTORY. Became PANAMAN 1951. Matson bought 1956, sold 1961. Renamed JOSEPH V, BATTLE CREEK 1966, and ST. JOAN 1968. Scrapped in Taiwan 1969.

CALIFORNIAN, 13,636 t C-4 ftr., blt. Vancouver, Wash., 1946 as MOUNT GREYLOCK. AmericanHawaiian SS Co. bought and renamed 1951. Lengthened 1954 for Ore Transports, Inc. Matson bought 1960, continuing to operate into 1980.

HAWAIIAN, 14,113 t C-4 ftr., also blt. 1946 at Vancouver and sold to American-Hawaiian, then to Ore Transports. Matson bought 1960, sold Oct. 1978 to Hawaiian Eileen Corp. Further history unclear.

HAWAIIAN LEGISLATOR, 11,178 t C-4 ftr., blt. Vancouver, Wash., 1946 as WILLIS VICTORY. Sailed as NEVADAN 1951 and COAST PROGRESS 1957. Matson bought 1963, sold January 1979.

ISLANDER, 3403 t barge (power never installed), blt. Beaumont, Tex. for Matson 1963. Still active 1980.

HAWAIIAN MONARCH, 17,807 t C-4 ftr., blt. Chester, Pa., 1944 as MARINE DRAGON. Matson bought 1965, renamed MAUNAWILI (#2) 1978. Still active 1980.

HAWAIIAN QUEEN, 17,504 t C-4 ftr., blt. Chester

1944 as MARINE DEVIL. Matson bought 1965, renamed MAUNALEI 1978. Still active 1980.

JOE SEVIER, 163 t motor tug, blt. Terminal Island, Calif., for Matson 1965. Transferred to Matson Services Co. 1969.

HAWAIIAN PRINCESS, 3874 t motor vessel, blt. Beaumont, Tex., 1966 for Matson. Still active in interisland service 1980.

SANFORD B. DOLE, 89 t tug, blt. Mermentau, La., 1967 for Matson. Transferred to Matson Services Co. 1969.

HAWAIIAN ENTERPRISE, 23,800 t (displacement) containership, blt. Sparrows Point, Md. 1970 for Matson. Renamed MANUKAI 1978. Still active 1980.

HAWAIIAN PROGRESS, identical history and specifications to HAWAIIAN ENTERPRISE. Renamed MANULANI 1978. Still active 1980.

KOPAA, 10,461 t bulk sugar carrier, blt. Sausalito, Calif., 1944 as T-2 tanker, MISSION SAN JUAN. Matson bought 1970 and redesigned. Still active 1980.

LURLINE (#5), 25,350 t (displacement) roll-on, roll-off ftr., blt. Chester, Pa., 1973. Leased to Matson. Still active 1980.

MATSONIA (#4), identical to LURLINE (#5), same history. Still active in 1980.

TRANSCHAMPLAIN, 7674 t ftr., blt. Sausalito 1944 as U.S.S. MASCONA (AO-83). Renamed SEATRAIN OREGON 1966. Matson leased 1974, returned to C.I.T. Corporation 1979.

TRANSONEIDA, 7666 t ftr., blt. Sausalito 1944 as U.S.S. COHOCTON (AO-101). Leased by Matson 1974, returned to C.I.T. Corporation 1979.

TRANSONTARIO, 7435 t ftr., blt. Sausalito 1944 as MISSION SOLEDAD (T-2 tanker). Renamed SEA-TRAIN CALIFORNIA 1966. Leased by Matson 1974, returned to Greyhound Leasing Corporation 1979.

MAUI (#2), 38,800 t (displacement) containership, blt. Bath, Maine for Matson 1977. Still active 1980.

KAUAI, similar to MAUI (#2), launched Chester, Pa., 12 Nov. 1979. Joined Matson fleet 1980.

OCEANIC VESSELS

(Listed chronologically by year when they were built for Oceanic or purchased. Some of the earliest likely were built for the Spreckels family and may have made some voyages before formal organization of the Oceanic Navigation Company, when they went under that flag. Following reorganization of the Oceanic Navigation Company as a Matson Navigation Company subsidiary in 1926, several trades were made between the fleets. Hence, a few ships are included in both the Oceanic and Matson lists, under names with which they served the South Pacific or Hawaiian trades.)

1869–1926

EMMA AUGUSTA, 284 t wood barkentine, blt. San Francisco 1867. Lost in Gulf of California, 24 Sept. 1889.

CLAUS SPRECKELS, 247 t wood brigantine, blt. San Francisco 1879 as 2 m sch. Rig changed 1884. Lost on Duxbury Reef, north of Bolinas Bay, Calif., 21 Jan. 1888.

JOHN D. SPRECKELS, 300 t wood brigantine, blt. San Francisco 1880, rerigged as 3 m sch. for Bering Sea cod fishery. Lost in collision with British SS STATESMAN 29 Mar. 1913.

CONSUELO, 293 t wood brigantine, blt. San Francisco 1880 for Oceanic, sold to Charles Nelson 1900, to Mexican owners 1902. Listed until 1922 as owned in Topolobampo, Mexico.

ANNA, 239 t wood sch., blt. San Francisco 1881 for Oceanic, sold to Pacific Marine Supply Co., San Francisco 1898. Lost on Sanak Island, Alaska, 3 Mar. 1901.

W. H. DIMOND, 390 t wood barkentine, blt. San Francisco 1881 for Oceanic, sold 1904 to Alaska Codfish Co. Wrecked on Bird Island, Alaska, 10 Feb. 1914.

WILLIAM G. IRWIN, 348 t wood brigantine, blt. San Francisco 1881 for Oceanic, sold 1901 to Tacoma & Roche Harbor Lime Co. Rerigged as 3 m sch. 1917, in copra trade. Burned for movie at Catalina Island, Calif., May 1926.

ROSARIO, 148 t, 2 m wood sch., blt. San Francisco c. 1879, bought by Spreckels Brothers 1882, transferred to Oceanic with value of $10,666, sold 1887. Crunched in ice at Point Barrow, Alaska, on whaling voyage 2 July 1898.

SUEZ, 2166 t steamer, blt. Low Walker, England, 1876. Chartered by Oceanic 1882–1883 from Nelson, Donkin & Co., London. Went on to Hong Kong and Atlantic. Later Turkish HODEIDAH. Lasted until about 1910.

ALAMEDA (#1), 3000 t iron ship, blt. Philadelphia 1883 for Oceanic. Sold to Alaska Steamship Co., 1910. Burned at Seattle pier 28 Nov. 1931.

MARIPOSA (#1), 3000 t iron ship, blt. Philadelphia

1883 for Oceanic, sold to Alaska Steamship Co. 1912. Sank after hitting Straits Island Reef, British Columbia, 18 Nov. 1917.

AUSTRALIA, 2737 t iron steamer, blt. Govan, Scotland, 1875, chartered to Oceanic 1886, received American registry 1890. Chartered to Russian Imperial Government, captured by Japanese cruiser SUMA 15 Aug. 1905. Scrapped in Japan 1912.

ZEALANDIA, 2737 t steamer, blt. Govan, Scotland, 1875, chartered by Oceanic 1886, became military transport under American registry 1898, returned to island service after war until 1902. Sold to Charles L. Dimon 1906, to U.S. Mercantile Corporation 1916. Lost on Mersey Bar, Liverpool, 2 Apr. 1917.

SELINA, 349 t wood brigantine, blt. San Francisco 1883. Operated by Oceanic, then chartered by Matson 1886–1887, piled ashore Paukaa, Hawaii, 11 Feb. 1887, no lives lost.

SIERRA (#1), 6076 t passenger liner, blt. Philadelphia 1900 for Oceanic. Sold 1920, operated by Polish-American Navigation Co. as GDANSK. Repurchased by Oceanic 1924, renamed SIERRA, sold to Japanese scrappers 1934.

SONOMA (#1), 6279 t passenger liner, blt. Philadelphia 1900 for Oceanic. Sailed 34 years, scrapped 1934.

VENTURA (#1), 6282 t passenger liner, blt. Philadelphia 1900 for Oceanic. Scrapped 1934.

1927–1970

MARIPOSA (#2), 18,017 t passenger liner, blt. Quincy, Mass., 1931 for Oceanic, sold 1953. Operated as Home Lines HOMERIC until galley fire c. 1969. Scrapped in Taiwan.

MONTEREY (#2) (see Matson sch., blt. 1887), sister ship to MARIPOSA, also blt. Quincy 1931 for Oceanic. Renamed MATSONIA (#3) in 1957, then LURLINE (#4) in 1963. Sold 1970, became Greek BRITANIS, operated as Caribbean cruise ship. Still listed by Lloyd's Register 1979–1980.

ALAMEDA (#2), 8218 t C-3 ftr., blt. Wilmington, N.C., 1944 as U.S.S. SHOSHONE (AKA-65). Bought by Oceanic 1947, traded to Matson 1961, renamed HAWAIIAN TRADER. Sold to Sea-Land Service, Inc., same year, renamed SHORT HILLS, COLO-RADO 1964, and U.S. MATE 1966. Scrapped in Taiwan 1971.

SIERRA (#2), 8178 t C-2 ftr., blt. Wilmington, N.C., 1944 as U.S.S. STOKES (AKA-68). Oceanic bought 1947, traded to Matson 1961, renamed HAWAIIAN BANKER. Sold 1961 to Sea-Land, renamed FAN-WOOD 1964, A & J, DOCTOR MAX, then FAN-WOOD again. Scrapped in Taiwan 1971.

SONOMA (#2), 8258 t C-2 ftr., blt. Wilmington, N.C. 1944 as WHITE SQUALL. Oceanic bought 1947, traded to Matson 1961. Renamed HAWAIIAN PILOT, sold 1962. Became SMITH PILOT, then U.S. PILOT. Scrapped in Taiwan 1970.

VENTURA (#2), 8175 t C-2 ftr., blt. Wilmington, N.C. 1944 as U.S.S. TODD (AKA-71). Oceanic bought 1947, traded to Matson c. 1961. Renamed HAWAI-IAN WHOLESALER, sold 1961. Renamed CHAT-HAM, scrapped in Taiwan 1972.

VENTURA (#3), 8413 t C-3 ftr., blt. Pascagoula, Miss., 1945 as U.S.S. HANOVER (AKA-116). Oceanic bought 1947, traded to Matson c. 1965. Matson sold 1970. Renamed ENTU 1972. Scrapped in Taiwan same year.

MONTEREY (#3), 9217 t ftr., blt. Sparrows Point, Md., 1952 as FREE STATE MARINER. Matson bought for Oceanic 1955, rebuilt as 14,799 t passenger liner. Sold 1970 to Pacific Far East Lines, laid up in 1978. Sold to Edward J. Daley, then (1979) to Royal Hawaiian Cruise Lines.

MARIPOSA (#3), 9217 t ftr., blt. Quincy, Mass., 1952 as PINE TREE MARINER. Matson bought for Oceanic 1956, rebuilt as 14,812 t passenger liner, sold 1970 to Pacific Far East Lines. Laid up 1978. Sold to Edward J. Daly, 1979. Sold to American World Line, 1980.

SIERRA (#3), 7920 t C-3 ftr., blt. Pascagoula, Miss., 1945 as SEA CENTAUR. Bought by Matson 1947, operated as HAWAIIAN BANKER, traded to Oceanic 1961. Sold 1970, renamed VANTAGE ENDEAVOR. Scrapped in Taiwan 1973.

SONOMA (#3), 8445 t C-3 ftr., blt. Pascagoula, Miss., 1944 as U.S.S. BURLEIGH (APA-95). Matson bought 1947, transferred to Oceanic 1961. Sold 1970 to Pacific Far East Lines. Resold 1972, renamed MONA. Scrapped in Taiwan 1973.

NOTES

CHAPTER ONE

Details of Captain William Matson's history before 1882 are elusive. If he wrote anything autobiographical, the record has not survived where I could find it; and he was so taciturn about his past that his daughter, Lurline Matson Roth, at the time of his death was unaware that he had been married twice and divorced once before marrying her mother, Lillie Low Matson, or that there were children of the first marriage.

Occurrence of the second marriage in May 1887 was unknown to the family until 1974, when the marriage certificate was located in San Mateo County, California; and confirmation of the bride's death, of unstated causes in the autumn of 1887, was found in San Francisco records. Mrs. Roth also was frustrated in attempting to confirm anything about her father's boyhood in Sweden. Nevertheless, her interview given in 1974 was the most useful source for material in this chapter.

Others included the obituary in the *San Francisco Chronicle* of October 13, 1917, and a Newcomen Society lecture delivered by John E. Cushing at the U.S. Coast Guard Academy, New London, Connecticut on October 4, 1949. Other biographies appeared in the *Matsonews,* a company publication, in December 1943; Felix Reisenberg's *Golden Gate;* the compendium *San Francisco—Its Builders, Past and Present;* John S. McGroarty's *Men of California* (1901) and *California Plutarchs* (1935); and William Camp's *San Francisco—Port of Gold.* Isaac Mar-

cosson's "Black Golconda" in the *Saturday Evening Post* and an interview with Rod G. Fischer added details.

Many of these sources disagreed with each other and with Mrs. Roth.

San Francisco Bay scow schooners were maritime oddities. Between the California gold rush, when they first began to be built in numbers, and 1910, the flat-bottomed scow schooner was developed to a high degree on San Francisco Bay and tributaries, where a shallow draft was often imperative. Square-ended, broad of beam, and shallow of hold, these were rugged, hard-working craft. Writing in the *Sea Letter* of the San Francisco Maritime Museum, Anita V. Mozley said of them: ". . . . the workboat that was developed to carry bulk goods and produce on the bay and its tributaries appeared in these waters even before the gold rush. . . . a flat-bottomed centerboard schooner with a square bow and stern . . . described by a deep-water sailor as 'a big square box with sails set' . . . often referred to as 'hay scows' and although that was not their only cargo it may have been their most picturesque one, with the five-high tiers of hay above the deck, the sails reefed up to accommodate it, and the man at the wheel on a raised platform so he could see over the load. . . .

"The scow schoonerman's life was hard . . . get up the [Sacramento] river with available wind and tide, pole or pull in harness when necessary, or run a line to a tree and winch up to it. At landing, the captain and his crew, one or two hands, loaded night and day until the scow was

full, then waited on the tide and wind for the return trip.
. . . the work was not lightened by the summer heat on
the upper stretches of the Sacramento. . . .

"In the workday routines . . . there were hazards of
getting stuck on the banks of a narrow slough when trying to tack at night; collisions, beats to windward up narrow channels and, certainly not the least, the possibility
of getting hit on the head with a chunk of coal in a hot
battle with another schoonerman for right-of-way up
Petaluma Creek.''

Names of the *Emma Claudina* partners were provided
by the National Archives, which listed owners for 1882
and 1886, adding, "Mr. Matson is not shown as an owner
on succeeding documents.''

Kenneth R. Hall, of the National Archives, in a letter
to the author on July 27, 1978, wrote:

"Masters of sailing vessels were first licensed by an
agency of the government in 1889. This applied only to
those commanding vessels over 750 tons. It is our understanding that before that date masters were licensed by
local shipmasters' associations.

"In 1882, Captain Matson should have had the Certificate of Registry for the *Emma Claudina* and one set of
shipping articles for the voyage on board when he sailed
for Hilo. Before departure he should also have completed
all reports, etc., required by the Bureau of Customs, the
U.S. Shipping Commissioner and the local port authority.''

Other information on the same subject is contained in
the U.S. Naval Institute Proceedings (a magazine) for
March 1976.

General Hawaiian history in this chapter is adapted
from several sources, including W. D. Alexander's *History
of the Later Years of the Hawaiian Monarchy;* Ralph S.
Kuykendall and A. Grove Day's *Hawaii: A History;*
Kuykendall's *Hawaiian Kingdom,* vol. 3; Thrum's
Hawaiian Almanac and Annual; Frederick Simpich, Jr.'s
Anatomy of Hawaii; Agnes C. Conrad's "Hawaiian
Registered Vessels" in the *Hawaiian Journal of History,*
vol. 13, and Edward Joesting's *Hawaii, an Uncommon
History.*

In addition, H. Austin Adams's *J. D. Spreckels;* Jacob
Adler's *Claus Spreckels—The Sugar King of Hawaii;* and
the Castle & Cooke history, *From Land and Sea,* by Frank
J. Taylor, Earl M. Welty, and David W. Eyre, provided
materials for this and other references to the Spreckels
family and its enterprises.

The unsanguine comment about Hawaii's import-
export problems was made by Lawrence S. Pricher, then
president of Alexander & Baldwin, in a July 12, 1977,
speech before the World Trade Association annual
meeting in Honolulu.

The pamphlet by C. J. Henderson concerning outer-
island conditions in the mid-1800s, entitled "The Agency
System: A Constructive Force in Hawaiian Business
Development,'' may be found in the University of
Hawaii's Hamilton Library.

CHAPTER TWO

The quotation from John C. Scott was published in the
Matson magazine, *Aloha,* in a special edition of February
1926, celebrating twenty-five years of incorporation. (This
was a totally different publication from the independent
quarterly, *Aloha,* now being published.)

Scott was widely known, and other references to his
history and connections with C. C. Kennedy appear in
several contemporary publications. Kennedy also is
mentioned in the 1899 publication, *Historical Hawaii,* in
connection with a biography of W. G. Irwin, and in an
article by Henry B. Restarick, president of the Hawaiian
Historical Society, in the *Honolulu Star-Bulletin* of
December 17, 1927.

Arrival of the *Emma Claudina* in Hilo on her first trip
was noted by the *Hilo Herald* and in Titus Coan's *Hilo
Shipping Lists.* The wreck of the *Selina* also was noted by
Hilo newspapers and in Thrum's *Hawaiian Almanac and
Annual,* which reported:

"Feb. 11, 1887: American brig *Selina* on trying to
make port of Hilo the wind died away and a heavy swell
setting in drove her ashore near Paukaa and became a
total loss. Passengers and crew and part of the cargo were
saved. She was chartered and wrecked on second trip.''

Commodore Peter Johnson's *Memoirs* were dictated to
a daughter and typed by her for use by the family. The
manuscript was privately printed by the Matson Navigation Company or W. P. Roth (the book gives no indication) in an edition of 200 copies in 1937. One or more
copies remain in the family's possession, one is owned by
Captain Harold D. Huycke, Edmonds, Washington, and
one (no. 114) owned by Matson is on permanent loan to
the University of Oregon. All Johnson quotations in this
book are from the *Memoirs.*

The marriage certificate of William Matson and Evadna
Knowles is on file at the office of the recorder for San

Mateo County, California. Confirmation of the bride's identity was provided by Frank W. Knowles, of Menlo Park, and Frances Knowles Hufbauer, of La Jolla, author of a history of the Knowles family. The grave of Evadna Knowles Matson was discovered in Greenlawn, Colma, having been moved there from the Odd Fellows Cemetery, San Francisco, in 1932. Records do not indicate the cause of death, but several diseases were epidemic in that area in 1887. B. Marian Norquard of the San Francisco Department of Health did this research.

David Kanakeawe Richards, Sr.'s, story of sailing with Captain Matson was printed by the *Honolulu Star-Bulletin* on May 3, 1941.

Details of the *Harvester*'s disappearance were confirmed by the late Dr. John Lyman, of Chapel Hill, North Carolina, internationally known maritime historian and authority on ship careers. He also confirmed all of the ship lists in the Appendixes of this book, worked out the discrepancies in the generally accepted story of the end of the first *Lurline*, provided details of the *Ada Iredale* abandonment and the subsequent career of the same ship as the *Annie Johnson*, and located records of Matson's purchase of the *Sumatra*. Agnes Conrad confirmed demise of this sad little vessel.

The quotation concerning the interest of Messrs. Scott and Kennedy in Matson's bills of lading was contained in a letter written by one ''TG'' on the letterhead of Theo. H. Davies & Company, in 1954, to Randolph Sevier.

The stories of the Pacific Mail and Oceanic steamship lines are compiled from several maritime sources: the Spreckels volumes; a Claremont, California, Graduate School Ph.D dissertation by Giles T. Brown; several magazines, and a ''History of The Oceanic Steamship Company,'' prepared by Frederick A. Stindt, of the Matson company, for members of a South Pacific tour group in the late 1940s. A personal interview with Captain William Meyer, veteran skipper of Oceanic passenger ships, also was valuable.

The remainder of the chapter came from general histories; the voluminous materials gathered by Captain Fred K. Klebingat and others for use with the *Falls of Clyde* as a museum ship at Honolulu; and from a long series of letters between Walter Giffard, of Honolulu; W. D. K. Gibson, of San Francisco; and Captain Matson. The Klebingat materials included a special section of the publication, *Oceans,* vol. 5, no. 5 (September–October 1972), prepared with the collaboration of Karl Kortum, Chief

Curator of the National Maritime Museum, San Francisco, and a long letter from Captain Klebingat to Dr. Roland Force, of the Bishop Museum. All of the Klebingat materials are available at the ship or the Bishop Museum, the Walter Le Montais Giffard Papers, at the University of Hawaii at Manoa Library.

The *Hilo Tribune* of June 24, 1899, reported the arrival of the *Falls of Clyde;* and the *Hilo Herald,* a day or so later, listed her varied cargo.

CHAPTER THREE

Principal sources for this chapter were the Johnson *Memoirs,* the interview with Lurline Matson Roth, and letters in the Irwin Collection. Newspapers and several marine histories were useful.

The story of William Crocker displaying the gold in his bank's coffers, very possibly apocryphal, appeared in David Warren Ryder's *Great Citizen,* published by Historical Publications, San Francisco. No trace has been found of this company; but a copy of the book was loaned by Emmett Solomon, longtime banker and Matson associate.

Incorporation of the Matson Navigation Company was reported in San Francisco and Hawaii newspapers. A few early records also survived the San Francisco fire and are retained by the company.

Assessments of William Matson's characteristics were made by Mrs. Roth, several unnamed associates quoted in the *Matsonews* historical issue of September 1943, and some persons interviewed.

Captains John Diggs and Charles Brocas, aged eighty-five and ninety-two, respectively, were interviewed together at Vista, California, in late 1974. Captain Brocas had driven his own automobile to the residence of John Diggs, Jr.

Some uncertainty exists about American registration of the steamer *Enterprise.* The *Rosecrans,* although built in England, had served as an American military transport, so undoubtedly had U.S. papers when Matson bought her; and the *Gagitano* was largely rebuilt after purchase, so legally could qualify for American registration when renamed *Hilonian;* but there is no ready explanation of how Matson managed to get the foreign-built *Enterprise* under the same colors unless installation of oil burners and tanks constituted enough rebuilding to make the change legal. Incidentally, the *Enterprise* was not precisely Matson's first steamer. Technically, that would have been the small *Daisy Kimball,* which Matson bought in 1894 and took to Hilo because he was unhappy with interisland service. As soon as the *Daisy Kimball* arrived, however, the Wilder Steamship Company bought her and promised improved service.

At this time, the Wilder line ran from Honolulu to Maui and the windward ports on Hawaii. Kauai and the Big Island's Kona and Ka'u ports were served by the Inter-Island Steam Navigation Company. The two were consolidated in 1905.

A distinction is necessary between William Matson's personal involvement in the oil business, which began with the Western Union Oil Company, and that of the Matson Navigation Company, beginning with installation of oil tanks in sailing ships and burners in steam vessels but involving no direct investment in production until later. These matters are discussed in letters in the Irwin Collection; *SpaN* [*sic*], a publication of the Standard Oil Company of Indiana, in 1973; the Marcosson *Saturday Evening Post* article; minutes of the Matson Company's annual meeting of December 18, 1911, and others.

The Castle & Cooke history entitled *From Land and Sea* is a partial rewrite of at least two earlier manuscripts commissioned but not published. Frank J. Taylor, first of the listed authors, actually died several years before publication. I taped portions of two earlier manuscripts supplied by Castle & Cooke President Malcolm Mac-Naughton in late 1974. Facts in the three versions are the same, but in some instances I preferred the earlier treatments.

CHAPTER FOUR

General histories of Hawaii thoroughly discuss the missionary arrivals. Honolulu libraries abound with them.

Descriptions of the second *Lurline* appear in several Matson publications. The company's reports to stockholders detail her activities, as well as negotiations for the Planters Line.

James Genge, of Sidney, B.C., provided information and newspaper photostats concerning his grandfather, R. P. Rithet. Additional materials in considerable quantity are in the British Columbia archives at Victoria. The story of Ripple Rock has been widely printed. Jim Gibbs' *Disaster Logs of Ships* is useful.

Some sources credit Captain Matson with exceptional foresight in the installation of 720,000-gallon fuel tanks in the *Wilhelmina* and correspondingly large oil capacity

in subsequent Matson passenger liners; others imply that the federal government either ordered or suggested that they be so fitted for possible conversion to armed cruisers in wartime. Be that as it may, they were so equipped.

Honolulu newspapers carried the story of the 1912 stormy voyage of the *Andrew Welch;* the *Marine Digest,* of Seattle, November 8, 1941, and letters from Dr. John Lyman provided other details about her eventual end.

CHAPTER FIVE

Dr. Westerberg's letters, in Swedish, were written between 1908 and 1917 to relatives in his home country. In 1974 copies were delivered by Fred Westerberg, of Mill Valley, California, to the Swedish Information Service, attached to the consulate of Sweden now housed in the San Francisco mansion Captain Matson built for his family. Mr. Westerberg agreed to publication of portions of the letters, and Ulla Wikander Reilly of the consulate did the translations. Originals are retained by the consulate, and English copies are at the University of Oregon.

Most of the history of the oil ventures was published in *Matsonews* of September–October 1957. Filing of the Crandall legal action was reported in the *San Francisco Examiner* of April 1, 1914. Follow-up stories appeared on March 16; April 9, 15, and 16, 1915; and June 30, 1917. Defense moves were discussed by one of the attorneys in an interview. He requested anonymity.

The late Captain William Meyer was helpful in explaining the competitive shipping situation of 1910–1914, and the Oceanic history and Matson annual reports also discuss it.

Information concerning molasses came in interviews with Matson personnel and molasses buyers, as well as some personal experience. I was among survivors of the wartime island rum. In 1980 the idle distillery was sold to California investors, who planned to produce beverage alcohol, suitable for rum and for vehicle fuel additives. An A&B subsidiary agreed to operate the pilot plant under contract.

Reports of the Matson party aboard the *Matsonia* were printed by both leading San Francisco newspapers on January 25, 1913.

Alaska misadventures of the older *Mariposa* were widely covered by newspapers and in regional maritime histories.

Contemporary newspapers also reported the developments when the German gunboat *Geier,* fleeing the British, was interned in Honolulu in 1914. Sixteen

German merchantmen also lay there with her until the United States entered the war in 1917. The German crews then attempted to burn the freighters and scuttle the *Geier* but were stopped by U.S. marines and sailors. The *Geier* was reconditioned and renamed the *Carl Schurz*. Sent to war on the U.S. side, she later collided with another vessel and sank in the Atlantic. It is not established, but probable, that Matson operated some of the German freighters for the government during the war.

Roth family history came from its members, Lurline Matson Roth, William Matson Roth, and Mrs. Frank Thompson, all interviewed in 1974.

Alexander G. Budge, retired from presidency of Castle & Cooke and from the Matson directorate, was interviewed at his home near Santa Rosa, California, also in the summer of 1974.

Captain K. W. Lindberg's personal history came from Matson records and reminiscences by Captain Diggs. Stories of the *Rithet* sinking were carried by San Francisco and Honolulu newspapers; and sailing ship courses were researched by W. H. Dole, of Gig Harbor, Washington.

CHAPTER SIX

Matson's activities during World War I were chronicled in part by Commodore Peter Johnson, in part in short company histories, and especially in a detailed but unpublished history of the *Wilhelmina*'s service, prepared from her logs.

"*A History of the Los Angeles Steamship Company*," a master's thesis by James M. Merrill, is concerned mainly with the early history of the company and the ships *Yale* and *Harvard*.

Competition in the Hawaii trade was covered by contemporary press reports and Matson internal materials. The story of the passenger discovering the *City of Honolulu* fire at sea was told to Captain William Meyer by the unnamed passenger when this survivor later was traveling on an Oceanic liner Meyer commanded. In a 1974 interview Meyer said, "He had come out from the East. He'd had a coal mine back there and they told him he'd die if he didn't get out of there. So he came out to Los Angeles to die and stayed about fifty years."

Meyer also was the authority for the statement that the transport *Thomas* was diverted from San Francisco to Los Angeles after picking up the passengers and crew of the *City of Honolulu*.

John Fischbeck was involved with Matson for decades,

first as a ship's officer and later in management of the Honolulu hotels. Retired, he was interviewed at his home in La Jolla, California, in 1974.

The Matson skippers all were well known in the fleet, and oddities of each were freely discussed by their peers. Not all the nicknames or anecdotes were printable. The late Commodore Hans O. Matthiesen gave hours of his time in retirement to interviews at the San Francisco Matson headquarters. About a year later, he was severely injured in an automobile accident and died of his hurts after long hospitalization.

The story of Captain Mely Gordenev was told by various acquaintances in as many versions. Captain Brocas told of the Kukuihaele cash payment. Captain Anatole Gordenev confirmed facts about his father, as well as some of his own notable adventures, when interviewed on a broiling day in Sacramento.

CHAPTER SEVEN

Fulton W. Wright, interviewed at his home in Pasadena on November 6, 1974, provided valuable information on Matson management.

The interview with Alexander Budge was the most useful source of information on the Royal Hawaiian Hotel construction, along with the Castle & Cooke manuscripts, Matson news releases, the *Matsonews* for March–April 1957, and Honolulu newspaper coverage. Joyce W. Curry, of the public relations department, Sheraton Hotels in the Pacific, confirmed several facts, including those about the hidden wines and the foundation pillars, and provided additional materials and photographs.

Peter Johnson's firsthand account of the *Malolo* accident and her maiden voyage to Honolulu was too good for any tampering, as was Budge's tale of the fainthearted booze smugglers.

CHAPTER EIGHT

The Harold Castle quotation is taken from the Castle & Cooke manuscripts.

Ship purchases and sales were copied from Matson records and confirmed by Dr. John Lyman. Mail contracts are matters of public record, reported in newspapers.

Hidden somewhere in Matson for nearly 100 years has been a series of small, hysterically happy disciples of confusion. It is these trolls who give identical names to five wildly different ships, award two or more names to one ship, and disguise twenty-four other ships with Hawaiian names beginning with the letter *M*. They arranged to have Oceanic Steamship Company sell out to The Oceanic Steamship Company and created a joint venture called Oceanic & Oriental Navigation Company.

Some of their best work was done in this last organization, which acquired ships mostly named "West Something" (e.g. *West Cajoot, West Conob*); renamed each of them "Golden Something" (*Golden Bear, Cloud, Sun,* etc.), and sold them eventually to the parent Matson Navigation Company, again renaming them—as *Kailua, Kohala, Kaimoku, Mauna Loa, Mauna Kea, Mokihana, Mahimahi, Lahaina, Waimea, Waipio,* and *Olopana.*

Nothing can be done about them.

It is inviting noisy dissent, but Matson management believes the Hawaiian names of its ships are spelled correctly as follows and have the indicated meanings. Personally, I never guarantee anything about the Hawaiian language.

The Matson list:

Ewa (crooked); *Hamakua* (back of the island); *Honomu* (gathering of the mu); *Kahuku* (the projection); *Kailua* (two currents of the sea); *Kainalu* (beautiful surf of the sea); *Kalani* (heavenly) or (the chief); *Kohala* (leaves of the hala tree, stripped and prepared for mat making); *Lahaina* (cruel sun); *Lihue* (goose flesh); *Liloa* (in honor of a Hawaiian king) or (to lie in the house); *Mahimahi* (dolphin, nearest thing to a dragon known to the Hawaiians); *Mahukona* (leeward smoke); *Makawao* (expansive view); *Makaweli* (fearful eye); *Makena* (mourning); *Makiki* (porous stone); *Makua* (parent); *Malama* (month); *Maliko* (budding season); *Mana* (satisfied condition); *Manini* (coral reef) or (fish); *Manoa* (thick); *Manukai* (sea bird); *Manulani* (heavenly bird); *Mapele* (variety of tree); *Maui* (demigod); *Maunalei* (wreath mountain); *Maunawili* (winding mountain); *Mauna Ala* (fragrant mountain); *Mauna Kea* (white mountain); *Mauna Loa* (long mountain); *Mokihana* (fragrance; odor); *Olopana* (person or place of high rank); *Onomea* (something palatable or sweet); *Waipio* (arching waters; waterfall); *Waimea* (misty, reddish waters).

CHAPTER NINE

Captain William Meyer, who told the story of the *Tahiti* rescues, had a file of newspaper clippings and photographs of the event; but their disposition after his death is unknown. New Zealand newspapers gave the most coverage.

The Dole pineapple stories came mainly from interviews with Alexander Budge; Malcolm MacNaughton; Frederick Simpich, Jr.; and J. Walter Cameron. The last two, both now deceased, were interviewed at Kula and Kahului, Maui, in late 1974. Background material was included in the *Reader's Digest* article by Frank J. Taylor and in reports of the involved corporations.

The *Fortune* magazine quote was from an article in the issue of September 1937, which also can be found in *American Biography,* vol. 40, p. 31.

Allen Wilcox, who has been president both of Matson and Alexander & Baldwin, discussed behavior of island families on shipboard. J. T. Cavanaugh, another former Matson official, described the company employees' ploy for obtaining top accommodations aboard ship and at the hotels. The letter describing experiences of one passenger with a monkey was written by Jane Hicks Markuson to Mary L. Worden.

CHAPTER TEN

Firsthand reports on several years of labor relations, especially valuable because he had been on both sides of the struggles, were provided by Jess A. Rose, who began a career as a longshoreman and ended it as Matson's stevedoring superintendent.

Charles P. Larrowe's *Harry Bridges, The Rise and Fall of Radical Labor in the United States,* from which Bridges' quotations are taken, gives good accounts of the long conflicts, as does William Burke's "On the Waterfront." It also helped me to have been an Associated Press editor in San Francisco and Tacoma during this period.

Matson's prewar interest in aviation was widely discussed in newspapers of the period. As a cable editor, I wrote some of the stories of the Pan American route surveys. It is important to note that the government's attitude toward the whole question of aviation was extremely fluid, including the reorganization and renaming of the controlling agency only two years after its establishment. The surviving agency, the Civil Aeronautics Board, had time for only a few decisions before World War II effectively put it out of business for four years.

The history of Matson's sea operations immediately before the war was obtained mainly from a résumé prepared by the company under the title, "The Matson Navigation Company in World War II," bound in looseleaf form but otherwise unpublished, and from direct reports of participants, of whom there were many. Fred A. Stindt, retired Matson veteran and a steamship and railroad historian, maintained excellent records, including those of the liner *Mariposa,* on which he sailed as chief purser.

Leslie Grogan's dramatic report of the radio traffic in the week before Pearl Harbor is given in an unpublished manuscript, of which both Matson and the author have copies. Slight discrepancies exist between Grogan's version of the *Lurline's* trip back to San Francisco and an official report by First Officer Edward Collins. In such instances, Collins' version has been used.

CHAPTER ELEVEN

The loss of the *Mauna Ala* was the most dramatic event in the long history of Christmas tree shipments to Hawaii, but far from the only one. Deck shipment was the best available method for years, but trees frequently were damaged by salt spray or dehydration, causing repetitive arguments with consignees and insurers. The advent of refrigerated containers in the last three decades improved that situation but brought new problems.

Street-corner salesmen in Honolulu quickly discovered that it was most efficient merely to have a refrigerated container hauled up to the sales lot and hooked to power lines. Thus, it became a temporary cold locker from which trees could be drawn only as sold. The dealers had to pay demurrage to Matson for keeping the containers so long, but that cost was far less than any other method of keeping trees cool and fresh in semitropical weather.

Matson officials never were enthusiastic about this practice, and matters reached a climax just before Christmas 1978 when a shortage of refrigerated containers for perishable foods developed. Matson notified some Christmas tree shippers they would have to revert to unrefrigerated cargo.

The resulting furore went on for days, mostly in the Honolulu newspapers, but with politicians rushing in to howl foul. Additional containers finally were borrowed but not until after a Honolulu dealer had solemnly charged that Matson was robbing Hawaii's children "of a *white* Christmas." Mercifully, no answer to this charge was printed.

Brief histories of all Matson vessels lost in the war appear in an undated booklet *Ships in Gray,* distributed by the Matson and Oceanic companies shortly after 1945. Several still are in circulation. Commodore Hans Matthiesen's story of the *Lahaina* sinking and the crew's lifeboat voyage, related in an interview, was matched by a carefully detailed account of the *Malama* scuttling and the

terrible prison experiences of her crew, prepared by Captain Malcolm Peters and Mate G. J. Pollard in 1945 from notes kept during their imprisonment. Pollard, who later became a captain and a Matson shore official, provided a copy of the report and added other facts during interviews in 1975.

With difficulty, Captain F. R. Trask managed to get through Australian censorship a complete report on the misadventures and loss of the *Mauna Loa* and the long travels of her crew. Captain A. G. Townsend, Matson's marine manager who received the Trask letter, also had a terse report from Captain W. G. Leithead concerning loss of the *Lihue* and possible sinking of a submarine by her gun crew. A short account and photos of the same event by Ensign Peter Wendt, the gun crew officer, appeared in *Life* magazine, March 30, 1942.

Harlan Soeten, curator of the San Francisco Maritime Museum (now the National Maritime Museum), wrote the article "Caribbean Convoy," quoted here, describing loss of the *Kahuku,* for *U.S. Naval Institute Proceedings,* July 1973.

The sinking of the *Honomu* was described by Alan L. Harvie, third engineer, in *Matsonews* for November–December 1959, and by Seaman "Sarge" Kolence in an interview with Charles Regal, printed by the *Seattle Post-Intelligencer,* December 7, 1942.

CHAPTER TWELVE

The two company manuscripts covering Matson's war activities were the principal sources for this chapter (see notes to Chapters 10 and 11). Fred A. Stindt, Captain R. J. McKenzie, and Captains William Meyer and Anatole Gordenev, in addition to those previously mentioned, added personal experiences.

I, too, had a brief wartime experience with Matson's 14,000-ton *Manulani,* one of the larger freighters in the prewar Pacific. Under navy orders as a civilian correspondent, I boarded the *Manulani* in San Francisco in late 1943, to share aft deckhouse quarters with a military medical corpsman; a newly uniformed and distinctly uneasy Hollywood photographer; a couple of others whom I don't remember; plus one rather small, still redhaired Alexander Budge, president of Castle & Cooke. The remainder of the deck was occupied by 100 cows, two or three spans of mules, and several crates of rabbits.

Shortly after we headed out through the Golden Gate and were picked up by a destroyer escort, the captain sent word that any passengers who wished could earn six or eight extra dollars a day by assisting the crew on the nine-day voyage to Honolulu. Nature of the needed assistance was not spelled out, nor did it need to be. Nobody volunteered.

At the time, I had no idea that *Manulani* meant "heavenly bird." Perhaps it was just as well.

Matson personnel made war history, both curious and heroic, on the payroll or off of it. Anatole ("Pete") Gordenev was an officer aboard a Matson vessel in Australia when he was called up by the army and put in charge of fleets of army vessels: tugs, refrigerator ships, power barges, and assorted small craft. Almost immediately, he was swamped by some 5,000 men, most of whom had never been to sea, sent out to operate them. Gordenev set up his own navigation and engineering school, which issued very official "papers" (masters, mates, engineers) to its graduates for more than a year. Many an army vessel operated throughout the war with no other indication that its officers had been trained for their jobs.

Gordenev went on to serve as an army cargo officer and won the Silver Star for rescuing shipmates on the British freighter *Auschun* when it was bombed and sunk at Milne Bay, New Guinea.

A civilian, Captain Nick Barbara, received the Merchant Marine Distinguished Service Medal for his actions in getting the ammunition ship *Buchanan* safely away when a Noumea dock blew up November 1, 1943, while the ship was loading. The *Buchanan* had one man killed.

Company records include the names of sixty-four employees killed during the war, including fifty-one crewmen on company-operated ships.

By way of contrast, Stellio Cherubini spent most of *his* war in an American stockade as an Italian internee, joining Matson after it was all over and eventually becoming one of the company's ship captains.

CHAPTER THIRTEEN

Most useful in collecting the story of Matson's postwar efforts in aviation were the legal briefs, current newspapers, and interviews with those closely involved. I relied on Matson's brief for the Civil Aeronautics Board docket no. 2537; the *Pacific Marine Review, Honolulu Star-Bulletin,* and *Honolulu Advertiser;* Captain Ernest Gann; J. Lee Jenkines; Neil Laidlaw; Arthur Matson; plus numerous company reports to stockholders and news releases.

Considerable personal observation was involved in connection with the Waikiki hotels during the war. Frank

Palmer; Arthur Rutledge of the Hotel and Restaurant Employees and Bartenders International Union; and Edward K. Hastings, a postwar manager for the Matson hotels, offered differing viewpoints.

Information concerning Frazer Bailey came from Matson company biographies, copies of Bailey's own speeches, Fulton Wright, and other Matson officials.

Paul Douglass, then Matson's local manager at Hilo and later involved in the frustrating Guam service, was most helpful with information about bulk-sugar handling and in demonstrating the facilities. Joe Kahee, of Hilo, and Kiyo Enomoto and John Bissen, of Kahului, also cooperated. Kahee is one of the comparatively rare full-blooded Hawaiians. Enomoto and Bissen were closely involved with the first bulk-sugar experiments.

CHAPTER FOURTEEN

Fulton W. Wright described the Walter Buck legal actions and John Cushing's efforts to put Matson operations on a paying basis.

Hawaiian longshoremen were discussed in a number of the interviews. Useful publications were Lawrence Fuchs' *Hawaii Pono;* Edward Johannessen's *Hawaii Labor Movement;* and Maxine du Plessix Gray's two-part article, "The Sugar Coated Fortress," in *The New Yorker* magazine.

Details of the financial problems just preceding Randolph Sevier's presidency and affecting it were taken primarily from Matson annual reports; a booklet, *Matson Navigation Company Pacific Coast–Hawaii Freighter Service, 1947–1964,* provided by former Matson Vice-President E. J. Bradley, and *A Digest and Complete Transcript of Proceedings of the Conference on Competition,* compiled by company officials. Reports of Sevier's speeches, an official biography, and several interviews were productive.

A good review of major Matson operations and financial history from 1942 to 1952 is contained in a Dean Witter & Company report for its clients, dated September 1952.

CHAPTER FIFTEEN

The hotel and ship turnaround problems were described by Hastings, Palmer, and others in interviews. Terry Parmiter, in the *Honolulu Star-Bulletin* of January 12, 1957, gave a good description of the process; and Frank J. Taylor, in the *Saturday Evening Post* of October 30, 1954, had a 5,000-word description of hula lessons on board the *Lurline,* with other details of the liner's operations.

Life was not exactly rugged for Royal Hawaiian Hotel guests. Suites had portable refrigerators and ice machines, and each floor had its own stamp dispenser. In 1955 the hotel served 387,243 meals, with the average check $3.70, of which 31 percent was the actual cost of the food.

The dinner menu for December 27, 1955, read:

Hors d'oeuvres

Ice Celery en Branche   Ripe and Green Olives   Chilled Tomato Juice
Supreme of Mandarins & Pineapple au Kirsch   Poi Cocktail
Hearts of Artichokes Piquante   Imported Italian Antipasto

Soups

Consomme with liver dumplings, Alsacienne   Cream of Corn, Maryland
Chilled Vichyssoise   Jellied Papaya Fruit Soup

Entrees

Supreme of Mahi Mahi, Mushrooms, White Wine Sauce, Bonne Femme	$5.75
Disjointed Spring Chicken, Sauté Sec, Timbale of Risotto à la Turque	$5.75
Old fashioned Veal Pot Pie, Young Vegetables, Butter Crust Ancienne	$5.75
Noisettes of Spring Lamb, Sauté, Sauce Bordelaise, Braised Celery	$6.00
Roast Guinea Squab, Chestnut Stuffing, Bread Sauce, Currant Jelly	$6.00
Bouquetiere of Fresh Vegetables with Cocoanut Muffins	$5.50
Broiled Prime Eastern Corn-Fed Minute Sirloin Steak, Escoffier Butter	$6.00
Cold: Breast of Chicken, Jeannette, Asparagus Tips Salad	$6.00
Veal and Ham Pie, Cucumber and Onion Salad in Cream	$5.75
Pineapple Cured Smoked Turkey with Your Favorite Salad	$5.75

Fresh Vegetables

New Green Peas, Cerfeuil   Kernel Corn Sauté in Butter
Baked Idaho or Dauphine Potatoes   Boiled Patna Rice

Salads

Hearts of Romaine   Sliced Tomato
(French, Lemon, Thousand Island, Lorenzo or Roquefort dressing)

Desserts and Cheese

Kona Coffee or Cocoanut Ice Cream   Passion Fruit or Guava Sherbet
Fresh Cocoanut Layer Cake   English Walnut Slice Delicieux
Mauna Loa Snowball, Crushed Pineapple   Parfait Framboisette

Camembert, Bel Paese, Swiss, Roquefort with Bents, Saltine or Ritz crackers

Cluster Raisins and African Dates   Fruits in Season, Demi Tasse

(Coffee and Liqueurs after dinner in the lounge)

CHAPTER SIXTEEN

Understandably, the Matson Navigation Company reorganization received wide coverage in Pacific Coast and Hawaii newspapers, as well as in several magazines. Material for this chapter was excerpted from these sources, speeches of Matson officials, and the company's reports to stockholders and employees. Useful references included the *Honolulu Star-Bulletin* for April 10, July 31, and October 14 and 22, 1959. A speech by Representative George P. Miller of California was inserted in the *Congressional Record* for July 9, 1959, and contains pertinent material.

Information on Matson's stevedoring and terminal

operations was obtained from several sources already mentioned. The interview with Jess A. Rose was the most instructive. Some personal observations were made at Los Angeles, Hilo, and Honolulu.

In 1956 the Matcinal Corporation was formed jointly by Encinal Terminals, Inc., and Matson to perform stevedoring and terminal operations in the East Bay area of California. Other operators protested to the Federal Maritime Board, however; and the new company, ruled in violation of antitrust regulations, was disbanded in 1958. Discussions of this and various other Matson terminal and seagoing operations were covered in a long question-and-answer interview with Robert J. Pfeiffer, who was vice-president and general manager of Matcinal, later held the same positions in Matson Terminals, Inc., and in 1973 was named president of the Matson Navigation Company. The interview was printed in the February 1974 issue of *Pacific Traffic* magazine.

CHAPTER SEVENTEEN

The Weldon group report was first printed in a Matson publication, *Operations Research,* vol. 6, no. 5 (September–October 1958), and was reprinted as a pamphlet, *Cargo Containerization in the West Coast–Hawaii Trade,* made available to the trade.

Conversion of piers and ships to handle containers, odd-sized cargo, and automobiles has been reported frequently in company and other marine periodicals.

Excellent reviews of Matson's entire operation were printed in a special summer edition of *Matsonews* in 1961. Included were Randolph Sevier's annual address to stockholders; his March 13 statement concerning fleet and rate situations given before a U.S. Senate subcommittee; and a more detailed discussion of the company's special role in ocean freighting, given at a joint hearing of the Hawaii House of Representatives Judiciary and Trade and Commerce Committees on March 22 of the same year. An additional statement was made on April 5 before a Hawaii State Senate committee.

"A First Hand Report on the New PMA-ILWU Pact," written by Wayne L. Horvitz, Matson director of industrial relations, appeared in *Matsonews* of November–December 1960. PMA is the Pacific Maritime Association, which represented most waterfront employers. The International Longshoremen's and Warehousemen's Union is the sole surviving organization following the long internecine strife between AFL and CIO longshore groups on the Pacific Coast.

Stanley Powell, Jr., certainly was one of the most-discussed chief officers in Matson history. His biography as used in this book was distributed, in part, in Matson news releases; but widely divergent opinions were offered by almost every one of his peers. Malcolm Blaisdell, his successor as company president, and Messrs. Hasenhauer, Laidlaw, Wilcox, Simpich, and Wright were among those commenting. Mr. Powell declined to be interviewed.

Details concerning the *Hawaiian Motorist* and *Lumberjack* were supplied by Dudley Burchard and other company officials closely concerned with those vessels.

Sources for various materials in this chapter included the *Sydney Morning Herald* and *Sydney Daily Telegraph* (Australia), both of March 17, 1963; *Business Week* of July 6, 1963 (mentioned in the text) and April 11, 1964; the *Honolulu Star-Bulletin* of February 7, 1964; and a Washington, D.C., wire story carried in the *San Jose* (California) *Post-Record* of July 27, 1964.

CHAPTER EIGHTEEN

More than elsewhere in this book, sources for material in Chapter 18 must remain largely anonymous. Many people who spoke freely still are connected with Alexander & Baldwin, Matson, or associated organizations; and their confidences must be respected.

All of the major developments, however, have been widely publicized in newspapers, company news releases and internal publications, promotional material (especially that concerning Wailea), Alexander & Baldwin quarterly and annual reports (Matson no longer publishes its own), and many public addresses.

The pineapple story mainly was told by Messrs. Cameron, Simpich, and Cadagan. George E. Goss outlined his Korea adventures.

This is a continuing story, even allowing some personal involvement. I was aboard *Lurline* (no. 5) as an observer on the westbound trip mentioned in the postscript, and was able to arrange photographs when the Kawaihae stop was inserted into her return voyage.

Matson history has not ended and is not likely to do so.

BIBLIOGRAPHY

GENERAL

Adams, H. Austin. *J. D. Spreckels.* Published by author, San Diego, 1924.

Adler, Jacob. *Claus Spreckels—The Sugar King of Hawaii.* Honolulu: University of Hawaii Press, 1966.

Alexander, William DeWitt. *History of the Later Years of the Hawaiian Monarchy.* Honolulu, 1896.

Andrews, Ralph W., and Kerwin, Harry A. *This Was Seafaring.* Seattle: Superior Publishing Company, 1955.

Benson, Richard. *Steamships and Motorships of the West Coast.* Seattle: Superior Publishing Company, 1968.

Brown, Giles T. "The Admiral Line and Its Competitors, 1916–1936." Ph.D. dissertation, Claremont Graduate School, Claremont, California, 1948.

———. *Ships That Sail No More.* Lexington: University Press of Kentucky, 1966.

Brown, Kenneth. "Across the Blue Pacific." Reprint from *Sea Breezes* [a journal of Commerce and Shipping Telegraph, Liverpool, England], October 1954, pp. 266–286.

Burke, William. "On the Waterfront." *Federal Reserve Bank Monthly Review.* San Francisco, October 1972.

Camp, William Martin. *San Francisco—Port of Gold.* Garden City, N.Y.: Doubleday, 1948.

"Charles T. Wilder." *Paradise of the Pacific,* November 1893, p. 168. A biographical sketch.

Coan, Titus. Hilo Shipping Lists, 1844–1882. Available at Hawaiian Mission Children's Society Library.

Conrad, Agnes C. "Hawaiian Registered Vessels." *Hawaiian Journal of History* 13 (1969):31–41.

Daugherty, Henry E. "Sailing Down from San Francisco." *Paradise of the Pacific,* 5 May 1941, pp. 13–17.

Davis, William Heath. *75 Years in San Francisco.* San Francisco: Howell Press, 1929.

Dean, Arthur L. *Alexander and Baldwin.* Honolulu: Advertiser Publishing Company, Ltd., 1950.

"Dividends from a $287 Million Venture." *SpaN.* Standard Oil of Indiana publication no. 1, 1973. Unsigned.

du Plessix Gray, Francine. "The Sugar-Coated Fortress." *The New Yorker,* 4 March 1972, pp. 41–79; 11 March 1972, pp. 39–81.

Fuchs, Lawrence. *Hawaii Pono.* New York: Harcourt, Brace & World, 1961.

Gann, Ernest. *Fate Is the Hunter.* New York: Simon & Schuster, 1961.

Gibbs, Jim. *Disaster Log of Ships.* Seattle: Superior Publishing Company, 1971.

Gilliam, Harold. *San Francisco Bay.* New York: Doubleday, 1957.

Hawaii Book, The. Chicago: J. G. Ferguson Company, 1961, pp. 164–167. A brief history, pictures of Captain William Matson.

Hufbauer, Virginia Knowles. *Knowles Genealogy.* Privately printed for the family. Possibly available from the author, La Jolla, California.

"In Memoriam" (Lillie Low Matson, d. 23 June 1930). *California Historical Society Quarterly* 1 (March 1931).

"Interview with Robert Pfeiffer, An" *Pacific Traffic Magazine,* February 1974.

"It Takes More than Ships." *Business Week,* 6 July 1963. Unsigned.

"Island 'Princes' Bow to New Ways." Ibid., 11 April 1964.

Jacobsen, Kim. "The Matson Monopoly." *Hawaii Business and Industry,* May 1961.

Joesting, Edward. *Hawaii, an Uncommon History.* New York: W. W. Norton, 1972.

Johannessen, Edward. *Hawaiian Labor Movement.* Boston: Bruce Humphreys, Inc., 1956.

Johnson, Peter. *Memoirs.* Privately published by W. R. Roth, San Francisco, 1937.

Kemble, John H. *San Francisco Bay—A Pictorial Maritime History.* Ithaca, N.Y.: Cornell Maritime Press, 1957.

———. "100 Years of the Pacific Mail." *American Neptune* 10 (April 1950): 123–143.

King, W. H. D. "Maritime History of Hawaii." Unpublished manuscript. Available at Hawaiian Historical Society Library.

Kuykendall, Ralph S. *The Hawaiian Kingdom.* Vol. 3. Honolulu: The University Press of Hawaii, 1967.

———, and Day, A. Grove. *Hawaii: A History.* Englewood Cliffs, N.J.: Prentice-Hall, Inc., 1961.

Larrowe, Charles P. *Harry Bridges, The Rise and Fall of Radical Labor in the United States.* New York: Lawrence Hill & Company, 1972.

Lubbock, Basil. *Downeasters—American Deep-Water Sailing Ships, 1869-1929.* Boston: Lauriat, 1929.

Lyman, John. "Pacific Coast Wooden Steam Schooners, 1884-1924." *Marine Digest,* 3 April 1943–17 July 1943.

———. "Pacific Coast-Built Sailers, 1850–1902." Ibid., 1 February 1941–4 October 1941.

———. "Pacific Coast-Owned Sailers That Were Built Elsewhere, 1900–1914." Ibid., 1 November 1941–4 April 1942.

Marcosson, Isaac. "Black Golconda." *Saturday Evening Post,* 5 April 1924.

"Matson Navigation Company." *Dean Witter and Company Report.* New York, September 1952.

McClellan, Edwin N. "American Ocean Lanes to Hawaii." *Paradise of the Pacific,* 2 February 1938.

McGroarty, John Steven, comp. and ed. *Men of California.* San Francisco: Pacific Art Company, 1901, p. 154.

———. *California Plutarchs.* Los Angeles: J. R. Finnell, 1935, pp. 43–44.

Merrill, James M. "History of the Los Angeles Steamship Company." Master's thesis. Claremont Graduate School, Claremont, California. Microfilm at University of Hawaii Library.

Mozley, Anita V. "Scow Schooners of San Francisco Bay." *Sea Letter.* San Francisco Maritime Museum publication, vol. 5, December 1973.

Nellist, George F., ed. *Men of Hawaii.* Vol. 3. Honolulu: Honolulu Star-Bulletin, Ltd., 1925.

Olmsted, Roger. "An Interview with Rod C. Fischer." *Sea Letter,* 4 June 1957.

Pacific Marine Review. Biography and picture of Captain William Matson (October 1917), p. 65; history of Matson Navigation Company (June 1932), p. 213; cover reproduction of first *Lurline,* vol. 35, no. 2 (February 1938); Matson airline story (August 1946), pp. 91–92.

Reinecke, John. *A History of Local 5.* Honolulu: The University Press of Hawaii, May 1970. Booklet.

Riesenberg, Felix, Jr. *Golden Gate.* New York: Tudor Publishing Company, 1940.

Ryder, David Warren. *Great Citizen.* A biography of W. H. Crocker. San Francisco: Historical Publications, 1962.

San Francisco—Its Builders Past and Present. Vol. 1. San Francisco: S. J. Clarke Publishing Company, 1913, pp. 65–68. No author listed.

Simpich, Frederick, Jr. *The Anatomy of Hawaii.* New York: Coward, McCann & Goeghegan, Inc., 1971.

———. *Dynasty of the Pacific.* New York: McGraw-Hill Company, 1974.

"Sitting Duck." *Forbes* magazine, 15 January 1969, p. 19.

Soeten, Harlan. "Caribbean Convoy." *U.S. Naval Institute Proceedings,* July 1973.

"Special Report: New Ideas from the Old Hawaiian Company." *Intermodal World,* vol. 8, no. 3 (December 1973):16–30. Unsigned.

"Stockholders Sue Directors of Matson Co." *Marine Digest,* 30 October 1948, p. 3. Unsigned. "Matson's New Service Will Benefit NW." Ibid., 7 December 1940, pp. 2–3. "Matson Files for a Direct Hawaii Route." Ibid., 19 July 1947, p. 4.

Taylor, Frank J. "Billion Dollar Rainbow." *Reader's Digest,* December 1954. Condensed from *Advertising Age.*

———. "Look! Ma's Dancing the Hula." *Saturday Evening Post,* 30 October 1954, p. 40.

_____. "Top Man on the Dock." *Nation's Business*,
    April 1952, p. 45.
_____. Welty, Earl M.; and Eyre, David W. *From Land
    and Sea—A History of Castle and Cooke*. San Fran-
    cisco: Chronicle Books, 1976.
Thomas, Gordon, and Witts, Max Morgan. *The San Fran-
    cisco Earthquake*. New York: Stein & Day, 1971.
Thrum, Thos. G. *The Hawaiian Almanac and Annual*.
    Also called *Thrum's Annual*. Honolulu. 1901, story
    on Captain Matson, p. 129; 1909, obituary James A.
    Low, p. 183; 1917, report on Rithet disaster; 1923,
    obituary Mrs. Eben Low, p. 153.
"With Matson Down to Melbourne." *Fortune* magazine,
    September 1937, p. 104.
Young, John P. *Journalism in California*. San Francisco:
    San Francisco Chronicle Publishing Company, 1915.

NEWSPAPERS

(Note: literally thousands of items concerning Matson
affairs have appeared in California and Hawaii newspapers
since 1882. Those listed here are for the most part concerned with major developments but make no pretense of
representing the whole of such materials available. In lieu
of cumbersome headlines, in most cases the content of
the article generally is briefly described.)

Hawaii Herald
    16 December 1897: Matson and Hilo trade.
    17 February 1898: more on Matson and Hilo trade.
    17 February 1898: regarding Spreckels and Wilder.
    22 July 1898 through 22 February 1901: assorted short
        items concerning ships arriving, passengers, and
        cargo.

Hilo Tribune
    10 November 1900: Matson manager fires all Hawaiian
        employees.
    22 February 1901 through August 1906: assorted local
        items, mostly concerning arrivals of *Falls of Clyde*,
        provided by Bishop Museum staff from collections
        not made available to researchers.
    20 May 1913: dope smuggler caught on ship.

Honolulu Advertiser (earlier called *Pacific Commercial
    Advertiser*)
    6, 8, 12 December 1896: *Lurline* ashore at Kahului.
    21, 25, 28 January; 9 February; 14 April; 6 June 1899:
        Falls of Clyde.

22 June 1900: fines for foreign ships carrying pas-
    sengers.
14 August 1900: hoodoo ships.
4 February 1914: history of Matson Line.
3 February 1917: Captain Matson's life story, photo.
11, 12 October 1917: Matson obituary.
17 January 1926: incidents of clipper ships.
8, 13 February 1931: Dillingham and importance of
    shipping.
3 November 1939: Maritime Commission disapproves
    Matson-Dollar agreement.
1 March 1941: "Jonah Ships of the Pacific" (Sunday
    Magazine).
10 March 1942: airline service decision.
3 November 1944: fleet of cargo ships to land after
    war.
7 July 1946: first Matson plane arrives.
7 February 1947: Tidewater, ex-Permanente.
17 October 1947: column "Thirty Years Ago."
25 October 1947: Royce appointed hotel head.
21 March 1948: *Matsonia*'s last trip.
25 December 1948: "Fifty Years Ago," *Lurline* arrival
    at Hilo with passengers and livestock.
24 August 1952: "Do You Remember?" by Jared G.
    Smith.
22 June 1958: Captains awarded World War II medals.
2 June 1977: "Waikiki Twenty Years Later; ex-Hotelier
    Can't Believe It."
28 June 1978: "Cox Selected as President of A & B,"
    by Kit Smith.
17, 18 October; 3, 4 November; 8 December 1978:
    Christmas tree stories.

Honolulu Star-Bulletin
    2 February 1914: sketch of Matson career. Special *Mat-
        sonia* issue.
    3 February 1914: Honolulu businessmen host luncheon
        for Captain Matson.
    6 August 1917: Rithet story, 3-column cut.
    17 December 1927: "How Some Hawaiian Greats
        Overcame Obstacles," by Henry B. Restarick.
    11 July 1934: historical notes on S. B. and Charles T.
        Wilder.
    29 November 1939: Matson reports thefts.
    5 March 1941: "Old Days with Captain Matson"
        (Richards interview).
    12 June 1946: Matson files brief with CAB.
    6, 30 December 1946: aviation stories.

8 January 1947: Matson refiles for air permit.

23 January 1947: Northwest supports Matson's request for air permit.

8 July 1948: Royce announces new hotel Surf Rider.

15 July 1949: Matson sues ILWU.

10 October 1949: Pioneer Lines to send freighters to Hawaii.

1 March 1950: story on Matson financial status.

12 January 1957: ''Lurline Day,'' by Terry Parmiter.

14 October 1957: ''Story Behind Matson Struggle,'' related articles.

22 November 1957: ''Matson's First Enterprise Sparked Local Oil Use.''

23 January 1958: Tacoma, ex-German supply ship, in use.

30 July 1958: Lurline offered for charter.

10 April 1959: Matson ''will remain in business'' but sign of possible merger seen.

14 October 1959: ''Story Behind Matson Struggle; Sales Forced by Stockholders,'' by Sidney P. Allen; ''Taxes Major Consideration Redemption Plan,'' by Ben Thompson.

25 October 1959: Matson delays Maui land decision.

31 July 1961: Company optimistic despite problems.

14 May 1962: ''New President [Sevier] Is Keen Judge of People.''

7 February 1964: ''Hawaii 'Big Four' Tell Matson's Story,'' by A. A. Smyser.

29 August 1974: ''Overdue for Review'' (editorial).

4 November 1974: Matson asks rate hike: ILWU-PMA contract talks.

28 October 1978: Cox cool in Alexander & Baldwin presidency.

17, 18 October; 4 November; 5 December 1978: stories on Christmas tree problems.

Maui News
22 July 1975: ''Lurline Calls, But It's a Different One.''

San Francisco Alta
30 June 1875: ''Oceanic Steamship Company.''

San Francisco Call
29 December 1894: Emma Claudina—record passage.

28 June 1910: ''Islais Creek Bonds Urged.''

30 December 1910: Matson gives Gillett banquet.

18 July 1911: Jeffery banquet.

28 July 1911: Barrett banquet.

8 November 1911: Chamber of commerce luncheon.

19 January 1912: Williams-Hill clash.

San Francisco Chronicle
21 February 1901: causes of assessment of Oceanic Steamship Company.

11 October 1901: loading of Annie Johnson.

4 May 1903: ''Lurline Ashore in Drake's Bay.''

6 May 1903: continuation of above.

18 July 1910: ''Sugar Interests in Hawaii,'' by Royal Mead.

24 December 1913: ''J. J. Dwyer Attacks.''

10 May 1914: ''Lurline Raises Flag for Swedish Pavilion.''

12 August 1915: ''Hawaiian Trade Fight.''

19, 29 March; 5 April; 19 June 1918: developments in estate settlements.

4 October 1918: World War I activities.

1 October 1934: Passenger recalls sailing on first Lurline.

30 July 1946: Matson's first flight to Honolulu.

17 April 1948: sailing of refurbished Lurline.

8 October 1957: Pacific Coast exchange prices.

San Francisco Daily Commercial News
14 May 1962: ''Bay Area Profile'' [Sevier], by Hugh Russell Fraser.

17 March 1975: ''Thirty Years Ago,'' about United Engineering.

20 November 1978: ''Hawaii Christmas Trees'' and ''Tempest in a Tree Pot.''

San Francisco Examiner
18 April 1912: Titanic statement by Matson.

22 May 1912: waterfront control plea.

27 August 1912: harbor control campaign.

14 February 1913: shipping interests discussed.

24 December 1913: J. J. Dwyer attacks Matson.

25 January 1914: banquet on Matsonia.

1 April 1914; 16 March 1915; 9, 15, 16 April; 30 June 1915: stories on Crandall suing Matson over oil stocks.

15 August 1917: marine column ''Along the Water-front.''

12 October 1917: Captain Matson's obituary and funeral.

16 October 1917: division of estate, terms of will.

26 October 1917: Roth to direct Matson Line.

30 October 1917; 1 November 1917: story on administration of Matson estate.

7 December 1917: distribution of Matson estate.

13 December 1917: "Will Admitted to Probate."

17 April 1948: *Lurline* Off to Aloha Land."

San Jose Post-Record

27 July 1964: "Consent Judgment to End Pacific Ship Domination."

Seattle Post-Intelligencer

7 December 1942: "Seaman Tells of War Terror in Arctic Sea," by Charles Regal.

Sydney Daily Telegraph, Australia

17 June 1963: "Sailing Through World's Most Romantic Islands."

Sydney Morning Herald, Australia

17 June 1963: feature on ships *Mariposa* and *Monterey.*

Victoria Daily Colonist, British Columbia

10 December 1916: "Firm Is Big Factor in Port's Development."

20 March 1919: "Mr. R. P. Rithet Is Called to Rest."

Wall Street Journal

9 July 1974: "Alexander & Baldwin See '74 Net Doubling."

17 December 1974: "Making Waves; Seafarers' Union Uses Its Muscle on Congress," by Jerry Landauer.

INTERVIEWS

(Most interviews were between July and December 1974, at the locations noted. Tapes of the interviews with Alexander Budge, Captains Charles Brocas and John Diggs, John Fischbeck, Edwin K. Hastings, Frank A. Palmer, Lurline Matson Roth, Frederick Simpich, Jr., and Fulton W. Wright, along with transcripts and firsthand notes on others are in the Worden Collection at the University of Oregon.)

Persons interviewed:

Jack Abramson, Honolulu; Captain James Beck, Rossmore, California; John Bissen, Kahului, Maui; Malcolm Blaisdell, San Francisco; E. J. Bradley, Del Mesa Carmel, California; Captain Charles Brocas, Vista, California; Captain Jonny Bruns, San Francisco; Alexander Budge, Santa Rosa, California; C. C. Cadagan, Del Mesa Carmel, California; J. Walter Cameron, Kahului, Maui; J. T. Cavanaugh, San Mateo, California; Charles DeBretteville, San Francisco; Porter Dickinson, Honolulu; Captain John Diggs, Vista, California; W. H. Dole, Gig Harbor, Washington; Paul Douglass, Hilo, Hawaii; Hobert Duncan, Honolulu; Frances Edwards, Honolulu (telephone); Kiyo Enomoto, Kahului; Jack Fischbeck, La Jolla, California.

Ernest Gann, Friday Harbor, Washington (telephone); Captain Anatole Gordenev, Sacramento; George E. ("Pete") Goss, Kahului; Raymond Hasenauer, Contra Costa County, California; Edwin K. Hastings, Honolulu; Captain Paul Heard, aboard *Lurline;* Captain Harold D. Huycke, Edmonds, Washington; J. Lee Jenkines, San Rafael, California; Joe Kahee, Hilo, Hawaii; Mrs. Stanley Kennedy, Sr., Honolulu; Captain and Mrs. J. C. Kleinschmidt, aboard *Falls of Clyde,* Honolulu; Frank K. Knowles, Menlo Park, California (telephone); Karl Kortum, San Francisco; Neil Laidlaw, San Anselmo, California.

Malcolm MacNaughton, Honolulu; Captain R. J. McKenzie, Honolulu; Arthur Matson, Lake Sammamish, Washington; Paul Matson, Los Angeles (telephone); Commodore Hans Matthiesen, San Francisco; Captain William Meyer, El Cerrito, California; Ernest Oribin, San Francisco; Frank A. Palmer, Jamestown, California; John Peters, San Francisco; Herman Phleger, San Francisco; Captain Gordon Pollard, San Francisco; Lawrence S. Pricher, Honolulu; Captain James Rasmussen, San Mateo, California; James Reid, Honolulu; Robert M. Richardson, San Francisco; Jess A. Rose, San Francisco; Lurline Matson Roth, Filoli, Woodside, California; William M. Roth, San Francisco; Arthur Rutledge, Honolulu; Frederick Simpich, Jr., Kula, Maui; Emmett Solomon, San Francisco; Thomas MacP. Stapleton, aboard *Lurline;* Barbara Thompson, Honolulu (telephone); Mrs. Frank Thompson, Honolulu; John Vidal, Contra Costa County, California; Allen Wilcox, Napoopoo, Hawaii; Fulton W. Wright, Pasadena, California; Lloyd Yates, San Francisco.

CORRESPONDENCE

(Only letters having direct bearing on the contents of the manuscript are listed. These are filed with the subjects on which they bear, not in a separate file. Some scores of letters of lesser importance, not listed here, are filed chronologically at the University of Oregon.)

Burchard, Dudley, 8 April 1975: regarding Palmer hotel stories.

————, 23 June 1975: regarding Thai costumes, port of Kawaihae, Japanese auto imports, Faxon Bishop.

Bush, Octavia, 26 June 1975: permission to quote Johnson *Memoirs*.

Cadagan, C. C., 7 May 1975: denying rumor of Brewer interest in buying Matson.

Conrad, Agnes C., 31 March 1976: sale of *Sumatra*.

Curry, Joyce W., 20 January 1978: confirming details of Royal construction.

Diggs, John, January, 1978: confirming health of father and Captain Brocas.

Genge, James, 20 December 1974: confirming history of R. P. Rithet.

Haines, Marion, 5 and 22 October 1975: regarding Commodore Johnson photographs.

Hall, Kenneth R., 27 July 1978: explaining history of master's licenses.

Hasting, Edwin K., 14 October 1974: hotel management comment.

Hemila, Gwen, 11 July 1978: also concerning master's licenses.

Holman, Mrs. R. L., to Matson Company, 1956 (copy): telling of voyage on first *Matsonia*.

Hufbauer, Virginia Knowles, 27 November 1974: regarding Evadna Knowles Matson.

Huycke, Harold D., 25 February 1975: regarding photos and sailing ships.

Jackson, Frances, 31 December 1974: answering questions about W. P. Alexander, Robert Wilcox, French Hawaii expedition, etc.

Kortum, Karl, 30 November 1977: discussion of scow crews.

Leithead, W. G., to Captain A. G. Townsend, 24 March 1942: report on *Lihue*.

Lyman, Dr. John, 27 January, 21 February, and 26 March 1975: histories of vessels.

Markuson, Jane, 7 October 1974 and 30 August 1975: story of trip on *Malolo* and permission to use.

Matthiesen, Commodore H. O., to Charles Regal, 12 July 1975: attempting to identify photos; comment on Commodore Johnson.

McCurdy, J. G., 13 June 1975: confirming *Santiago* history.

Najita, Joyce M., 17 June 1975: permission to quote from Reinecke history.

Park, Mrs. Henry R. (Carol), 24 November 1974: relating efforts to trace her Matson connections.

Pollard, Captain G. J., 17 September 1975: history of *Malama* sinking and crew imprisonment.

Regal, Charles, 17 June 1975: reporting on permission to quote Crocker biography (one of scores of Regal letters bearing on every facet of this book project and covering more than five years).

Reilly, Ulla Wikander, 20 January 1975: discussing Westerberg letters.

Richardson, Robert M., 19 November 1977: general comments after reading manuscript; some personal history.

_____, 16 May 1978 (to Charles Regal): more comments on manuscript.

Robinson, Eleanor B., 1 February 1979: request for Grogan diary (provided 6 February).

Roth, Lurline Matson, to R. J. Pfeiffer, 17 November 1978: comments on manuscript; some deletions.

Schneider, Emil A., to Gregg Perry, 26 April 1976: attaching galley proofs on Castle & Cooke book.

Simpich, Frederick, Jr., to Dudley Burchard, 18 September 1974: suggestions following interview.

_____, 5 November 1974 and 14 January 1975 (circa): comments, mainly on Dole problems; W. Russell Starr letter enclosed.

Spaulding, John, 29 January and 11 February 1975: answers to questions on Kukuihaele.

Stindt, Fred A., 26 December 1974: early history of American-Hawaiian and Pacific Mail lines (one of several letters on various related subjects).

Trask, Captain F. R., to Captain A. G. Townsend (copy), 11 March 1942: relating adventures of *Mauna Loa* and crew.

Waterhouse, J. T.: undated comments on manuscript, via Gregg Perry, 29 April 1976.

Westerberg, Fred, 26 November 1974: history of father and connection with Matson.

MATSON COMPANY PUBLICATIONS, REPORTS, MISCELLANEOUS

Aloha (Company magazine published during the 1920s.)

| February 1926: | John A. Scott (posthumous), "Captain Matson's Early Days in Hilo." |
| February 1928: | Matt J. Lindsay, "Matson Freight Service in the Old Days." (Unsigned), "The Matson Fleet: Eighteen Fine Ships." |

Matsonews (Company publication, first published in 1939 in magazine form, later as monthly in newspaper format; renamed *Matson Log* in 1978.)

November 1939: "Oldest Matson Employee" (W. H. Sellender). "Up from the Ranks" (Commodore Charles A. Berndtson).

December 1939: "Second Oldest Employee in Years of Service" (Captain James P. Rasmussen).

January–February 1940: "Hawaii's Christmas Ship from Pacific Northwest." "Up from the Ranks" (Captain T. F. McManus).

March–April 1940: "Three Decades with Matson" (Captain Konrad Hubbenette).

May–June 1940: "Four New Freighters Within a Year."

July–August 1940: "Heroic Mission Saves Six in Storm." "Matson Men Convert *Waimea* to Bulk Cement Carrier."

November–December 1940: "Heroic Men of the S.S. *Maliko*."

December 1943 (Historical Issue): "Early Days." "First Ships." "From Sail to Steam." "World War I." "The Man." "Values." "Epoch of Progress." "Shoreside." "World War II." "In Retrospect."

March–April 1957: "Royal Hawaiian Celebrates Thirtieth Anniversary."

September–October 1957: "Mixing Oil and Water."

September–October 1959: Hugh Gallagher, "Origin of Matson Flag Revealed."

November–December 1959: "World War II Sinking of *Honomu* Recalled by Matson Chief Engineer" (unsigned interview with Alan L. Harvie).

November–December 1960: Randolph Sevier, "The Ocean Liner in a Hurrying World." "First Ocean-Going Automobile Ship." Wayne L. Horvitz, "A First Hand Report on New PMA-ILWU Pact."

Summer 1961: Randolph Sevier, "Annual Report to Stockholders." "Hawaii's Floating Warehouse." "Matson's Role in Ocean Freight." "Containers . . . Competition . . . Subsidy?"

April 1974: "Seatrain Withdraws from Hawaii, Guam."

November 1974: "Matson Adds Service" (ro-ro). "Change in Guam" (personnel; terminals).

October 1975: "Guam 'Feeder' Service."

December 1975: "Majuro Service Launched."

Matson's Pacific News (1967 brochure): "Matson Observes 85th Anniversary."

Matson Log

December 1978: "Pfeiffer Reports on L.A. Terminal."

March 1979: "Overhead Crane System in L.A."

July 1979: "Richmond Terminal Nears Completion."

Ampersand (Alexander & Baldwin quarterly magazine.)

Fourth Quarter 1973: "Outsize Cargo Gets a Break."

First Quarter 1974: "Are Those Assets Well Employed?" "A Watchful Situation at Matson."

Summer 1977: "S.S. *Maui* Taking Shape."

Spring 1978: "20 Years of Containerization in the Pacific."

Winter 1978/79: "To the Rescue" (World War II). "From Matson—A New Concept in Container Handling."

Cargo Containerization in the West Coast-Hawaii Trade. Reprint from *Operations Research,* vol. 6, no. 5 (September–October 1958). Pamphlet for internal use and customers, published by Matson.

Digest and Complete Transcript of Proceedings of the Conference on Competition, A. Pamphlet for internal use, published by Matson, 1954.

"History of the Oceanic Steamship Company," by Frederick Stindt, circa 1948. Unpublished manuscript prepared for South Pacific tour parties.

"History of the U.S.S. *Wilhelmina*." Unpublished manuscript, undated, prepared from ship's logs, circa 1919.

Matson Annual Reports. Reports for 1916 and 1959

through 1967 used most often. Complete files maintained at company headquarters, San Francisco.

Matson Introduces Intermodal Surface Transportation between North America and the Far East. Sales brochure, undated.

"Matson Line History." Unpublished manuscript, written in 1927, unsigned.

Matson Navigation Company Pacific Coast–Hawaii Freighter Service, 1947–1964. Loose-leaf report for use in rate hearings, circa 1965.

"Matson Navigation Company in World War II." Unpublished loose-leaf manuscript, circa 1947, unsigned.

Ships in Gray: The Story of Matson in World War II. Booklet, published by Matson, circa 1946. Privately distributed.

We're Rolling, On and Off. Sales brochure for Matson ro-ro ships, 1974.

LETTER COLLECTIONS

Dillingham Collection. Bishop Museum, Honolulu: this collection is generally not available, but some letters from it were provided for this project.

Irwin Collection. University of Hawaii: several scores of letters between Walter M. Giffard, William Matson, W. D. K. Gibson, and William Irwin, covering the period of 1892 through 1907, concerning cargoes, the *Falls of Clyde,* the Oceanic Line, and various business affairs.

Klebingat, Captain Fred K., to Dr. Roland Force. Bishop Museum, 20 October 1965: résumé of *Falls of Clyde* restoration project, with reprint from *Petroleum Today* (Spring 1965); also reprint from *Oceans* (September–October 1972).

Westerberg, Dr. Frederick, to Swedish relatives, 1908–1917 (in Swedish). At Swedish consulate, San Francisco.

SPEECHES

Cushing, John E.   Newcomen Society lecture. "Captain William Matson, from Handy Boy to Shipowner." New London, Connecticut, 4 October 1949. Reprinted by Princeton University Press, January 1951.

Matson, William.   Address as president of the Chamber of Commerce of San Francisco to trustees of that organization, 25 October 1911. Pamphlet at California Historical Society Library, San Francisco.

Miller, Hon. George P. (of California).   To House of Representatives, Washington, D.C. Entered in *Congressional Record* of 9 July 1959.

Pricher, Lawrence S.   "Hawaii's One-Way Lifeline." Delivered to World Trade Association annual meeting, Honolulu, 12 July 1977.

By agreements with Matson Navigation Company and the library of the University of Oregon, tapes, transcriptions, and notes on interviews and research, along with the vital *Memoirs* of Commodore Peter Johnson, photostats of newspapers and magazine materials, working copies of the manuscript, correspondence, and key editions of Matson publications and reports to stockholders have been sent to the library, to be added to other papers previously supplied. There is no formal name, but references to the Worden Collection will serve to locate these materials.

Complete financial histories of the company, from 1906, are kept at Matson headquarters in San Francisco. Alexander & Baldwin, Inc., maintains recent records at its Honolulu offices.

INDEX

🏛 *Production Notes*

This book was designed by Roger Eggers and typeset on the Unified Composing System by The University Press of Hawaii.

The text and display typeface is Garamond No. 49.

Offset presswork and binding were done by Halliday Lithograph. Text paper is Glatfelter Hi-Opaque Offset, basis 55.